ROBIN GINTHER VENNERI

OSTARA

A Book of Rituals and Celebrations for the Springtime Sabbat

KIPS Publishing LLC
Rochester, PA

Ostara Guide: Rituals and Celebrations for the Springtime Sabbat
© 2023 by Robin Ginther Venneri

Print ISBN 13: 979-8-987-55910-9
Second Edition, 2024
10 9 8 7 6 5 4 3 2
KIPS Publishing LLC
Rochester, PA
All rights reserved.
www.kipspublishingllc.com

LEGAL DISCLAIMER

We, KIPS Publishing, and the author, Robin Ginther-Venneri, are not herbal experts by any means and are not medical professionals. The products available, along with statements, opinions, views expressed, ideas, notes, procedures, and suggestions in this book, on the blog, on the website, in e-books, on Facebook, Pinterest, and Twitter pages, and any follow-up comments on-site or by email, are opinions and are meant for informational purposes only. They are not meant to be used to diagnose, treat, prescribe, prevent, or cure any disease or to administer in any manner to any physical ailments. They are not intended as a substitute for the medical advice of a trained health professional. We cannot be held liable for your decisions and choices and the outcome of those decisions and choices. You are encouraged to do your own research and consult your healthcare professional before treating yourself or anyone else.

The information in this book, on the blog, on the website, in e-books, on Facebook, Pinterest, and Twitter pages, and any follow-up comments on-site or by email are general and not specific to individuals and their circumstances. You must study herbs thoroughly and talk with a healthcare practitioner before you treat yourself or anyone else. I would like you to know that all matters regarding your health require medical supervision. Please consult your health care professional before adopting the statements, opinions, views expressed, ideas, notes, procedures, and suggestions in this book, on the website, in e-books, on Facebook, Pinterest, and Twitter pages, and any follow-up comments on-site or by email, as well as about any condition that may require diagnosis or medical attention.

Herbs are very powerful, and if they are misused, they can be harmful. Herbs can also cause allergic reactions and interfere with traditional medications by blocking their effectiveness, increasing their effectiveness, or reacting with them harmfully. Always check with your health care professional before using herbs or herbal products!

Do not use herbal products of any kind if you are nursing, pregnant, taking medications, or undergoing treatment for any medical condition without consulting your health care professional.

Any plant substance, whether used as food or medicine, externally or internally, can cause an allergic reaction in some people. Neither KIPS Publishing nor the author Robin Ginther-Venneri can be held responsible for claims arising from the mistaken identity of any herbs or the use of any remedy or healing regime or because you did not first seek the advice of a trained healthcare professional as recommended. Do not try self-diagnosis or self-treatment for serious or long-term problems without consulting a healthcare professional. Do not undertake self-treatment while undergoing a prescribed course of medical treatment without seeking professional advice. Always seek medical advice if symptoms persist.

We, KIPS Publishing, and Robin Ginther-Venneri disclaim any liability arising directly or indirectly from using this book, on the website, on the blog, in e-books, a class, class notes, follow-up email contacts, or of any products available or mentioned herein.

Additionally, the FDA has not evaluated the statements on the website, blog, e-books, Facebook, Pinterest, and/or Twitter pages, and any follow-up comments on these sites or by email. The information on this site is not intended to diagnose, treat, or cure any disease.

Thank you,
KIPS Publishing LLC

Expressing Gratitude and the Value of Mistakes in Research

Robin understands that making mistakes is an integral part of the learning process. They are grateful for the valuable lessons they have learned and the infinite knowledge that is yet to be discovered.

As you read Robin's work, it's important to acknowledge the effort put into it, while also understanding that it is the result of a rigorous, yet imperfect process. Robin is excited to share both the final polished research and the raw, unrefined process that led to it. Together, we can appreciate the evolution of ideas and the remarkable journey of seeking knowledge.

With humility and gratitude,
Robin

Book Blessing and Protection Spell

Supplies:
The book you wish to bless and protect
A small white candle
A sprig of Rosemary
Clear quartz crystal or amethyst (optional)
A quiet and sacred space

Preparation: Choose a time when you can be undisturbed and when you feel calm and focused. Place the book, the candle, the Rosemary, and any optional crystals on a clean and sacred surface.

Cleanse the Space: Light the white candle. As it flickers, visualize its flame clearing and purifying the energy around you. Pass the book and the Rosemary through the candle flame, visualizing any negative or stagnant energies being cleansed.

Invoke Divine Energy: Close your eyes and take a few deep breaths to center yourself.
If you work with specific deities, call upon them for blessings. Otherwise, you can invoke the universal energies of light, wisdom, and protection.

Blessing the Book: Hold the book in your hands and visualize a warm, golden light surrounding it.

Say aloud or in your mind: "By the light of this flame and the wisdom it contains,
I bless and protect this book and its knowledge to sustain. May it be a source of insight, growth, and grace, Guarded by the energies of this sacred space."

Infuse with Rosemary: Take the sprig of Rosemary and gently wave it over the book. Feel the protective energies of Rosemary infusing the book.

Say: "Rosemary, herb of wisdom and protection. Guard this book with your magical reflection. Shield it from harm, keep its pages pure, Infuse it with the knowledge that will endure."

Optional Crystal Blessing: If you have a clear quartz crystal or amethyst, hold it in your hands. Visualize the crystal radiating a protective energy field around the book.

Say: "Crystal clear, amplify this protective sphere, Guard this book, keep it ever dear. May its energies be enhanced and pure, Infusing it with magic to endure."

Closing: Thank the divine energies, deities, or universal forces you invoked. Blow out the candle, visualizing the protection lingering around the book.

Placement: Keep the book in a safe and sacred space. You may choose to keep the rosemary sprig with the book for continued protection.

Remember to perform this spell with respect, intention, and a focused mind. The energies you infuse into the book will contribute to its positive atmosphere and long-lasting protection.

Acknowledgments

Writing this book has been a transformative journey, and I am immensely grateful to those whose unwavering support and encouragement have made it possible.

First and foremost, I extend my deepest gratitude to my mentors, Colby and Jamie. Your guidance, wisdom, and belief in my abilities have been the compass that guided me through the intricate paths of this creative endeavor. I am truly fortunate to have had the privilege of learning from you both.

To my pillar of strength, my husband Jeff, and our beautiful daughter Caitlan—your love and understanding have been my constant inspiration. Your unwavering support, even during the busiest of times, has been the bedrock upon which this project stands.

A special mention goes to my adorable grandchildren, Lylah and Beau. Your laughter and innocence brought light to my writing days, reminding me of the joy that truly matters.

I want to express my gratitude for the hard work of my editor. Thank you for your thoughtful guidance and assistance. Any mistakes are mine alone.

To all my friends and family who stood by me with words of encouragement and endless patience, I am profoundly thankful. Each of you has contributed in unique ways, shaping not only the book but also the author behind the words.

This journey wouldn't have been the same without you, and for that, I am forever grateful.

Map to Start Your Spiritual Journey

Get Organized

Start by making space
Make lists (shopping, to-do, bills, home repair, etc.)
Create a schedule
Create a budget
Organize your living space
Get rid of stuff (less stuff - less anxiety)

Self-Reflection

Know thyself, Ask yourself
Who am I, really?
Am I living authentically?
Are my beliefs supporting my spiritual growth?
Am I spending my time wisely?

Be Still

Quiet your mind. Hear your soul.
Commit 15 min a day
to sitting in silence and solitude.
Allow your thoughts to pass w/out
judgment, bring your attention back to your breath, and slowly see your mind clear.

Ostara Blessings

Blessed Ostara, herald of spring's renewal,
As the earth awakens from its wintry slumber,
May your spirit be filled with the warmth of the sun,
And your heart blossoms with the promise of new beginnings.

Under the gentle gaze of the growing light,
May you find harmony and balance within,
May the seeds of your intentions take root,
Blossoming into abundance and fulfillment.

As the earth bursts forth with life once more,
May you feel connected to the cycles of nature,
May the joys of rebirth and growth
Fill your days with beauty and inspiration.

Blessed be on this sacred day of Ostara,
May its blessings shine upon you,
May you walk in harmony and grace
With the ever-turning wheel of the seasons.

Ostara Altar Blessing

In the burgeoning of springtime, when the earth begins to stir,
As the buds burst forth in bloom and new life begins to birth,
We gather 'neath the dawning sun,
where the day and night align,
bless this altar with your fertility as the wheel of life entwines.
By the crocus' golden hue,
by the hare's playful leap,
May this space be filled with abundance as we celebrate
Ostara's sweet sleep.
With growth and renewal, to the goddess of the dawn,
bless this sacred space as the earth's rebirth is drawn.

CHAPTER 1

The Wheel of the Year Explained

The Wheel of the Year, also known as the Wheel of Life, symbolizes the Earth's cycles and the cycle of life itself. Our ancestors used it to mark the turning of the seasons and years, for farmers to plan their work, and for modern pagans to reconnect with nature's rhythms.

The Wheel of the Year consists of eight holidays or festivals, also known as holy days. These festivals follow the cyclical calendar of the sun and moon and the natural world's rhythms. Four of them are solar festivals or lesser Sabbats, which are associated with the sun and God. The other four are season-change festivals, or Grand Sabbats, related to the Earth and Goddess.

The Wheel of the Year has two halves: a dark half marking Autumn/Winter and a light half marking Spring/Summer. Each half has two lesser Sabbats and two Grand Sabbats. The lesser Sabbats are Yule, the Winter Solstice; Ostara, the Spring Equinox; Litha, the Midsummer Solstice and Equinox; Litha, the Midsummer Solstice, and Mabon, the Autumn Equinox. The two annual equinox solstices are the solar festivals or lesser Sabbats. The equinoxes occur when we have a day and night of almost equal length because the sun is directly over the equator. The solstices occur when we have the shortest day (June) and the longest day (December), related to the Earth's tilt. The exact date varies each year by a few days due to the Earth's rotation around the sun in 365.25 days, while our calendar is set for 365 days. Hence, we have a leap year every four years to balance the calendar.

Wheel of the Year

Pagan Sabbats

A pagan sabbat is a seasonal festival celebrated by some Pagan and Wiccan traditions. There are eight sabbats in a year, marking key points in the solar cycle. These include Samhain, Yule, Imbolc, Ostara, Beltane, Litha, Lammas, and Mabon. Each sabbat has its own significance, rituals, and traditions. For example, Samhain is often associated with honoring ancestors and the thinning of the veil between worlds, while Beltane is a celebration of fertility and the coming of summer. These festivals are a way for practitioners to connect with nature, celebrate the changing seasons, and honor spiritual beliefs.

Light and Dark

Sabbat Dates

Sabbat	Northern Hemisphere Date	Southern Hemisphere Date
Imbolc	February 1-2	August 1-2
Ostara	March 19-21	September 20-23
Beltane	May 1	October 31
Litha	June 20-22	December 20-23
Lammas	August 1-2	February 1-2
Mabon	September 21-24	March 20-22
Samhain	October 31	April 30
Yule	December 20-23	June 20-22

CHAPTER 2

Ostara

Ostara, a pagan sabbat, celebrates the vernal equinox, marking the arrival of spring. Rooted in ancient traditions, it symbolizes balance, fertility, and the awakening of nature after winter's slumber. Practitioners often engage in rituals and festivities to honor the rebirth of life and embrace the increasing light of the season.

Ostara, also known as the Spring Equinox, is a pagan sabbat with roots in various ancient cultures, most notably Germanic and Celtic traditions. The name "Ostara" is believed to be derived from the Germanic goddess Eostre, who is associated with spring, fertility, and the dawn. The celebration typically falls around March 20th-23rd in the Northern Hemisphere, marking the equinox when day and night are of equal length.

Historically, Ostara has been linked to agricultural cycles and the celebration of new life. Ancient communities engaged in rituals to welcome the return of longer days and the promise of fertile fields. Eggs, symbolizing fertility and renewal, were commonly incorporated into these festivities.

In Norse mythology, the goddess Idunn, guardian of the golden apples representing eternal youth, is often associated with Ostara. The Saxon goddess Eostre, mentioned by the Venerable Bede, is another inspiration for this celebration, with traditions like the lighting of bonfires and the honoring of hares, symbols of fertility.

Modern Ostara celebrations draw from these historical roots, blending them with contemporary pagan practices. Common customs include decorating eggs, creating altars adorned with symbols of spring, and participating in outdoor activities to connect with nature. Some rituals involve the planting of seeds or the lighting of candles to symbolize the increasing sunlight.

Overall, Ostara stands as a time to honor the changing seasons, embrace the energy of renewal, and connect with the natural cycles of life and growth. It's a celebration that bridges ancient wisdom with modern pagan practices, fostering a deep connection to the Earth and its ever-turning wheel.

Modern pagan and Wiccan communities primarily celebrate Ostara. It is observed by those who follow earth-based spiritual traditions, including practitioners of various neopagan paths. While less widely recognized than some mainstream holidays, Ostara has gained popularity among individuals who seek to connect with nature, honor the changing seasons, and embrace the symbolism of renewal and fertility. Celebrants may include Wiccans, Druids, Heathens, and other neopagan or eclectic spiritual practitioners who incorporate the sabbat into their yearly rituals.

Ostara - Spring Equinox

As we contemplate the shifting seasons with the pagan observance of Ostara, the spring equinox draws near. It's a moment for introspection, acknowledging the evolving cycles of nature and the emergence of new life. Prepare for late spring plantings by turning the soil and starting seeds indoors for a thriving herb garden. Celebrate the delicate balance of light and dark during this time as the sun begins to tip the scales, signaling the imminent return of new growth. Take a moment to stroll in nature, observing the myriad beginnings unfolding around you. Meditate on the ever-turning Wheel of the Year and revel in the beauty of seasonal change.

May the gentle touch of spring's awakening grace your days during Ostara. May the balance of light and dark bring harmony to your spirit. As nature blooms, may your heart blossom with joy and renewed vitality. Embrace the fertile energy of this season, and may your endeavors flourish like the flowers in the fields. Blessed Ostara to you with the promise of growth, warmth, and the beauty of the ever-turning Wheel of the Year.

On this vernal equinox, as day and night find equilibrium, may your life be touched by the gentle hand of balance. May the essence of renewal and new growth infuse your days with hope and possibility. Like the blossoming flowers and budding leaves, may your aspirations and endeavors flourish. May the energy of spring bring harmony to your heart, and may you embrace the beauty of the evolving seasons with gratitude. A blessing for the spring equinox, where balance and new growth intertwine in the dance of life.

CHAPTER 3

Ostara at a Glance

Ostara

Ostara

I blossom as nature
unfolds her leaves.
I am rooted in the
fertile soil of Mother Earth.
I am filled with the life-giving light of the sun.
I am fresh and renewed with the coming of spring.

Ostara at a Glance

Ostara - March 20 - 21

Ostara - the Vernal Equinox - begins on March 20th (September in the Southern Hemisphere). At precisely this moment, the sun reaches its zenith and is directly over the equator. While this date can occasionally fall between March 20th and 21st due to a six-hour shift each year, Ostara marks the official start of spring in the Northern Hemisphere, even if many locations still experience cold temperatures and snow cover.

Though the phrase "equinox" literally means equal night, there is a discrepancy regarding how much daylight and nighttime people experience. People see more daylight than darkness near the equator despite it being an equinox. Alternately, those in higher latitudes can often be subject to less sunshine at this time of year. The most important notion here isn't so much the variation in light of day but rather that all over the world, the sun hits its zenith at the same time on an equinox. This universal phenomenon happens regardless of latitude and should remind us that we are connected, no matter where we reside on our planet.

On the day of the Spring Equinox, the sun is perfectly aligned with the equator. This marks a symbolic and physical moment when the light triumphs over darkness, ushering in a new season. Whether in America or Australia, this unique moment can be experienced everywhere.

There is no right or wrong way to celebrate any of the Sabbats. Pagans base their celebrations on cultural traditions, historical practices, and inclinations.

So live and let live!

Quicky Ostara Correspondences

Heroes, Deities and Goddesses
Amalthea (Greek)
Aphrodite / Venus (Greco-Roman)
Blodeuwedd (Welsh)
Eos (Greek)
Eostre (Germanic)
Epona (Celtic)
Flora (Roman)
Freya (Norse)
Gaia (Greek)
Guinevere (Welsh / Arthurian)
Libera (Roman)
Maia (Greek)
Persephone (Greek)
Rati (Hindu)
Renpet (Egyptian)
Umai (Russian)
Vila (Slavic)

Gods
Aengus/ Macan Og (Irish)
Cernunnos/ Herne (Anglo-Celtic)
The Dagda (Irish)
Eros/Cupid (Greco-Roman)
the Green Man (European / North American)
Kama (Hindu)
Mabon (Anglo-Welsh)
Osiris (Egyptian)
Pan (Greek)
Thor (Norse)

Archetypes
Female
Goddess of fertility;
Mother of the Earth;
the Goddess in the form of the Maiden.

Male
God in the form of a young, lustful man who will soon become the father;
God of the wild, the Green Man.

Shadow Work Tea Blend

Nettle Leaf
Papaya Leaf
Mugwort
Sage
Elderberry

Herbs for Dreaming

Drink a tea made from one or a combination of these herbs before sleeping to induce beautiful dreams.
Mugwort is for lucid dreaming and astral travel.
Lavender for a peaceful, relaxing, and restful sleep.
Cloves are for protected dreams free from nightmares.
Rose Petals are used for dreams of self-love, happiness, and good fortune.

Ostara Altar Items

Egg Shells for Rebirth

Bright-colored flowers

Use Rose Petals for Love and Protection

Milk and honey offering

Moss Agate to aid New Beginnings

Bulbs, seeds and fruit

Moss provides Prosperity Strength

Crystals for joy and rebirth

Black and white candles

Spring decorations

On this Spring Equinox, I set forth my spiritual intentions for the season of rebirth and growth. I embark on a journey of purification, cleansing my being of stagnant and old energy to make way for the fresh vitality that spring offers.

With a heart full of zeal, I embrace the positive intense energy that surrounds me, channeling it into motivation for personal and spiritual growth. I seek balance in all aspects of my life, navigating the transitions with grace and resilience.

In this season of birth and revitalization, I open myself to the flow of good fortune and evolution. My intentions are rooted in kindness and joy, fostering a spirit of fertility that nurtures hopeful intentions for the days to come.

May this Spring Equinox be a time of profound transformation and the manifestation of all my positive and spiritual aspirations.

Flowers

Apple blossom, columbine, crocus, daffodil, daisy, honeysuckle, jasmine, jonquil, lilac, narcissus, orange blossom, primrose, rose, tulip and violets

Trees

Alder, apple, and hawthorn

Crystals

Agate, aquamarine, and bloodstone

Metals

Silver

Incense

Apple blossom, clean crisp air, columbine, crocus, daffodil, daisy, honey, honeysuckle, jasmine, jonquil lilac, narcissus, orange blossom, primrose, rose, and any spring floral scent, rain

Herbs

Broom, high john root, irish moss, and lemon grass

Animals, Totems, and Mythical Creatures

Bees, boar, chicks, hedgehog, horse, phoenix, pooka, rabbit, ram and robin

Symbols and Tools

Baskets, eggs, hare, and seeds

Food

Asparagus, dill, eggs, honey, lamb, lettuce, radishes, seafood, and spring onions

Drinks

Mead

Colors

Green, light blue, pink, silver, violet, white, and yellow

Activities and Traditions of Practice

Blessing seeds, cascarones, coloring eggs, egg hunts, home blessings, making plans for the year, painting or carving runes to represent new ideas or qualities you want to bring into your life, preparing a garden spring cleaning, start seedlings, and starting garden plants indoors

Acts of Service

Assisting with the homeless (as most temporary shelters will soon be closing), litter pick-up (as the snow melts, the garbage is unburied!) and doing community gardening or community farming

Alternate Names for Ostara in Other Pagan Traditions

Alban Eiler (Celtic, meaning the "Light of the Earth")
Festival of Summer Finding (Asatru)
Vernal or Spring Equinox

Holidays or Traditions Occurring During Ostara in the Northern Hemisphere:
Religious

Dionysus or Bacchus Day (Greco Roman, March 16-17)
Annunciation of the Blessed Virgin Mary or Lady Day (Catholic, March 25th)
Palm Sunday (Christian, the Sunday before Easter)
Good Friday (Christianity, the Friday before Easter)
Easter (Christian, the first Sunday after the first full moon after the Spring Equinox)
Passover (Jewish, fifteenth day of Nisan, which begins on the night of the full moon after the northern Vernal Equinox)

Secular

St. Patrick's Day (while originally the Catholic Feast Day of a Saint, it is celebrated more as a secular holiday in the United States on March 17th)

Holidays or Traditions Occurring During Ostara in the Southern Hemisphere:
Religious

Feast of Jupiter, Juno, Minerva (Nova Roma)
Michaelmas (Catholic Christians)
Birth of the Virgin Mary (Catholic Christian, September 8th)

Secular

Floriade (largest flower festival in the Southern Hemisphere)

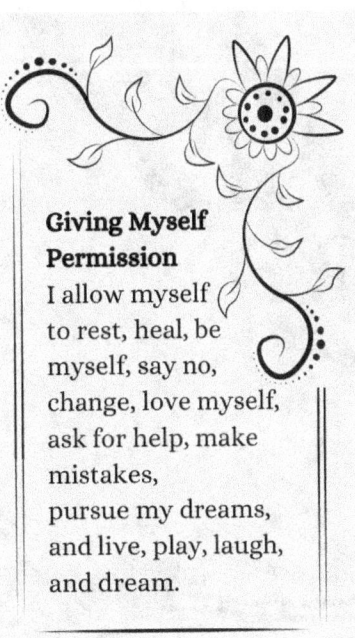

Giving Myself Permission
I allow myself to rest, heal, be myself, say no, change, love myself, ask for help, make mistakes, pursue my dreams, and live, play, laugh, and dream.

CHAPTER 4

Ostara
Activities

Ostara Activities

Here are some ways to celebrate Ostara

Decorate Eggs
Coloring and decorating eggs is a classic Ostara activity symbolizing fertility and new life. You can use various natural dyes and symbols or even create intricate designs.

Plant Seeds
Ostara is associated with growth and fertility. Planting seeds or tending to a garden during this time symbolically aligns with the season's energy.

Spring Cleaning
Clearing out clutter and performing a thorough spring cleaning is a common Ostara tradition. It symbolizes making space for new energy and opportunities.

Altar Decorations
Set up an altar with items representing the elements of spring – flowers, fresh greens, colored candles, and symbols of fertility like eggs and seeds.

Feast
Prepare a festive meal using fresh, seasonal ingredients. Include foods that symbolize fertility and growth, such as eggs, sprouts, and leafy greens.

Light a Candle
Light a candle on your altar or throughout your home to represent spring's returning light and longer days.

Outdoor Activities
Spend time in nature, whether walking in the park, hiking, or simply sitting in your garden. Connect with the season's energy and observe the signs of new life.

Crafts and Artwork
Engage in creative activities like crafting or artwork that reflects the themes of Ostara. This could include making your own spring-themed decorations.

Divination
Use divination tools such as tarot cards, runes, or scrying to gain insights and guidance for the coming season.

Celebrate with Others
If you're part of a Pagan or Wiccan community, consider joining or hosting a gathering to celebrate Ostara together. Share rituals, stories, and the joy of the season.

Offerings

Make offerings to the Earth or any deities you work with. Pouring libations or burying offerings in the soil can be a way to give thanks for the returning life.

Create a Spring Wreath

Craft a wreath using fresh or artificial flowers, ribbons, and symbols of the season. Hang it on your door, or use it as a centerpiece.

Attune to Nature's Rhythms

Observe the changing natural rhythms around you. Notice the blooming flowers, the return of migratory birds, and the longer daylight hours.

Express Gratitude

Take a moment to express gratitude for the abundance in your life and the opportunities for growth and renewal.

Remember that personalization is key in any celebration. Feel free to adapt these ideas to align with your own spiritual or cultural practices. Ostara is a time to honor the awakening of the Earth and embrace the energy of renewal and growth.

Ostara, Bestow upon us your gifts of hope and growth. Guide me in the ways of light, unveiling the path of illumination as I embark on the journey to transcend into enlightenment. Shedding my cold winter skin, I activate my sanctity, burning away what no longer serves me. Emerging from hibernation, I awaken dormant energy, blossoming with the arrival of spring. Amen, A'ho, so it is.

Ostara Simmer Pot

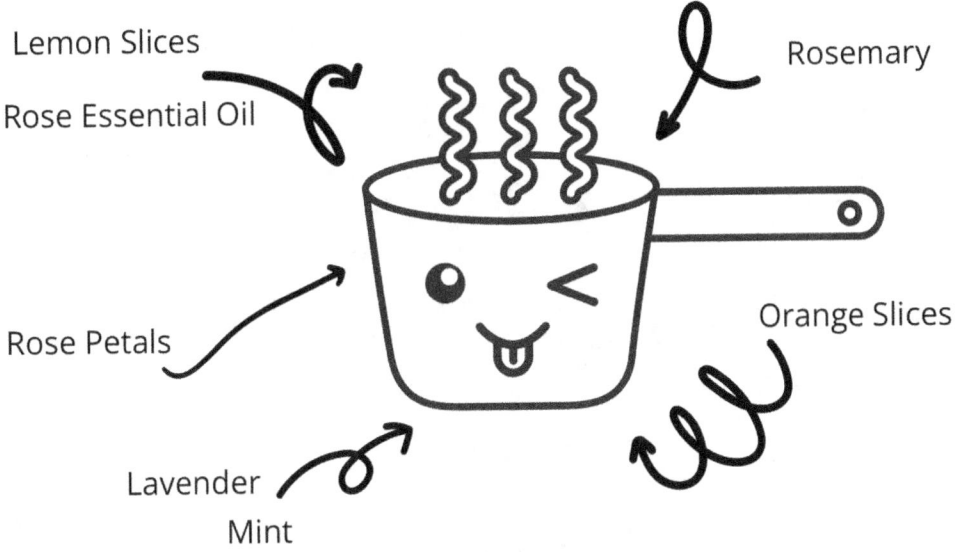

Lemon Slices

Rose Essential Oil

Rosemary

Rose Petals

Orange Slices

Lavender

Mint

Ostara Mini Altar

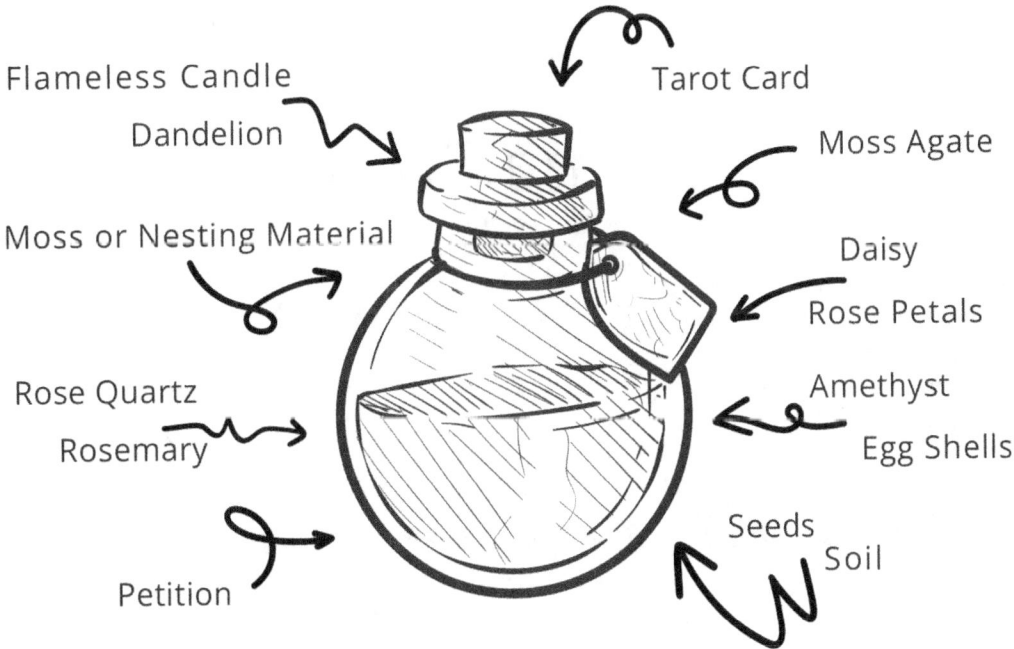

Flameless Candle

Dandelion

Tarot Card

Moss Agate

Moss or Nesting Material

Daisy

Rose Petals

Rose Quartz

Rosemary

Amethyst

Egg Shells

Petition

Seeds

Soil

Ostara Wish Jar

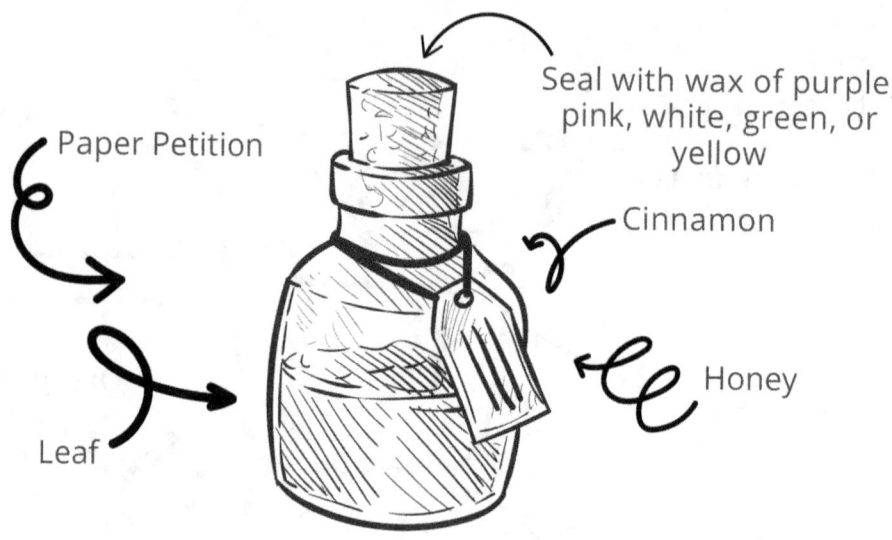

Paper Petition

Leaf

Seal with wax of purple, pink, white, green, or yellow

Cinnamon

Honey

Ostara Egg

On Ostara night, write your intentions
on an egg: fertility, prosperity,
health, love, happiness.
Then bury it and plant a seed
or flower above the egg and
watch it grow.

Spring Bath

3 Drops of Ylang Ylang
3 Tablespoons of Dried Thyme
Marjoram Sprigs
1 Cup of Himalayan Salt
1 Cup of Epson Salt

Place your crystals around the tub and light your candles

Ostara Diffuser Blends

Spring Clean

3 Drops of Lime
2 Drops of Lavender
3 Drops of Lemon
2 Drops of Rosemary

Sweet Sunshine

5 Drops of Wild Orange
3 Drops of Lemongrass
1 Drop of Peppermint

Witch's Garden

1 Drops of Basil
2 Drops of Peppermint
2 Drops of Lime

Stay Grounded

4 Drops of Grapefruit
3 Drops of Frankincense
2 Drops of Lemongrass

Ostara Blessings

2 Drops of Tangerine
2 Drops of Spearmint
3 Drops of Lemongrass

Flower Blossoms

1 Drop of Clary Sage
2 Drops of Geranium
2 Drops of Lavender
1 Drop of Ylang Ylang

Ostara Celebration

2 Drops of Geranium
2 Drops of Ylang Ylang
2 Drops of Vetiver
2 Drops of Patchouli

Ostara Ritual

2 Drops of Geranium
5 Drops of Lime
3 Drops of Wild Orange

Easter Egg Magic

Eggs dyed were given as gifts during or after the festivals of Spring Equinox in ancient Egypt, Greece, Ireland, and Rome. Modern Pagans also use colored eggs as powerful Easter Talismans

 Red Eggs: Power of Resurrection, Passion, and New Life

 Orange Eggs: Attraction and Good Luck

 Yellow Eggs: Happiness and Inspiration

 Green Eggs: Abundance and Good Health

 Blue Eggs: Peace and Spirituality

 Purple Eggs: Mystical and Magical Powers of Spring

CHAPTER 5

Ostara
Celebrations

Neo-Pagans

Neo-pagans celebrate Ostara, the vernal equinox, in various ways, often blending modern interpretations with diverse pagan traditions.

Common practices
Rituals and Ceremonies: Neo-pagans may perform rituals that focus on themes of balance, renewal, and the emergence of life in spring. These rituals often involve invocations, casting circles, and symbolic actions.

Altar Decorations: Altars are adorned with symbols of spring, such as flowers, colored candles, and representations of animals associated with fertility, like hares or butterflies. Eggs, often decorated with meaningful symbols, are also common altar additions.

Egg Decorating: The symbolism of eggs as a universal symbol of fertility and rebirth is embraced by neo-pagans. Decorating eggs with colors, symbols, or intentions is a creative and symbolic practice.

Outdoor Activities: Connecting with nature is integral to neo-pagan spirituality. Celebrants may engage in outdoor activities like nature walks, picnics, or communal gatherings in natural settings.

Feasting: Neo-pagans celebrate Ostara with festive meals featuring fresh, seasonal foods. The focus is often on locally sourced ingredients and dishes that symbolize the energies of spring.

Seed Planting: Planting seeds or participating in gardening activities is a symbolic way to connect with the agricultural aspects of Ostara, representing growth, renewal, and the cycle of life.

Music and Dance: Some neo-pagans incorporate music and dance into their celebrations to express the vibrancy and energy associated with the arrival of spring. This can include traditional or modern music and dance forms.

Meditation and Reflection: Neo-pagans may use Ostara as a time for personal reflection and meditation. Setting intentions for personal growth and renewal is a common aspect of this practice.

Community Gatherings: Many neo-pagans celebrate Ostara in community settings, participating in group rituals, feasts, and shared activities. This fosters a sense of kinship and connection among practitioners.

It's important to recognize that neo-paganism encompasses a diverse range of beliefs and practices, and individual celebrations of Ostara may vary based on personal preferences, traditions, and the specific pagan path followed.

Heathens

Heathens celebrate Ostara, also known as Eostre or Vårblot, in various ways, often drawing inspiration from Norse and Germanic traditions.

Blóts and Rituals: Heathens may perform blóts (sacrificial offerings) or other rituals to honor specific deities associated with spring, such as Freyja, Ostara, or Idunn. These rituals often involve prayers, invocations, and symbolic acts to welcome the season.

Altar Decorations: Altars are adorned with symbols of spring, fertility, and rebirth. This can include flowers, fresh greens, eggs, and representations of animals like hares or chicks.

Symbology of Eggs and Hares: Eggs and hares symbolize fertility and renewal, and Heathens incorporate these symbols into their celebrations. This may involve decorating eggs, creating hare-themed crafts, or incombining these symbols into rituals.

Feasting: Heathens celebrate Ostara with communal feasts that feature seasonal and locally sourced foods. This may include dishes with newly sprouted plants, fruits, and other offerings.

Honor to Land Spirits: Some Heathens pay homage to land spirits or wights during Ostara, recognizing the importance of nature and the spirits that inhabit the land. Offerings such as food, drink, or crafted items may be given to these spirits.

Community Gatherings: Heathen communities often come together for Ostara celebrations, fostering a sense of kinship. These gatherings may include communal rituals, storytelling, and shared activities.

Outdoor Activities: Given the emphasis on nature, Heathens may engage in outdoor activities during Ostara, such as nature walks, hikes, or working together on communal outdoor projects.

Craftsmanship and Art: Some Heathens express their spirituality through craftsmanship and art, creating items that reflect the themes of Ostara. This can include handmade decorations, artwork, or tools related to agricultural activities.

It's important to note that Heathenry is diverse, and practices can vary among different Heathen individuals and groups. Personal interpretations of historical sources, regional influences, and individual preferences contribute to the varied ways Heathens celebrate Ostara.

Druids

Druids, like other neopagan traditions, celebrate Ostara in ways that honor nature, the changing seasons, and the principles associated with this sabbat. While practices can vary among individuals and groups, some common ways in which Druids might celebrate Ostara include:

Nature Communion: Druids often celebrate Ostara by spending time in nature, connecting with the season's energy. This can involve nature walks, meditation, or rituals held in natural settings.

Spring Equinox Rituals: Druids may perform rituals to mark the arrival of spring, acknowledging the balance between light and dark on the equinox. These rituals might include invocations, prayers, or symbolic actions representing renewal and growth.

Altar Decorations: Altars are adorned with symbols of spring, such as flowers, budding branches, and representations of animals associated with fertility. Eggs and other seasonal items may also be part of the altar setup.

Seed Planting: Some Druids engage in practical activities like planting seeds or participating in community gardening projects to symbolize Ostara's growth, renewal, and agricultural aspects.

Storytelling and Lore: Druids often value storytelling and the passing down of lore. During Ostara celebrations, they might share myths and legends associated with the season or specific spring-related deities.

Community Gatherings: Ostara is sometimes celebrated in community settings, where Druids come together to share their experiences, perform rituals, and strengthen their connection to the natural world.

Feasting: Sharing a meal with fresh, seasonal foods is a common practice during Druidic celebrations. This can include locally sourced fruits, vegetables, and other items per the principles of honoring nature.

Music and Dance: Druids may incorporate music and dance into their Ostara celebrations, using these artistic expressions to celebrate the energy and vitality associated with the arrival of spring.

It's important to note that individual Druidic traditions and practices can vary, so not all Druids may observe Ostara similarly. The emphasis is often on fostering a deep connection with nature and celebrating the cycle of life and growth.

Druid's Alban Eilir

Ancient cultures cherished agricultural holidays as some of their most significant events. In the modern Druidic community, the Wheel of the Year connects eight seasonal festivals, each tied to the Earth's rhythms. These festivals, which include equinoxes, solstices, and fire festivals, provide meaningful opportunities to honor the changing seasons and the interconnectedness of all life.

Alban Arthan, the Winter Solstice, occurs in the heart of winter when darkness prevails and transitions to light with the arrival of spring during Imbolc. Alban Eiler, the spring equinox, marks a time of rejuvenation and growth, leading to the lively celebrations of Beltane and the radiant Alban Hefin, the Summer Solstice. Lughnasadh and Alban Elfed bridge the gap between light and dark, while Samhuinn guides the way back to Alban Arthan, completing the cycle.

Within this sacred wheel, themes of composting, growth, rebirth, and harvest resonate deeply, mirroring the eternal cycle of life and death. Rooted in Druidic tradition, these celebrations serve as powerful reminders of our connection to nature and the cyclical rhythms shaping our lives.

Similar to the Wiccan tradition of Ostara, Alban Eilir – translating to "Light of the Earth" – symbolizes joy and renewal during the spring equinox. Druids embrace rejuvenation through planting, nurturing, and creativity. Through communal gatherings, rituals, and environmental stewardship, they honor the Earth's abundance and reaffirm their commitment to living harmoniously with the natural world.

As Druids find solace and inspiration in the Earth's timeless wisdom, they embark on a journey of self-discovery, growth, and interconnectedness. In celebrating Alban Eilir and beyond, they immerse themselves in nature's embrace, humbled by its beauty and uplifted by its enduring presence.

Wiccans

Wiccans celebrate Ostara with rituals and activities that focus on renewal, balance, and the awakening of nature.

Rituals and Ceremonies: Wiccans often conduct rituals to honor the seasonal transition. This may involve casting circles, invoking deities associated with fertility and spring, and performing spellwork related to growth and new beginnings.

Decorating Altars: Altars are adorned with symbols of spring, such as flowers, fresh greens, and colorful eggs. Representations of animals like hares or chicks, which symbolize fertility, might also be included.

Egg Symbolism: Eggs are a central symbol of Ostara, representing fertility and the potential for new life. Wiccans may decorate eggs, incorporate them into rituals, or even participate in egg hunts as part of their celebrations.

Outdoor Activities: Connecting with nature is emphasized during Ostara. Wiccans might engage in outdoor activities like planting seeds, taking nature walks, or simply spending time in natural settings to appreciate the changing season.

Feasting: A festive meal with fresh, seasonal foods is often shared among Wiccans during Ostara celebrations. This can include dishes made with spring vegetables, fruits, and other symbolic foods.

Candle Lighting: As Ostara represents the balance between day and night, Wiccans may light candles to symbolize spring's increasing light and warmth.

Honor Deities: Wiccans may choose to honor specific deities associated with spring and fertility during their Ostara celebrations. This can vary depending on individual beliefs and traditions.

These practices are diverse, and individual Wiccans may incorporate different elements into their Ostara celebrations based on personal preferences and the specific traditions they follow.

CHAPTER 6

Other Holidays

Ostara Holidays

Numerous holidays and festivals grace the months of March and April, including:

Saint David's Day
Baba Marta Day
Bolludagur
Öskudagur
Hina Matsuri
Ceadda's Day
Ægir Sea
Purim
Holi
Forty Saints
Ides of March
St. Patrick's Day
Sheelah's Day
Saint Joseph's Day
Ostara
Alban Eiler
Bacchanalia
Lady Day
Nowruz
Prince Kuhio Day
Borrowed Days
Ramadan
April Fools Day
Hanshi Festival
Qingming Festival
Passover
Chaul Chnam Thmey
Easter
Earth Day
Eid al-Fitr
Walpurgisnacht

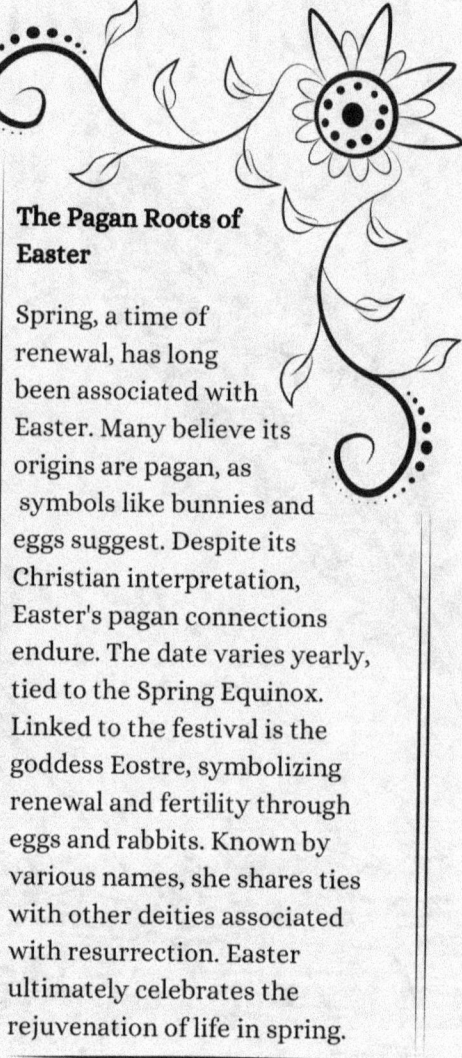

The Pagan Roots of Easter

Spring, a time of renewal, has long been associated with Easter. Many believe its origins are pagan, as symbols like bunnies and eggs suggest. Despite its Christian interpretation, Easter's pagan connections endure. The date varies yearly, tied to the Spring Equinox. Linked to the festival is the goddess Eostre, symbolizing renewal and fertility through eggs and rabbits. Known by various names, she shares ties with other deities associated with resurrection. Easter ultimately celebrates the rejuvenation of life in spring.

Purim

Date: Purim is a Jewish holiday celebrated on the 14th day of the Hebrew month of Adar.

Historical Context: It commemorates the events described in the Book of Esther, where the Jewish people in Persia were saved from a plot to annihilate them.

Story of Esther: Queen Esther and her cousin Mordecai play key roles in the Purim story.

Villain: Haman, the royal vizier, plots to destroy the Jewish people.

Events Leading to Purim: King Ahasuerus: The Persian king, unaware of Esther's Jewish identity, marries her.

Haman's Plot: Haman convinces the king to issue a decree to exterminate the Jews.

Esther's Courage: Esther's Revelation: Esther reveals her Jewish heritage to the king and pleads for her people.

The intervention of Mordecai: Mordecai's previous act of loyalty is acknowledged, and Haman is eventually hanged on the gallows he prepared for Mordecai.

Celebration of Purim: The Scroll of Esther (Megillah) is read in synagogue services.

Joyful Atmosphere: Purim is marked by joy, feasting, and celebration.

Traditions and Customs: Dressing in costumes is a common Purim tradition, symbolizing the hidden nature of miracles.

Gifts (Mishloach Manot): People exchange food packages to foster unity and friendship. Charitable Giving (Matanot LaEvyonim): Giving to the less fortunate is encouraged.

Special Foods: Hamantaschen, Triangular pastries filled with sweet fillings, representing Haman's three-cornered hat.

Festive Atmosphere: Carnivals and Parades, Many communities organize lively events, including carnivals, parades, and contests.

Religious Significance: Thanksgiving and Gratitude. Purim is a time of expressing gratitude for the survival of the Jewish people.

Conclusion: Relevance Today, Purim remains a significant and joyous holiday in the Jewish calendar, symbolizing the triumph of good over evil and the importance of courage and faith.

Holi

Date: Holi is a Hindu spring festival celebrated on the last full moon day of the lunar month Phalguna.

Timing: It typically falls in March, marking the arrival of spring.

Festival Origin

Mythological Significance: Holi commemorates various legends from Hindu mythology, primarily focusing on the victory of good over evil.

Rituals and Traditions

Holika Dahan: The night before Holi, a bonfire is lit to symbolize the burning of Holika, a demoness. This ritual signifies the triumph of good (Holika's nephew Prahlad) over evil.

Playful Celebrations: The main day of Holi involves people playing with colored powders and water, singing, dancing, and celebrating with friends and family.

Water Balloon Fights: Pichkari and Water Balloons, Water guns (pichkaris), and water balloons add a playful element to the celebrations, allowing people to drench each other.

Colors and Powders

Gulal and Abeer: Participants smear each other with vibrant colored powders known as "gulal" and "abeer."

Traditional Sweets

Gujiya: A popular sweet dish made during Holi, especially in North India.

Social Harmony

Equality in Celebration: Holi is known for breaking social barriers and bringing people together, as everyone, regardless of age, gender, or social status, participates in the festivities.

Regional Variations

Different Names: Holi is celebrated under various names across India, such as Rangwali Holi, Basanta Utsav, Dol Jatra, and more.

Diverse Customs: Different regions have unique customs and traditions associated with Holi.

Modern Celebrations

Community Events: Holi is not only celebrated in homes but also through community events, parties, and festivals.

International Recognition: Holi has gained recognition and is celebrated by people of various cultures around the world.

Cultural Significance: Holi marks the arrival of spring, symbolizing renewal, joy, and the triumph of positivity.

Conclusion

Joyful Celebration: Holi is a festive occasion characterized by vibrant colors, cultural traditions, and a spirit of joy that transcends boundaries. It continues to be one of the most widely celebrated and recognized festivals globally.

Ides of March

Date: The Ides of March is observed on March 15th.

Historical Origin: The term "Ides" originates from the Roman calendar, signifying the middle of the month.

Historical Significance: The Ides of March gained prominence due to the assassination of Julius Caesar in 44 BCE. He was stabbed to death by a group of Roman senators, including his close associates.

William Shakespeare's Play: "Julius Caesar". The events surrounding Caesar's assassination are famously depicted in William Shakespeare's play titled "Julius Caesar," where the phrase "Beware the Ides of March" is uttered.

Roman Calendar

Ides Definition: In the Roman calendar, the Ides marked the midpoint of the month, occurring on the 15th of March, May, July, and October, and the 13th for other months.

Superstitions

Cautionary Phrase: The phrase "Beware the Ides of March" has taken on a superstitious connotation, warning of impending danger or doom on this day.

Observances

Cultural References: The Ides of March is often referenced in literature, arts, and popular culture as a symbol of betrayal and political intrigue.

Contemporary Usage

Metaphorical Meaning: The phrase "Ides of March" is sometimes used metaphorically to signify a time of caution or awareness regarding potential dangers or challenges.

Other Months with Ides

Occurrences: While the Ides of March is the most famous, in the ancient Roman calendar, each month had an Ides. For the months of March, May, July, and October, the Ides fell on the 15th day. In every other month, the Ides fell on the 13th day.

Legacy and Impact

Literary Influence: The events of the Ides of March and Julius Caesar's assassination have left a lasting impact on literature, drama, and historical narratives.

Historical Turning Point: The Ides of March represents a critical historical juncture with the assassination of Julius Caesar, and its echoes continue to resonate through various forms of artistic expression and cultural references.

Nowruz

Cultural Celebration: Nowruz, meaning "New Day" in Persian, is an ancient celebration marking the Persian New Year.

Zoroastrian Roots: Nowruz has Zoroastrian origins and has been celebrated for over 3,000 years.

Date and Timing: Spring Equinox. Nowruz is observed on or around the vernal equinox, typically falling on March 20th or 21st.

Solar Calendar Basis: It symbolizes the rebirth of nature and the beginning of the solar year.

Traditional Preparations

Cleaning and Arranging: Houses are thoroughly cleaned, and new clothes are often worn to symbolize renewal and freshness.

Haft-Seen Table: A central tradition is setting up the Haft-Seen table, adorned with seven symbolic items starting with the Persian letter 'S.'

Haft-Seen Table Items

Sabzeh: Sprouted wheat, barley, or lentils representing rebirth.

Samanu: A sweet pudding symbolizing power and strength.

Senjed: Dried oleaster fruit, symbolizing love and compassion.

Seer: Garlic cloves representing medicine and health. Seeb: Apples symbolizing beauty and good health.

Somāq: Sumac berries representing the sunrise and patience.

Search: Vinegar symbolizes aging and patience.

Ceremonial Customs

Chahārshanbe Suri: A prelude to Nowruz, it involves jumping over bonfires to cleanse the spirit and ward off evil.

Visiting Relatives: Nowruz is a time for family gatherings and visiting relatives and friends.

Religious Significance

Zoroastrian Roots: Originally a Zoroastrian festival, Nowruz has evolved and is celebrated by various communities, including Iranians, Central Asians, and others.

UNESCO Recognition: Nowruz is recognized as an Intangible Cultural Heritage by UNESCO, highlighting its global cultural significance.

Duration of Celebrations

13 Days: Nowruz celebrations last for 13 days, culminating in Sizdah Bedar, a day when people spend time outdoors.

Cultural Symbolism

Nature and Renewal: Nowruz reflects the harmony with nature, emphasizing renewal, hope, and the triumph of light over darkness.

Conclusion: Nowruz stands as a cross-cultural celebration of renewal and hope, fostering a sense of unity and shared heritage among diverse communities.

Saint David's Day

Celebration of Saint David
Date: Saint David's Day is celebrated annually on March 1st.
Honoring Patron Saint: The day commemorates Saint David, the patron saint of Wales.
Saint David's Life
Date of Birth: Saint David is believed to have been born in the 6th century, with his death traditionally dated on March 1st.
Monastic Life: He was a Welsh bishop and the founder of several monastic communities in Wales.
Cultural and National Significance
National Day of Wales: Saint David's Day is a national day in Wales, celebrated with pride and a sense of Welsh identity.
Symbols of Wales: The day is marked by the display of Welsh symbols, including the national flag with the red dragon.
Traditional Customs and Observances
Wearing of Leeks and Daffodils: Traditional customs involve wearing leeks or daffodils, both symbols of Wales.
Welsh Costumes: Some people don traditional Welsh costumes as part of the celebrations.
Religious Observances: Saint David's Day is observed with church services, prayers, and special events.
Pilgrimages: Pilgrimages to Saint David's Cathedral in Pembrokeshire are common, paying homage to the saint.
Traditional Foods: Cawl, a traditional Welsh soup, often made with lamb or bacon, leeks, and vegetables, is a popular dish during the celebrations.
Educational and Cultural Activities
School Celebrations: Many schools in Wales organize special activities, performances, and educational events to mark Saint David's Day.
Concerts and Festivals: Cultural events, concerts, and festivals are held to celebrate Welsh heritage and music. Some towns and cities host parades featuring traditional Welsh music, dance, and costumes.
Community Gatherings: Local communities come together for celebrations, including music, poetry, and traditional performances.
Welsh Diaspora: Saint David's Day is also celebrated by the Welsh diaspora worldwide, maintaining a connection to Welsh culture and heritage.
Recognition and Integration: Cultural Identity, Saint David's Day is a reflection of Wales' cultural identity and serves as an opportunity for communities to celebrate their shared heritage.
Conclusion: Saint David's Day is a day of cultural pride for the people of Wales, fostering a sense of community and honoring the legacy of Saint David, a revered figure in Welsh history.

Bolludagur

Icelandic Tradition: Bolludagur, meaning "Bun Day," is an Icelandic tradition celebrated on the Monday before Lent.

Pre-Lenten Celebration: It marks the beginning of the pre-Lenten festivities. Culinary Focus: Bollur, the central element of Bolludagur is the consumption of "bollur" or cream-filled buns.

Sweet Treats: Bollur are often sweet pastries filled with whipped cream and sometimes jam.

Symbolism and Origin

Indulgence Before Lent: Bolludagur is a day for indulgence before the fasting period of Lent.

Symbolic Farewell to Winter: It is also considered a symbolic farewell to winter.

School Tradition: Whipping with Buns, traditionally, children engage in a playful custom known as "bolludagurssveinar" or "bun-throwing boys." They playfully spank their friends with bollur, usually in schools.

Playful Customs: Dressing Up. Children often dress up in costumes or wear masks while participating in the bun-throwing activity. Bolludagur is associated with light-hearted and playful customs, bringing joy to the community.

Commercial Celebrations

Bakery Offerings: Bakeries play a significant role in Bolludagur, offering a variety of bollur with different fillings and toppings.

Specialty Buns: Some bakeries create specialty bollur with unique flavors to mark the occasion.

Community Participation

Social Gathering: Bolludagur is often celebrated as a community event where people come together to enjoy the festive atmosphere.

Coffee Houses: Coffee houses and cafes may also join in the celebration, offering special treats for the occasion.

Link to Lenten Season

Countdown to Lent: Bolludagur is part of the countdown to Lent, a period of fasting and reflection leading up to Easter. It signifies the transition from festive celebrations to the more reflective and contemplative season of Lent.

Cultural Identity

Unique Icelandic Tradition: Bolludagur is a unique Icelandic tradition that reflects the cultural identity of the country.

Community Bonding: The shared enjoyment of bollur fosters a sense of community and cultural pride.

Conclusion: Bolludagur serves as a festive prelude to the Lenten season in Iceland. The joyous celebration, centered around sweet treats and playful customs, brings communities together to enjoy the spirit of the occasion before the solemnity of Lent begins.

Oskudagur

Icelandic Tradition: Öskudagur, also known as Ash Wednesday, is an Icelandic tradition celebrated on the Wednesday that marks the beginning of Lent.

Post-Bolludagur Celebration: It follows Bolludagur, the Bun Day celebration, and is part of the pre-Lenten festivities.

Cultural Significance: A transition to Lent, Öskudagur serves as a transition from the joyous and indulgent pre-Lenten celebrations to the more reflective period of Lent.

Religious Observance: Ash Wednesday is the first day of Lent in many Christian traditions.

Customs and Activities

Bun Tradition: Similar to Bolludagur, Öskudagur involves the custom of children dressing up and going door to door, singing songs, and receiving buns or other treats. Penny-for-a-Bun Tradition, children may also carry small decorated sticks and ask for pennies in exchange for a bun.

Costumes and Masks: Children often dress up in costumes or wear masks during Öskudagur, adding a playful and festive element to the celebration.

Parades and Events: Some towns organize parades or events, and participants may wear imaginative costumes. Öskudagur is a community-oriented celebration where neighbors, friends, and families come together to share in the festivities.

Social Bonding: The exchange of treats, dressing up, and engaging in playful activities contribute to social bonding.

Religious Observances: In addition to the secular traditions, Öskudagur is observed as Ash Wednesday within the Christian context. Some Christians attend church services where a cross is marked on their foreheads with ashes.

Business Involvement: Local businesses, especially bakeries and shops, may actively participate by offering special Öskudagur-themed treats. Some businesses may run promotions or offer discounts during the Öskudagur celebrations.

Festive Atmosphere: Öskudagur maintains a joyful and lighthearted atmosphere, allowing people to enjoy the last moments of festivity before the reflective period of Lent begins.

Celebratory Treats: Traditional Icelandic treats, including buns and other pastries, play a central role in the festive atmosphere.

Cultural Identity: Öskudagur reflects the cultural identity of Iceland, blending elements of pre-Lenten celebrations with unique customs and communal participation. The celebration contributes to the preservation of cultural traditions passed down through generations.

Conclusion: Öskudagur provides a festive farewell to the pre-Lenten celebrations in Iceland. With its blend of playful activities, communal engagement, and cultural significance, Öskudagur marks the transition from the exuberance of Bolludagur to the contemplative period of Lent.

Hina Matsuri

Celebrations in Japan: Hina Matsuri, also known as Doll's Day or Girls' Day, is a traditional Japanese celebration. It is observed annually on March 3rd.

Symbolism and Customs

Dolls Display: A central custom of Hina Matsuri involves displaying a set of dolls known as "Hina Ningyo." These dolls represent the imperial court of the Heian period.

Hierarchy of Dolls: The dolls are arranged on multiple tiers, with the emperor and empress at the top, followed by court musicians, ministers, and attendants.

Purification Rituals: Some customs involve the purification of evil spirits by placing peach blossoms and other items in a bowl of water.

Prayer for Good Fortune: Families may pray for the well-being and good fortune of their daughters during Hina Matsuri.

Traditional Foods

Hishimochi: Special tri-colored rice cakes called "hishimochi" are often consumed during Hina Matsuri. The three colors represent the peach blossoms, snow, and grass.

Doll Festival Parades: Some regions organize parades and community events featuring traditional costumes, music, and dance. In certain areas, processions of Hina Ningyo dolls are showcased during parades.

Musical Tradition: Special songs, known as "Hinamatsuri Uta," are sung during the celebration. These songs express good wishes for the well-being of girls.

Traditional Attire

Kimono: Families often dress up their daughters in traditional kimonos during Hina Matsuri. Some girls wear a special ceremonial kimono called "hina-ginu" for the occasion.

Regional Variations

Diverse Customs: Hina Matsuri customs may vary across regions in Japan, with unique local traditions and practices. Some areas host local festivals and events to celebrate Hina Matsuri.

Family Celebrations: Families decorate their homes with the Hina Ningyo dolls and other symbolic items. It is a time for families to come together, celebrate, and share special foods. Hina Matsuri has a significant influence on Japanese popular culture, with its motifs appearing in various forms, including art, anime, and merchandise.

Craftsmanship: The creation and craftsmanship of Hina Ningyo dolls have become an art form, with artisans crafting intricate and detailed dolls.

Conclusion: Hina Matsuri is a celebration deeply rooted in Japanese culture, emphasizing traditions, family, and the well-being of girls. The display of Hina Ningyo dolls and the various customs associated with the festival contributes to its rich cultural significance in Japan.

Ceadda's Day

Historical Figure: Saint Ceadda, also known as Saint Chad, was an Anglo-Saxon bishop and abbot in the 7th century.

Date of Commemoration: Ceadda's Day is celebrated on March 2nd, marking the anniversary of his death.

Ecclesiastical Role

Bishop of Mercia: Ceadda served as the Bishop of Mercia and later became the Bishop of the Northumbrians.

Monastic Leadership: He played a significant role in monastic life and held positions of leadership.

Christian Missionary Work

Conversion Efforts: Ceadda was involved in Christian missionary activities, contributing to the spread of Christianity in Anglo-Saxon England. He played a crucial role in the conversion of the Mercians.

Relationship with St. Cedd: Ceadda had a brother, Cedd, who was also a prominent figure in the Christianization of Anglo-Saxon England. Both brothers worked together on missionary endeavors.

Feast Day Observance: Ceadda's Day is observed annually on March 2nd in the liturgical calendar. The day serves as a commemoration of Saint Ceadda's life, his contributions to Christianity, and his death.

Religious Observances: On Ceadda's Day, churches may hold special services, prayers, and commemorations in honor of the saint. Monastic communities and religious institutions with connections to Ceadda may observe the day with particular solemnity.

Legacy and Influence: Ceadda is remembered for his historical importance in the early Christianization of England. His legacy has had a lasting impact on the cultural and religious history of the region.

Artistic Representations

Religious Art: Ceadda is sometimes represented in religious art, iconography, and stained glass windows in churches.

Depictions in Literature: His life and contributions are also depicted in literature, hagiographies, and historical writings.

Regional Observances: Ceadda's Day may be celebrated more prominently in regions with historical ties to the saint, such as Mercia and Northumbria. Some communities may have local traditions or events to mark the day.

Conclusion: Ceadda's Day is a day of commemoration honoring the life and contributions of Saint Ceadda, a figure who played a crucial role in the early Christianization of Anglo-Saxon England. The observance is marked by religious services, cultural acknowledgments, and recognition of his historical significance.

Ægir

Norse Mythology: The Sea Personified

Ægir's Realm: In Norse mythology, Ægir is a sea jötunn (giant) associated with the sea and ocean. He is often considered a benevolent deity, representing the unpredictable yet vital nature of the sea.

Role and Family

Sea God: Ægir is specifically recognized as a god of the sea and its elements.
Brother of Loki: In some accounts, Ægir is portrayed as the brother of Loki, the trickster god.

Gatherings at Ægir's Hall: Himminbjorg, Ægir is said to dwell in a hall named Himminbjorg beneath the ocean waves. He is known for hosting gatherings for the gods, particularly the Æsir, in his hall.

Brewer of Mead: One of Ægir's notable attributes is his skill in brewing ale and mead. He is described as hosting grand feasts where the gods gather to enjoy his crafted beverages.

Wife and Children: Ægir is often married to Rán, a sea goddess associated with the treacherous aspects of the sea.

Nine Daughters: According to some sources, Ægir and Rán have nine daughters, often personifications of waves.

Nautical Symbolism: Ægir's role extends to the symbolism of the sea in navigation and the unpredictable nature of maritime endeavors.

Offerings for Safe Voyages: Sailors might make offerings to Ægir for safe and prosperous journeys at sea.

Primary Sources: The primary sources for the mythology of Ægir are found in the Poetic Edda and Prose Edda, written in Old Norse.

Influence in Norse Literature:

Skaldic Poetry: Ægir is frequently mentioned in Skaldic poetry, reflecting the cultural significance of the sea and seafaring in Norse society.Cultural Imagination: His portrayal contributes to the Norse cultural imagination surrounding the sea and its dual nature.

Modern Adaptations

Literary and Artistic Works: Ægir continues to be featured in modern adaptations, including literature, art, and popular culture.
Symbol of the Sea: As a symbol, Ægir remains an embodiment of the sea's power and mysteries.

Conclusion: Deity of the Deep, Ægir, the Norse sea god, embodies the complexities of the sea—both its nurturing and unpredictable aspects. His role in hosting divine gatherings and crafting mead highlights the importance of the sea in Norse mythology and its enduring influence on cultural representations.

The Forty Saints

Origin and Significance: The Forty Saints, also known as the Holy Forty Martyrs, are venerated in Coptic Christian tradition.

Historical Period: They were Christian soldiers martyred during the reign of Emperor Licinius in the early 4th century.

The Forty Martyrs of Sebaste: The most well-known group of Forty Saints is the Forty Martyrs of Sebaste, a Roman province in modern-day Turkey.

Date of Martyrdom: They were martyred around 320 AD during the persecutions of Christians.

Martyrdom under Licinius

Winter Persecution: The Forty Martyrs faced persecution during winter and were exposed to extreme cold conditions as a form of punishment.

Refusal to Renounce Faith: Despite the harsh conditions, they refused to renounce their Christian faith.

Miraculous Intervention: According to legend, a warm bathhouse appeared miraculously to one of the martyrs who was wavering. Seeing this, the others chose to remain steadfast in their faith.

Survival of the Fittest: Only 39 of the original forty died, as one of the soldiers succumbed to the temptation and entered the warm bath, forfeiting his place among the martyrs.

Veneration and Feast Day: The Forty Saints are commemorated in the Coptic liturgical calendar, and their feast day is celebrated on Hathor 25 (around December 17 in the Gregorian calendar). The veneration of the Forty Saints extends to local Christian communities with a particular emphasis on Coptic Christianity.

Symbol of Christian Perseverance: The story of the Forty Martyrs symbolizes Christian perseverance in the face of adversity and the triumph of faith over worldly comforts. Their steadfastness serves as an inspiration for believers facing challenges to uphold their religious convictions.

Iconography and Art: The Forty Saints are often depicted in religious art, showcasing their endurance in the cold and their miraculous intervention.

Visual Representation: Iconography may feature the saints standing together In unity or entering the warm bath.

Coptic Pilgrimages: Pilgrimages to sites associated with the Forty Saints may be part of local traditions in Coptic Christian communities. Devotees may engage in prayers and rituals to honor the memory of the Forty Saints.

Martyrdom Symbolism in Christianity: The concept of martyrdom, as exemplified by the Forty Saints, is a universal theme in Christian traditions, emphasizing the sacrifice for one's faith. The Forty Saints, particularly the Forty Martyrs of Sebaste, have left an enduring legacy in Coptic Christian tradition. Their story of resilience and commitment to their faith continues to inspire believers and is commemorated annually as a testament to the triumph of spiritual convictions over temporal challenges.

St. Patrick's Day

Historical Celebration: St. Patrick's Day is celebrated annually on March 17th.

Patron Saint of Ireland: The day honors St. Patrick, the patron saint of Ireland, who is credited with bringing Christianity to the country.

St. Patrick's Life: St. Patrick was born in Britain, possibly in the late 4th century, and was captured by Irish raiders at the age of 16.

Escape and Religious Calling: After escaping captivity, he returned to Britain, received religious training, and had a vision calling him to convert the Irish to Christianity.

Missionary Work: St. Patrick is known for his missionary work in Ireland, baptizing converts and establishing churches.

Legends and Symbols: St. Patrick is often associated with the shamrock, which he used to explain the concept of the Holy Trinity (Father, Son, and Holy Spirit).

Driving Out Snakes: Legend suggests that St. Patrick drove snakes out of Ireland, symbolizing the expulsion of paganism.

Religious Observance

Feast Day: St. Patrick's Day is originally a feast day in the Catholic Church, commemorating St. Patrick's death.

Religious Services: Some observe the day with religious services, prayers, and processions.

Global Celebration: Irish Diaspora, St. Patrick's Day has become a global celebration, especially in countries with a significant Irish diaspora.

Parades and Festivals: Cities worldwide host parades, festivals, and events featuring Irish music, dance, and culture. Wearing green clothing and accessories is a popular tradition associated with St. Patrick's Day.

Festive Foods and Drinks: A traditional St. Patrick's Day meal is corned beef and cabbage. Celebrations often include Irish drinks, including stout, beer, and whiskey.

Irish Identity: St. Patrick's Day is a source of cultural pride for the Irish, fostering a sense of identity and heritage. The celebration provides an opportunity to showcase Irish music, dance, literature, and traditions.

Public Celebrations: Parades are a central feature of St. Patrick's Day celebrations, featuring floats, marching bands, and cultural displays.

Street Festivals: Street festivals with music, dance performances, and food stalls are common.

Commercialization: St. Patrick's Day has become commercialized with the sale of themed merchandise, decorations, and apparel. The day attracts tourists, and landmarks may be illuminated in green to mark the occasion. People of various backgrounds celebrate St. Patrick's Day, and it is not limited to those of Irish descent.

Conclusion: St. Patrick's Day combines religious observance with cultural celebrations, uniting people in the commemoration of Ireland's patron saint and the expression of Irish identity and heritage. The festivities have transcended national borders, making St. Patrick's Day a widely recognized and celebrated occasion around the world.

Saint Joseph's Day

Date: March 19th, Saint Joseph's Day is celebrated annually on March 19th.

Religious Significance: The day honors Saint Joseph, the earthly father of Jesus Christ, in Christian tradition.

Saint Joseph in Christian Tradition: Saint Joseph is a key figure in the New Testament and is described as the husband of Mary, the mother of Jesus. He is recognized for his role as the guardian and caretaker of Jesus during his childhood.

Liturgical Celebration: Saint Joseph's Day is a liturgical feast day in the Catholic Church. It is often celebrated with solemnity, especially in Catholic-majority regions.

Patron of Workers: Saint Joseph is recognized as the patron saint of workers, reflecting his role as a carpenter.

Protector of the Holy Family: He is also considered the protector of the Holy Family, providing care and guidance to Mary and Jesus.

Traditions and Customs

Altars: A notable tradition on Saint Joseph's Day is the creation of elaborate home altars dedicated to Saint Joseph. The altars are adorned with candles, flowers, statues, and symbolic items, often including a statue of Saint Joseph.

Fasting Tradition: Some communities observe a tradition of fasting on Saint Joseph's Day. The day culminates in a feast, often featuring traditional foods and special dishes.

Special Foods

St. Joseph's Day Bread: A specific type of bread, often shaped like a staff or a cross, is prepared for the occasion.

Zeppole: Zeppole, a type of Italian pastry, is a popular treat associated with Saint Joseph's Day.

Religious Services: Churches hold special masses and religious services in honor of Saint Joseph. Devotees may participate in prayers and devotional practices dedicated to Saint Joseph. Italian and Spanish Influence: Saint Joseph's Day is particularly celebrated with enthusiasm in Italian and Spanish cultures.

Community Gatherings: Some communities organize parades, processions, and cultural events to mark the day.

Symbolism and Reverence

Symbol of Fatherhood: Saint Joseph symbolizes fatherhood, humility, and dedication in Christian teachings. He is respected and revered as a model of virtue and obedience in fulfilling his role in the Holy Family.

Conclusion: Saint Joseph's Day serves as a time for spiritual reflection on the virtues associated with Saint Joseph, emphasizing his role in the Christian narrative and his influence as a patron saint. The day is marked by a combination of religious observances, cultural traditions, and communal celebrations, particularly in regions with a strong Catholic or Christian heritage.

Alban Eiler

Druidic Celebration: Alban Eiler, also known as the Spring Equinox, is a Druidic celebration observed by some modern Druids and Celtic neopagans. It is rooted in nature-based spirituality, emphasizing the significance of the spring equinox in the natural cycle.

Celtic Calendar

Four Fire Festivals: Alban Eiler is one of the four fire festivals in the Celtic calendar, representing the midpoint between the winter solstice and the summer solstice. Connection to Equinox: The festival aligns with the time when day and night are approximately equal, marking the balance between light and darkness.

The symbolism of Alban Eiler

Rebirth and Renewal: Alban Eiler symbolizes the themes of rebirth, renewal, and the awakening of nature after the dormancy of winter.

Fertility and Growth: The celebration is associated with fertility, growth, and the emergence of life in the natural world.

Rituals and Practices

Druidic Rituals: Druids and Celtic neopagans may perform rituals to honor the changing season and the energies associated with Alban Eiler. Many practitioners prefer to celebrate outdoors, connecting with nature and observing the signs of spring. Observing the changing landscape, blossoming flowers, and the return of wildlife are common activities during Alban Eiler.

Symbolic Offerings: Offerings to nature, such as planting seeds or making symbolic gestures, are part of the celebration.

Seasonal Altar: Altars may be decorated with symbols of spring, including flowers, fresh greens, and representations of eggs or hares.

Candle Lighting: Candles are often lit to symbolize the increasing strength of the sun.

Gatherings and Festivities: Some Druidic communities organize gatherings, festivals, or communal celebrations to mark Alban Eiler. Sharing meals and communal feasts are common, fostering a sense of community and connection.

Personalized Practices: Practices and interpretations of Alban Eiler may vary among individuals and Druidic traditions. Some modern celebrations may incorporate contemporary elements while maintaining the essence of Druidic spirituality.

Continued Relevance: Alban Eiler continues to be observed by modern Druids and those following Celtic neopagan paths. Practitioners may adapt traditional rituals to suit their contemporary understanding and context.

Conclusion: Alban Eiler reflects a nature-centric spirituality, embracing seasonal changes and the symbolic significance of the spring equinox in Druidic traditions. The celebration underscores the interconnectedness between the natural world and spiritual practices, fostering a sense of harmony and reverence for the cycles of nature.

Bacchanalia

Bacchanalia Origins: The Bacchanalia was an ancient Roman festival dedicated to Bacchus, the god of wine, fertility, and revelry. It was associated with mystery cults and involved secretive and ecstatic rites.

Date and Participants: Bacchanalia was celebrated in March, specifically during the Roman month of Bacchus. Initially, it was attended by women only, but over time, men also became part of the festivities.

Rituals and Practices

Dionysian Influences: The Bacchanalia drew inspiration from Greek Dionysian traditions involving wild and ecstatic rituals. Central to the festival was the consumption of wine to induce a state of intoxication, symbolizing the uninhibited nature of the celebration.

Secretive Nature

Mystery Cult Practices: Bacchanalia had an air of secrecy, with initiates participating in rituals that were not disclosed to outsiders.

Initiation Rites: Initiates underwent various rites of initiation, contributing to the mystique surrounding the festival.

Social and Sexual Freedom

Libertinism: Bacchanalia provided an opportunity for participants to indulge in social and sexual freedom. During the festival, normal social conventions were set aside, and participants engaged in behaviors that would be frowned upon in regular Roman society. Suppression by the Roman Senate, the Bacchanalia faced accusations of excess, immorality, and political conspiracies. In 186 BCE, the Roman Senate issued a decree (Senatus consultum de Bacchanalibus) suppressing the Bacchanalia due to concerns about its potential subversive nature.

Prohibitions: The Senate's decree included strict prohibitions against the Bacchanalia, limiting the number of participants and imposing penalties for those who defied the ban.

Prosecutions: Authorities actively prosecuted individuals associated with the Bacchanalia, leading to arrests and the dismantling of Bacchic groups.

Historical Sources: Livy, the Roman historian, provides a detailed account of the Bacchanalia and the Senate's actions in his work "History of Rome."

Varied Perspectives: Different historical sources may offer varying perspectives on the nature and significance of the Bacchanalia.

Cultural Impact: The Bacchanalia has left its mark on literature, arts, and later cultural representations, often serving as a symbol of unrestrained revelry.

Conclusion: The Bacchanalia, while initially a religious celebration, became controversial due to accusations of excess and conspiracy. Its suppression by the Roman Senate reflects the tension between religious freedom and concerns about social and political upheaval in ancient Rome.

Prince Kuhio Day

Hawaiian Holiday: Prince Kuhio Day is a state holiday in Hawaii commemorating the birth of Prince Jonah Kuhio Kalaniana'ole.

Date of Celebration: It is observed annually on March 26th.

Born into Royalty: Prince Kuhio (1871–1922) was a member of the Hawaiian royal family and a prince in the Kingdom of Hawaii.

Advocate for Hawaiians: He became a notable political figure, advocating for the rights and well-being of Native Hawaiians.

Legacy and Contributions: Prince Kuhio served as the congressional delegate for Hawaii, representing the territory in the United States Congress.

Efforts for Hawaiians: He worked to improve conditions for Hawaiians, focusing on issues such as land rights, education, and health care.

Hawaiian Homelands Act: Prince Kuhio was a key figure in the passage of the Hawaiian Homes Commission Act of 1920, also known as the Hawaiian Homelands Act. The act aimed to provide Native Hawaiians with designated lands for agricultural and residential purposes.

Celebration and Observance

Cultural and Civic Events: Prince Kuhio Day is marked by various cultural and civic events across Hawaii. Schools and community organizations often organize educational programs to highlight Prince Kuhio's contributions.

Traditional Observances

Hula Performances: Traditional Hawaiian hula performances may be part of the celebrations.

Ceremonies and Gatherings: Ceremonies, gatherings, and commemorations take place at important sites associated with Prince Kuhio.

Recognition of Hawaiian Culture:

Preserving Heritage: Prince Kuhio Day serves as a day to honor and preserve Hawaiian heritage, traditions, and the cultural identity of Native Hawaiians. It fosters a sense of cultural pride and unity among the people of Hawaii.

Statewide Holiday: Prince Kuhio Day is a state holiday, and government offices, schools, and some businesses in Hawaii may be closed in observance.

Conclusion: Prince Kuhio Day stands as a tribute to the life and legacy of Prince Jonah Kuhio Kalaniana'ole, recognizing his efforts in advocating for the rights and well-being of Native Hawaiians. The holiday is a testament to his enduring impact on Hawaiian culture, governance, and land reform.

Borrowed Days

Celtic Folklore: Borrowed Days is a traditional weather lore observed in Celtic folklore, particularly in Ireland and Scotland.

Spring Equinox Connection: It is associated with a period of borrowed or stolen days around the time of the spring equinox.

Time of Occurrence: Late March to Early April. Borrowed Days are said to occur from late March to early April.

Shift in Weather Patterns: It marks a period when there can be a noticeable shift in weather patterns.

Folk Belief

Borrowing Days from April: The folklore suggests that the last three days of March borrow or steal days from the month of April. The weather during these borrowed days is believed to influence the coming weeks.

Weather Predictions: Borrowed Days are associated with unpredictable weather patterns, with days alternating between winter-like conditions and glimpses of spring. Frost and Sunshine: Folklore suggests that frosty or wintry conditions may occur during these days, followed by sunshine.

Observation in Folk Calendar: The concept of Borrowed Days is part of the folk calendar, where specific dates are associated with agricultural and seasonal observations.

Agricultural Implications: Farmers and communities may take note of the weather during this period for its potential impact on crops and planting.

Transition from Winter to Spring: Borrowed Days symbolize the transitional phase between winter and spring.

Nature's Unpredictability: The lore reflects the unpredictability of nature during this time, with lingering winter conditions and the emergence of spring.

Folk Rhyme Tradition: Borrowed Days are often referenced in a traditional rhyme: "March borrowed from April Three days, and they were ill; The first was frost, the second was snaw, The third was cauld as ever't could blaw."

Agricultural Practices

Impact on Planting: Farmers may consider the weather during Borrowed Days when planning spring planting. The lore may caution against premature planting due to potential late frosts.

Regional Interpretations: Variations of the Borrowed Days lore exist in different regions, with local communities adapting the tradition to their specific climate and agricultural practices.

Conclusion: Borrowed Days offers cultural insights into the way communities historically interpreted and navigated the transitional period between winter and spring. Rooted in folklore, this tradition reflects the observance of nature's nuances and the importance of weather predictions in agricultural practices.

Ramadan

Islamic Holy Month: Ramadan is the ninth month of the Islamic lunar calendar.
Holiest Month: It is considered the holiest month in Islam.
Fasting (Sawm): The most prominent aspect of Ramadan is fasting, known as Sawm.
Abstaining from Food and Drink: Muslims refrain from eating and drinking from dawn (Fajr) until sunset (Maghrib).
Self-Discipline: Fasting is a practice of self-discipline, self-control, and empathy for the less fortunate. Ramadan is a time for increased spiritual reflection, prayer, and devotion.
Quranic Revelation: Ramadan is believed to be the month during which the first verses of the Quran were revealed to Prophet Muhammad.
Night of Power (Laylat al-Qadr): Laylat al-Qadr, or the Night of Power, falls within the last ten nights of Ramadan and is considered highly significant.
Suhoor: The pre-dawn meal before fasting begins at Fajr.
Iftar: The meal to break the fast is called Iftar, and it is done at Maghrib.
Increased Acts of Worship
Tarawih Prayers: Special nightly prayers called Tarawih are performed during Ramadan. Muslims aim to read the entire Quran during the month.
Charity and Generosity
Zakat and Sadaqah: Muslims are encouraged to increase acts of charity, including giving Zakat (obligatory almsgiving) and Sadaqah (voluntary charity). Ramadan emphasizes community support and caring for those in need.
Eid al-Fitr: Celebration at the End: Ramadan concludes with the celebration of Eid al-Fitr. Muslims gather for prayers, feasts, and festivities to mark the end of fasting.
Fasting Exceptions: Certain individuals, such as the sick, elderly, pregnant women, and young children, are exempt from fasting.
Makeup Fasts: Those unable to fast due to valid reasons may compensate by fasting at a later time.
Worldwide Participation: Ramadan is observed by Muslims worldwide, creating a sense of unity and shared devotion. Cultural and regional variations exist in how Ramadan is observed, but the core principles remain consistent.
Personal Development: Ramadan is seen as an opportunity for personal growth, increased piety, and strengthening one's connection with Allah.
Renewal of Intentions: Muslims use the month to renew their intentions, seek forgiveness, and purify their hearts.
Conclusion: Holistic Spiritual Experience: Ramadan provides a holistic spiritual experience for Muslims, encompassing fasting, prayer, charity, and community. It is a time of self-improvement, increased devotion, and a deepened connection to the teachings of Islam.

April Fool's Day

Date: April Fools' Day is observed annually on April 1st.

Origin and History: The exact origin of April Fools' Day is uncertain and has various historical explanations.

Historical Traditions: It has been linked to different cultural traditions, including changing the New Year's date and medieval festivals.

Practical Jokes: April Fools' Day is known for the tradition of playing practical jokes and pranks on friends, family, and colleagues.

Humorous Intent: The pranks are typically harmless and intended to be humorous rather than harmful.

Global Observance: April Fools' Day is observed in many countries worldwide, each with its own variations of pranks and customs.

Media Participation: Media outlets, companies, and individuals often participate by creating elaborate hoaxes or jokes.

Fool's Errands: Traditional activities include sending someone on a "fool's errand," a task with no real purpose.

Unusual Stories: Spreading false or unusual stories to deceive others is a common element.

Morning Pranks: In some cultures, pranks are played only in the morning, and if someone falls for a prank after noon, the prankster may be considered the fool.

Famous Hoaxes

Media Hoaxes: Over the years, media outlets have orchestrated famous April Fools' Day hoaxes, including fictitious news stories and announcements.

Creative Pranks: Companies and individuals engage in creative and imaginative pranks to capture attention.

Different Traditions: While the essence of pranking remains consistent, different countries may have specific traditions and customs associated with April Fools' Day. Regional Preferences: The nature and acceptance of pranks can vary across cultures.

Online Pranks: With the rise of social media, online pranks and hoaxes have become prevalent on April Fools' Day.

Digital Jokes: Companies and internet users often share humorous content, and some online platforms may feature special features for the day.

Prank Etiquette: The general etiquette for April Fools' Day pranks is to keep them good-natured and avoid causing harm or distress.

Revealing Pranks: It is customary to reveal the prank by saying "April Fools!" after the joke is played.

Conclusion: April Fools' Day is a light-hearted and playful tradition where people engage in pranks and jokes for amusement. The day is characterized by a sense of humor and a willingness to participate in playful activities with a spirit of fun and laughter.

Qingming Festival

Date Spring Equinox: The Qingming Festival, also known as Tomb-Sweeping Day, typically falls around April 4th or 5th of the Gregorian calendar.

Solar Terms: It is based on the solar terms and usually aligns with the spring equinox.

Cultural Significance: Qingming is a traditional Chinese festival with cultural and historical significance. The primary purpose is to honor ancestors by visiting their gravesites and performing rituals.

Tomb-Sweeping Rituals: Families visit the graves of their ancestors to clean and sweep the tombstones and surrounding areas.

Offerings: People offer food, incense, and other symbolic items as a sign of respect to their deceased loved ones.

Outdoor Activities: Qingming is also a time when people engage in outdoor activities, enjoying the arrival of spring.

Kite Flying: Flying kites is a popular activity during Qingming, with many regions hosting kite festivals.

Historical Roots: Qingming has ancient roots, with practices dating back over 2,500 years. It was originally known as Jingtian, a day for purification and the start of spring plowing.

Regulations on Fire and Air Travel: Some regions may have regulations on open-air burning during Qingming to address environmental concerns. In certain areas, restrictions on flying kites and lanterns may be implemented to avoid accidents.

Traditional Foods

Qingtuan: A traditional food associated with Qingming is qingtuan, a glutinous rice ball filled with sweet red bean paste or other fillings.

Cold Foods: Eating cold foods is a tradition linked to Qingming, symbolizing the transition from winter to spring.

Cultural Customs: In some regions, people may wear willow branches to ward off evil spirits and promote good health. Swinging on swings is another custom in certain areas during Qingming.

Modern Observance

Public Holiday: The Qingming Festival is a public holiday in China, and many people take the day off to pay respects to their ancestors. Some local governments organize official ceremonies to commemorate historical figures.

Conclusion: The Qingming Festival embodies cultural reverence for ancestors and the transition to spring. The combination of tomb-sweeping rituals, outdoor activities, and traditional customs makes it a significant and widely observed festival in Chinese communities.

Passover

Religious Significance: Passover, also known as Pesach, is a major Jewish festival.

Biblical Origins: It commemorates the liberation of the Israelites from slavery in ancient Egypt, as narrated in the Book of Exodus.

Spring Festival: Passover is observed in the spring, typically in March or April of the Gregorian calendar.

Eight Days: In Judaism, Passover is observed for eight days, but in Israel and for some Jewish denominations, it lasts for seven days.

Seder Meal: The central event of Passover is the Seder, a ritualistic meal held on the first night (and sometimes the second night) of the festival.

Haggadah: The Haggadah, a guidebook, is read during the Seder, recounting the Exodus story and detailing the symbolic foods.

Symbolic Foods

Matzah: Unleavened bread, known as matzah, is a key element, symbolizing the haste with which the Israelites left Egypt.

Maror and Charoset: Bitter herbs (maror) and a mixture of fruit and nuts (charoset) represent the bitterness of slavery and mortar used in the building.

Dietary Restrictions: During Passover, leavened products (chametz) are prohibited. Only unleavened bread is consumed.

Kosher for Passover: Foods must be certified as "Kosher for Passover" to adhere to dietary restrictions.

Exodus Story

Ten Plagues: The narrative includes the ten plagues inflicted upon Egypt, culminating in the Passover event.

Bedikat Chametz: Before Passover begins, a ritual called bedikat chametz involves searching for and removing any remaining leavened products from the home.

Burning Chametz: Chametz found during the search is traditionally burned.

Family and Community Observance

Home Celebrations: Passover is often celebrated at home with family and friends participating in the Seder. Some communities organize communal Seders, and synagogues may host special services.

Universal Theme: Passover's theme of liberation resonates universally, symbolizing freedom from oppression.

Social Justice Emphasis: The festival is often associated with social justice, promoting empathy and compassion for those experiencing oppression.

Conclusion: Historical and Religious Significance: Passover holds profound historical and religious significance in Judaism, commemorating the Exodus and emphasizing themes of freedom, redemption, and the importance of justice. The rituals and traditions associated with Passover continue to be observed by Jewish communities worldwide.

Chaul Chnam Thmey

Cambodian New Year: Chaul Chnam Thmey, also known as Khmer New Year, is the traditional Cambodian New Year celebration.

April Celebration: Chaul Chnam Thmey is typically celebrated in April, marking the end of the harvest season.

Theravada Buddhist Influence: The festival is deeply rooted in Theravada Buddhist traditions.

Solar New Year: The festival coincides with the Solar New Year. Chaul Chnam Thmey is a three-day celebration, though festivities may extend beyond this period in some regions.

Spiritual and Cultural Practices: The festival includes various Buddhist rituals, prayers, and visits to pagodas for spiritual merit.

Cleansing Ceremonies: Houses and public spaces are cleaned to symbolize the purification of the old year.

Water Festival: Water plays a significant role in the celebration, symbolizing purification and the washing away of sins and bad luck. People engage in water-throwing activities, similar to the Songkran Festival in Thailand.

Traditional Foods and Offerings: Traditional Khmer dishes are prepared for the celebrations, and families come together for festive meals.

Offerings to Ancestors: Offerings are made to ancestors, and prayers are dedicated to seeking blessings for the upcoming year.

Ceremonial Observances: Candle processions are held at pagodas and in communities, symbolizing the dispelling of darkness and ignorance.

Robam Tep Apsara: The traditional Apsara dance may be performed during celebrations. Festivities include traditional Khmer music, dance performances, and cultural events. Parades featuring vibrant costumes and traditional music are common.

Family-Centric: Chaul Chnam Thmey is a time for family reunions and gatherings, fostering a sense of unity and shared joy.

Respect for Elders: Younger generations pay respects to elders, seeking their blessings.

National Holiday: Chaul Chnam Thmey is a national holiday in Cambodia, and businesses, schools, and government offices may close during the celebrations.

Countrywide Observance: The festival is observed throughout Cambodia, with both urban and rural communities participating.

Conclusion: Chaul Chnam Thmey is a celebration rich in cultural and religious traditions, reflecting the importance of spirituality, family, and community in Cambodian society. The festivities bring people together to welcome the new year with joy, gratitude, and a sense of renewal.

Easter

Central Christian Festival: Easter is a central and significant festival in Christianity, commemorating the resurrection of Jesus Christ from the dead.

Resurrection Sunday: The primary focus is on the resurrection, believed to have occurred on the third day after Jesus' crucifixion.

Spring Observance: Easter is celebrated in the spring, typically between March and April.

Moveable Feast: The date varies each year and is a moveable feast in the Christian liturgical calendar.

Lead-up to Easter: Holy Week precedes Easter and includes events such as Maundy Thursday (Last Supper), Good Friday (Crucifixion), and Holy Saturday (Jesus' burial).

Liturgical Observances: Christian denominations observe Holy Week with special liturgical services.

Resurrection Narrative: The resurrection is narrated in the New Testament of the Bible, with the Gospels providing details of the empty tomb and the appearances of Jesus to his disciples.

Symbol of Victory: Easter symbolizes victory over sin and death, emphasizing hope and redemption.

Symbolism and Traditions: Eggs symbolize new life and are often associated with Easter. Decorated eggs and egg hunts are common traditions.

Easter Bunny: The Easter Bunny is a secular symbol of the holiday, often depicted bringing Easter eggs to children.

Sunrise Services: Many Christian communities hold sunrise services on Easter Sunday, symbolizing the dawn of the Resurrection. Churches conduct special Easter services, including the proclamation of the Resurrection.

White and Gold: Liturgical colors for Easter include white and gold, symbolizing purity, joy, and the glory of the Resurrection.

Symbol of Christ: The Paschal Candle, often lit during Easter services, symbolizes the presence of Christ as the light of the world. It is also associated with themes of renewal and baptism.

Easter Foods: Traditional Easter meals often include ham, lamb, or other festive dishes. Different cultures have special Easter breads, each with its own significance.

Public Holidays: Easter is a public holiday in many countries, with businesses and schools closed.

Parades and Festivities: Some regions host parades, festivals, and cultural events during the Easter weekend.

Conclusion: Easter holds profound spiritual significance for Christians, representing the core of the Christian faith—the resurrection of Jesus. Alongside religious observances, it has become a cultural and secular celebration marked by various traditions and symbols.

Walpurgisnacht

Cultural and Folklore Tradition: Walpurgisnacht, also known as Walpurgis Night or the Night of the Witches, is a cultural and folklore tradition celebrated on the night of April 30th.

Historical and Folkloric Origins: The tradition is named after Saint Walpurga, an 8th-century Christian missionary. The date corresponds to the eve of her feast day.

Pagan Roots: Walpurgisnacht has roots in pre-Christian, pagan celebrations that marked the arrival of spring and the expulsion of winter spirits.

Beltane Connection: The celebration is often associated with Beltane, an ancient Celtic festival marking the beginning of the warmer season.

Warding Off Winter Spirits: Walpurgisnacht is believed to involve rituals and activities to ward off the last remnants of winter and evil spirits.

Folk Customs and Practices: Bonfires are a central element of Walpurgisnacht, symbolizing the cleansing and protective power of fire.

Costumes and Masks: Participants may wear costumes and masks, often depicting witches or other supernatural beings.

Dancing and Revelry: Festivities include dancing, singing, and general merrymaking, often in outdoor settings.

Folk Beliefs

Witchcraft and Spirits: Walpurgisnacht is associated with superstitions about witches gathering to engage in rituals and mischief. Some communities perform protective rites and rituals on this night to guard against malevolent forces.

Regional Variations

Northern and Central Europe: Walpurgisnacht is particularly celebrated in Northern and Central European countries, including Germany, Sweden, Finland, and the Czech Republic.

Local Traditions: Different regions may have unique customs and local variations of the celebration.

Cultural Event: In modern times, Walpurgisnacht is often celebrated as a cultural event and an opportunity for community gatherings. Certain locations with strong traditions, such as the Harz Mountains in Germany, attract tourists for special Walpurgisnacht celebrations.

Fictional Representations: Walpurgisnacht is featured in various literary works and cultural references, often depicting mystical and supernatural elements.

Contemporary Significance: While rooted in historical and folkloric traditions, Walpurgisnacht is also embraced as a celebration of the arrival of spring and the triumph of light over darkness.

Conclusion: Walpurgisnacht is a blend of historical Christian elements and pre-Christian pagan traditions. It continues to be celebrated in diverse ways, blending folklore, superstitions, and community festivities in various regions.

CHAPTER 7

Crafts

Ostara Eggs to Decorate

Eggs have long been symbolic in various cultures, and Ukrainian folk art offers some of the most exquisite examples of ceremonial egg decoration. This tradition, passed down from mothers to daughters, involves two primary forms of decoration, Krashanka and Pysanka.

Krashanka eggs are dyed in a single brilliant color, derived from the word "kraska," meaning "color." These eggs were not only consumed but also believed to possess talismanic properties. They were used as defensive charms against high winds and were even buried to protect crops from disruptive weather.

Pysanky, on the other hand, are elaborately decorated with symbols and colors, derived from the word "pysaty," meaning "to write." These eggs were not eaten but displayed in households, worn as talismans, or given as gifts. Pysanky were believed to offer protection from fire and lightning, and according to tradition, they held sway over the destiny of the world.

To make your own krashanka, begin by hard-boiling eggs and then dyeing them using natural vegetable dyes. For red, try beets; for light blue, yellow onion skins; for green, spinach skins; and for orange, cabbage. Allow the eggs to soak in the dye overnight for vibrant colors, and then dry them in an egg carton.

Pysanky-making is a more intricate process. These eggs are decorated raw and are not intended for consumption. Symbols and motifs are inscribed onto the eggshell using wax before dyeing. Special tools called kistky are used to apply the wax designs. While krashanka eggs can be disposed of after use, it is believed to be bad luck to discard them carelessly. Burning or casting the shells into running water is the traditional way to dispose of them respectfully.

The tradition of Ostara egg decoration is both beautiful and rich in cultural significance, offering a glimpse into Ukrainian folklore and craftsmanship.

Pysanky

Pysanky, rooted in Ukrainian folklore and cultural traditions, are intricately decorated Easter eggs with deep mythological significance. Pysanky symbolizes various aspects of life and nature. Common symbols include the sun, which represents life and warmth, and the rooster, symbolizing protection against evil spirits.

Ancient Origins: The tradition of creating pysanky dates back thousands of years, with evidence suggesting its existence in ancient times. The eggs were initially associated with spring rituals, fertility, and protection.

Pre-Christian Beliefs: Pysanky making was part of pre-Christian spring rituals. The eggs were believed to possess magical properties, offering protection from misfortune and ensuring fertility and abundance.

Adoption of Christian Symbolism: With the spread of Christianity, pysanky became intertwined with Christian symbolism. The cross, fish, and other Christian motifs found their way onto the decorated eggs, blending ancient and Christian beliefs.

Technique and Materials: Pysanky are created using a wax-resist method. Beeswax is applied to the eggshell, covering areas that the artist wants to remain the egg's original color. The egg is then dipped in dye, and the wax is reapplied to preserve the existing colors or create new patterns.

Color Symbolism: Different colors on pysanky carry specific meanings. For instance, yellow represents wealth and fertility, while red symbolizes the passion and the joy of life.

Regional Variations: Various regions in Ukraine have distinct pysanky styles and color palettes. These regional variations often reflect the local folklore, traditions, and cultural influences.

Pagan Roots: Many pysanky designs trace their origins to pagan beliefs. The geometric patterns and symbols on the eggs were thought to harness the power of nature and protect against evil.

Modern Celebrations: Pysanky making remains a cherished tradition in Ukrainian communities, especially during the Easter season. Workshops, exhibitions, and festivals showcase the artistry and cultural significance of pysanky.

Cultural Heritage: Pysanky are not only artistic expressions but also a reflection of Ukrainian cultural heritage. The intricate designs and symbolism embedded in these eggs continue to be passed down through generations, preserving a rich and ancient tradition.

Creating pysanky involves a traditional wax-resist method, resulting in beautifully decorated eggs. Here are the basic instructions.

Ingredients:
White eggs (raw)
Beeswax
Pysanky dyes or food coloring
Small containers for dyeing
Kistka (stylus for applying wax)
Candle or electric wax pen
Pencil or light pencil marks (optional for design guidelines)

Instructions:
Prepare the Eggs: Start with clean, white eggs. Ensure they are at room temperature. If using pencil marks for design guidelines, lightly sketch your design on the egg.
Apply Beeswax: Heat the beeswax in a small container using a candle or an electric wax pen until it becomes liquid.
Using the kistka, apply the melted wax to areas where you want to preserve the egg's white color.
First Dye Bath: Dip the egg into the lightest dye color. The wax will resist the dye, protecting the covered areas. Allow the egg to dry completely.
Additional Wax Application: Apply wax to areas where you want to retain the first color. These are the parts that will remain the color of the first dye.
Second Dye Bath: Dip the egg into the next darker dye color. The wax will once again protect the covered areas. Allow the egg to dry completely.
Repeat the Process: Continue applying wax and dyeing the egg in a sequence of colors, going from lighter to darker shades. Each time you apply wax, you're preserving the colors underneath.
Final Wax Application: For the last color, cover the entire egg with wax to preserve the final color.
Final Dye Bath: Dip the egg into the darkest dye color. Allow the egg to dry completely.
Remove Wax: Gently heat the egg (using a candle flame or warm oven) to melt and wipe away the wax, revealing the intricate, multicolored design.
Seal and Polish: Optionally, seal the egg with a clear sealant to protect the colors. Polish the egg with a soft cloth for a glossy finish.
Display or Gift: Your pysanka is now ready to be displayed or given as a meaningful and artistic gift.

Note: Exercise caution when working with hot wax, and ensure proper ventilation when using dyes. This recipe provides a basic guide, and you can explore various design techniques and color combinations based on your creativity and cultural influences.

Colored Egg Traditions

Coloring eggs is a cherished tradition observed across diverse cultures worldwide, frequently entwined with distinct festivals and celebrations. From vibrant Easter eggs in Western traditions to intricately decorated pysanky in Ukrainian culture, the practice of coloring eggs holds significant cultural and symbolic significance, reflecting the rich tapestry of global customs and rituals.

Greece: In Greece, red eggs are a significant part of Easter celebrations. The eggs are dyed red to symbolize the blood of Christ and the renewal of life.

Iran: In Iran, particularly during Nowruz (Persian New Year), colored eggs are part of the Haft-Seen table setting, symbolizing fertility and new beginnings.

Germany: Germans celebrate Easter by decorating eggs, often using vibrant colors and intricate patterns. These eggs are then hidden for children to find in Easter egg hunts.

Poland: Poland has a rich tradition of decorating eggs, known as pisanki. Similar to Ukrainian pysanky, these eggs are often adorned with intricate designs and vibrant colors.

Balkan Countries: Various Balkan countries, including Bulgaria and Romania, have traditions of coloring eggs for Easter. Red is a common color symbolizing joy and happiness.

Egypt: In Egypt, it's customary during the spring holiday of Sham El Nessim to color and decorate eggs. The eggs are often part of picnics and celebrations.

China: During the Chinese Spring Festival, eggs are often dyed red for good luck and prosperity. The red color is considered auspicious.

Armenia: Colored eggs are also part of Armenian Easter celebrations. Similar to other traditions, the eggs are often red and symbolize the blood of Christ.

United States: While not tied to a specific cultural or religious tradition, coloring eggs is a common practice during the Easter season in the United States. Families often engage in egg dyeing activities.

Seed Packet Cards

Embrace the spirit of spring by ushering in the planting season with a touch of magic – Seed Packet Greeting Cards. Whether you have a sprawling garden or just a few pots in your kitchen, the joy of growing your own plants is unparalleled.

Seeds embody the promise of new life, and what better way to share this promise than through seed packet greeting cards? These charming cards make for delightful surprises during Ostara, reviving the almost-forgotten art of sending personalized greetings. Your loved ones will not only cherish the handwritten notes received during this sabbat but will also find themselves tempted to embark on a gardening journey, especially if they haven't explored it before.

Materials You'll Need:
Envelopes
Pre-cut blank greeting cards
Seed packets
Pens and markers
Glue stick
Various craft supplies

Directions:
Create a list of recipients and choose a packet of seeds for each card.
Attach the seed packet to the front of the card, using a small amount of glue to ensure it's securely fastened without touching the seeds.

Craft an upbeat message on the inside of the card using a pen or marker. Feel free to embellish the surrounding area with glitter and other art supplies.

Once the glue is dry, place the cards into envelopes marked with the recipient's name.

While gifting seed packets for Ostara is a wonderful way to connect with friends and family, there's no need to wait for a special occasion. Sending these cards throughout the year, for birthdays or other significant moments, is a thoughtful gesture that transcends seasons. After all, the joy of planting seeds knows no bounds and can be shared anytime, making these greeting cards a heartwarming and versatile expression of care.

CHAPTER 8

Hot Cross Buns

Hot cross buns are a delicious pastry that people have enjoyed for years.

Ingredients:

Dough

3 cups of flour

¾ cup of sugar

1 cup of whole milk

¼ cup of melted butter or margarine

⅛ teaspoon of salt

1½ teaspoons of cinnamon

¼ teaspoon of allspice (this ingredient is optional)

1 cup of raisins (this ingredient
is also optional)

1 cup of walnuts (also optional)

28 grams of dry yeast

¼ cup of hot water to dissolve the dry yeast

1 large egg, well-beaten Frosting:

1 cup of orange juice

1 tablespoon of milk

2 cups of confectioner's sugar

Instructions:

Preheat the oven to 375 degrees

Combine all of the dough ingredients except the hot water, egg, and yeast.

Add the hot water to the yeast and let it dissolve.

After the yeast dissolves, add the egg and the mixture.

After mixing the dough's ingredients, cover it with a cloth and leave it for an hour to rise in a warm place.

Now that the dough is ready, shape them into round balls about 3 inches across.

Place the balls about 3 inches apart on a lightly greased cookie sheet or a jelly roll pan.

Now, put the dough sheet in the oven. Wait for about 5 to 8 minutes.

Open the oven and remove the buns.

Cut ¾ of an inch down into the dough using a knife and carve equilateral crosses on top. After you are done, put the buns back in the oven and leave them to bake for about 15 to 20 minutes.

When they turn to a brown-gold color, they are done, and you can remove them from the oven.

During the 20 minutes, when the buns are in the oven, you can start making the frosting. Mix all of the frosting ingredients and beat them until they are smooth and consistent.

After removing them from the oven, add the frosting on top of the buns.

It is important to drizzle the frosting when the buns are still hot.

Ostara Peep Ambrosia

Ostara peep ambrosia is a dessert that is very easy to make. It is the perfect dish for the Ostara celebration.

Ingredients:
2 cans of pineapple tidbits
2 cups of shredded coconut flakes
2 cans of mandarin oranges
2 bananas, chopped
1 package of 12 marshmallow peeps
1 jar of maraschino cherries
1.75 grams of cottage cheese
1.5 grams of any dessert topping

Instructions:
Cut the peeps into small pieces
Squeeze the juice from the fruits mentioned in the ingredients.
Combine and mix all of the ingredients together
Leave the mixture in the fridge for a few hours
Take it out of the fridge and serve it as a dessert

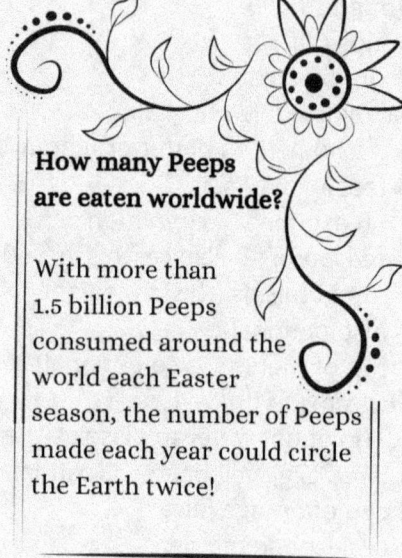

How many Peeps are eaten worldwide?

With more than 1.5 billion Peeps consumed around the world each Easter season, the number of Peeps made each year could circle the Earth twice!

Bath for Peacefulness

This soothing and comforting bath soak blend is meant to bring you peace of mind but also to awaken your psychic abilities, making it an excellent way to end a long day and prepare for ritual and magic.

Just so you know, essential oils are called for in this recipe, which you should be careful about if you have sensitive skin. Also, coconut oil can make for a slippery bathtub, so step carefully and give the tub a good wipe-down after your bath.

You will need:
1 to 2 cups whole milk or oat milk
2 cups Epsom salts
1 tbsp. coconut oil
1 tbsp. aloe vera gel
13 drops of sandalwood essential oil
13 drops of jasmine essential oil

Directions:
Draw the water and slowly add all the ingredients into the tub.
To heighten this experience, consider lighting candles and adding a piece or two of moonstone to the water before you get in.

CHAPTER 9

Spells

Ostara Egg Spell

Renewal and Abundance

Ingredients
Decorated Ostara egg (preferably hand-painted or adorned with symbols of fertility and growth)
Fresh spring flowers (such as daffodils, tulips, or hyacinths)
A small bowl of water
Spring herbs (like lavender, rosemary, or mint)
A green candle
Optional: crystals associated with renewal and abundance (such as green aventurine, clear quartz, or citrine)
Instructions:

Prepare Your Sacred Space: Find a quiet and undisturbed area where you can work your spell. Set up your altar or workspace with the spring flowers, herbs, bowl of water, and the decorated Ostara egg placed at its center. Arrange the crystals around the egg if you choose to use them.

Light the Green Candle: As you light the candle, focus on its flame and visualize it as a beacon of growth, renewal, and abundance. Feel its warmth and energy radiating throughout your space.

Invoke the Spirits of Spring: Call upon the spirits of spring, fertility, and growth to join you in your spell. You can use your own words or a simple invocation like:
"Spirits of spring, I call to thee,
Bring forth renewal and fertility.
As the earth awakens from its sleep,
Bless this egg that I now keep."
Repeat this invocation three times, allowing the energy to build with each repetition.

Dip the Egg in Water: Gently dip the egg into the bowl of water, symbolizing the cleansing and purifying influence of spring rains. As you do this, visualize any stagnant or negative energy being washed away, leaving behind only pure, fertile energy. Arrange the spring herbs and flowers around the egg, creating a vibrant and colorful display. As you do this, visualize the energy of spring infusing the herbs and flowers, filling your space with their life-giving essence.

Closing: Take a moment to express gratitude to the spirits of spring for their presence and assistance in your spell. You can extinguish the candle, but keep the decorated Ostara egg as a symbol of renewal and abundance throughout the season.

Ostara Spring Equinox Spell

Renewal
Ingredients
White, green, and yellow candles
Spring flowers and herbs
Bowl of water
Optional: crystals associated with the equinox

Instructions
Set up altar with candles in a triangular formation.
Light candles, invoking energies of spring.
Center yourself and connect with equinox energy.

Invoke spirits of spring with a simple invocation.
"As Ostara approaches,
I call upon the energies of spring,
Renewal, growth, and abundance it will bring.
With balance and harmony, let new beginnings start,
Bless this sacred space and open my heart."

Charge the water with spring energy.
Infuse herbs and flowers with intentions for renewal.
Set intentions for growth and abundance.
Express gratitude and blow out candles.
Optionally charge crystals with spell energy.
Carry spell's energy with you through spring.
Remember, intent and connection are key to the spell's potency.

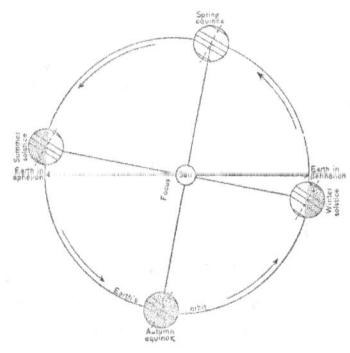

Windy Wishing Spell

This spell is a simple one to try out when you have a wish you'd like to send out into the universe. You can do this spell when you need to, but if you want to time it with astrology magically, you can perform it on a Wednesday or when the Moon is in Gemini, Libra, or Aquarius.

Ingredients:
A mixing bowl
Dandelion seeds (from one or two dandelions)
1 tsp. fennel seeds
1 tsp. lavender herbs
1 tsp. thyme herbs
Optional: crystal quartz

Directions:
Mix all the herbs and seeds in the mixing bowl.
Place the mixed contents in a bag with crystal quartz. Take the bag to a high-lookout point or a windy location where you will have privacy. Hold the bag in your hands and consider the wish you would like to have granted. What would help you right now? You can use your mind to see the results of having that wish granted.
Take a moment to take deep, slow breaths, feeling the air move through your body.

Say the following incantation:
"Air moves through me; magic flows on the breeze. May divinity in the sky hear my wish and support me. My wish is: (say your wish)."

Take a small handful of the ingredients from your bag and blow it into the wind. Repeat this three times.

Tobacco Water

This water is said to protect property from any that would do harm to your property.
Warning: This tincture is highly flammable. Burn outside in a fire safe area only.
Glass Bottle (Cleansed), Dried Red Rose Tobacco (Sweet cigar, crumbled), Alcohol (Rubbing) or any flammable liquid. Enchant each ingredient as you place it in the bottle. Seal bottle. Shake. Let it sit for nine days. Pour mixture on concrete at the house entrances and light on fire. Fire activates the spell.

Saturn Protection Ring

This simple spell calls on the protective energies of Saturn and the symbolism of this planet's infamous rings. Hematite rings absorb negativity and protect the wearer from negative energy and harm. They are affordable and easy to find in metaphysical shops. You will need just one hematite ring for this spell, which is best performed on a Saturday.

Cleanse your hematite ring of any unwanted energies by running it through purifying smoke or leaving it in direct sunlight for a few hours.

When you're ready to charge it for use, hold the ring in your hand and say the following incantation: "Ring of Saturn, protect me from negative energy and harm!" Say this as many times as you would like to. When you feel the ring is sufficiently charged, put it on.

Note: Hematite is a brittle stone that can break more easily than other crystals used in jewelry. This property works in our favor, however, as it's said that a hematite ring will break when it has absorbed all the negativity it can. If and when this happens, take the broken ring and bury it. Replace with a new one if you would like to, and repeat this spell.

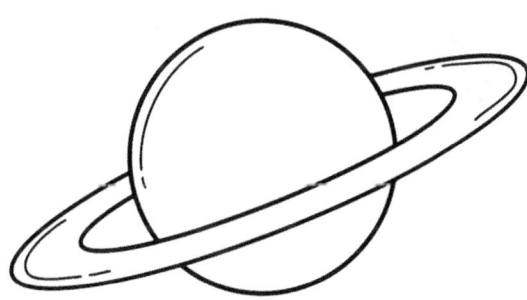

Doorstep Rice Spell

Fill a jar with raw white rice without sealing it. Place the jar by the front door for protection. Remember that rice absorbs negative energy rather than repelling it. Replace the rice with fresh raw rice weekly. Avoid bringing old rice back into your home or cooking it. Dispose of it outside your home by burning, scattering, or throwing it away.

Anti-Anxiety Spell Jar

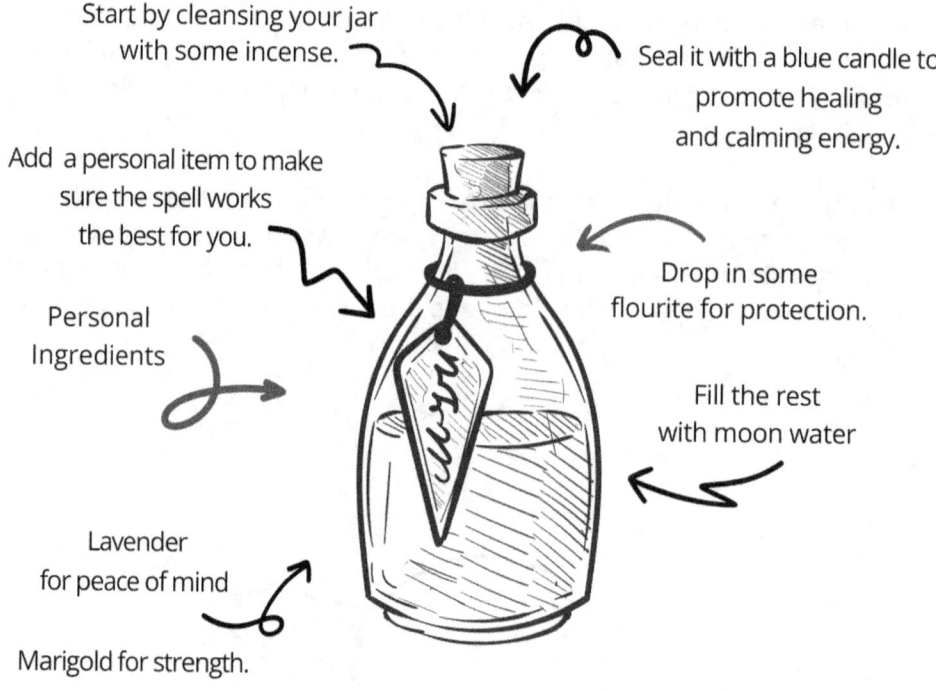

Start by cleansing your jar with some incense.

Seal it with a blue candle to promote healing and calming energy.

Add a personal item to make sure the spell works the best for you.

Drop in some flourite for protection.

Personal Ingredients

Fill the rest with moon water

Lavender for peace of mind

Marigold for strength.

Banishing Spell

Write down the name of the person or thing you want to banish on a piece of paper. Write your own name over the top of what you want to banish so your name crosses out theirs. Say this chant three times: "I cover you, I cross you, I command you, compel you, [name of person], get out of my life!" Burn the piece of paper with the names on it in the flame of the candle. Dress a black candle with banishing oil and light it. Let the candle burn out completely. Dispose of the remains in the trash as a symbol of banishment.

Banishing Candle Dressing

Mix equal parts of:
Black pepper
Cinnamon
Paprika
Salt
Cayenne pepper
Then add a little vinegar to make a paste.
Rub the paste around the candle to dress it

Door Protection Sachet

Create a small sachet or pouch using fabric or a small bag.
Fill it with protective herbs such as rosemary, sage, and basil.
As you fill the sachet, visualize a protective barrier forming around your home.
Once the sachet is filled, tie it securely with a knot.
Hold the sachet in your hands and focus your intention on protection and safety for your home and those within it.
Place the sachet near your front door or doorstep, either hanging it on the doorknob or tucking it discreetly nearby.
As you do so, recite a simple incantation, such as:
"By earth and air, by fire and sea, Protect this home, so mote it be. May all who enter find peace and light, Warding off darkness with gentle might."
Visualize the protective energy of the herbs surrounding your home like a shield, keeping negativity and harm at bay.
You feed the sachet periodically, refreshing it with new herbs and repeating the spell to maintain the protective energy around your doorstep.

New Moon Spell

Setting Intentions

During the New Moon, the sky is dark, representing new beginnings and potential. This is an ideal time for setting intentions for the upcoming lunar cycle.

Ingredients

White candle
Pen and paper
Essential oil (such as lavender or sandalwood)
Clear quartz crystal

Instructions

Begin by cleansing your space with the essential oil and lighting the white candle.
Sit in a comfortable position and take several deep breaths to center yourself.
Write down your intentions or goals on the paper, focusing on what you wish to manifest during this lunar cycle.
Hold the clear quartz crystal in your hand and visualize your intentions coming to fruition.
Place the paper under the candle and let it burn while you continue to meditate on your intentions.
Once the candle has burned down, bury the ashes outside or keep them in a special place as a reminder of your goals.

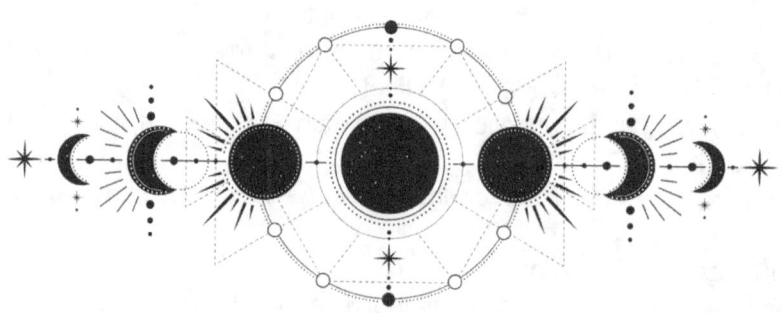

Waxing Moon Spell

Growth and Manifestation
The Waxing Moon phase is a time of growth and expansion. Use this spell to amplify your intentions and manifest your desires.

Ingredients
Green candle
Bay leaves
Pen and paper
Patchouli essential oil

Instructions
Anoint the green candle with patchouli oil while visualizing your goals of growing and expanding.
Write your intentions or desires on the bay leaves using the pen and paper.
Light the candle and place it in front of you.
Hold each bay leaf over the flame, allowing it to catch fire briefly, and then drop it into a fireproof container.
As the leaves burn, visualize your intentions manifesting with each flame.
Once all the bay leaves have burned, extinguish the candle and give thanks for the abundance that is coming your way.

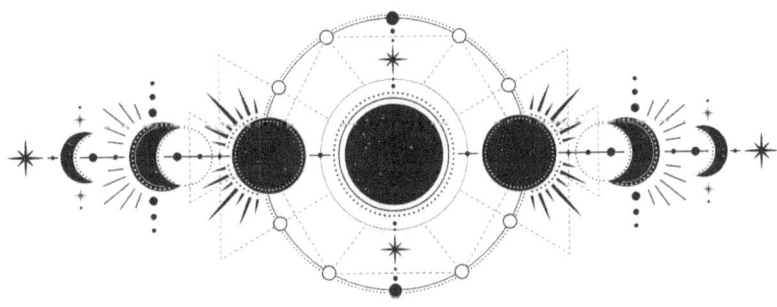

Full Moon Spell

Release and Gratitude
The Full Moon is a powerful time for releasing what no longer serves you and expressing gratitude for what you have.

Ingredients
White sage or palo santo for cleansing
A small bowl of water
Black candle
Rose quartz crystal

Instructions
Begin by smudging your space with white sage or palo santo to cleanse the energy.
Fill the small bowl with water and place it in front of you.
Light the black candle and sit quietly, reflecting on what you wish to release.
Write down anything you want to let go of on a piece of paper.
Hold the paper over the flame of the candle and say aloud what you are releasing.
Drop the paper into the bowl of water to extinguish the flame, symbolizing the release of those energies.
Hold the rose quartz crystal in your hand and express gratitude for the blessings in your life.
Place the crystal next to the candle and let it burn down completely, absorbing and transmuting any remaining negative energy.

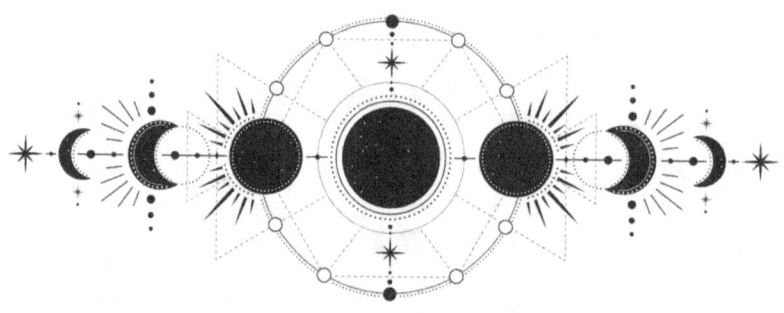

Waning Moon Spell

Banishing Negativity
The Waning Moon phase is ideal for banishing negativity and obstacles from your life.

Ingredients
Black candle
Smoky quartz crystal
Patchouli or cedarwood essential oil

Instructions
Anoint the black candle with patchouli or cedarwood oil while focusing on banishing negativity.
Light the candle and place it in front of you.
Hold the smoky quartz crystal in your hand and visualize any negative energies leaving your body.
Repeat a banishing incantation or affirmation, such as "I release all that does not serve me" or "I banish negativity from my life."
Allow the candle to burn down completely, visualizing the negativity being consumed by the flame.
Once the candle has burned out, bury the leftover wax away from your home to symbolize the permanent removal of negativity from your life.

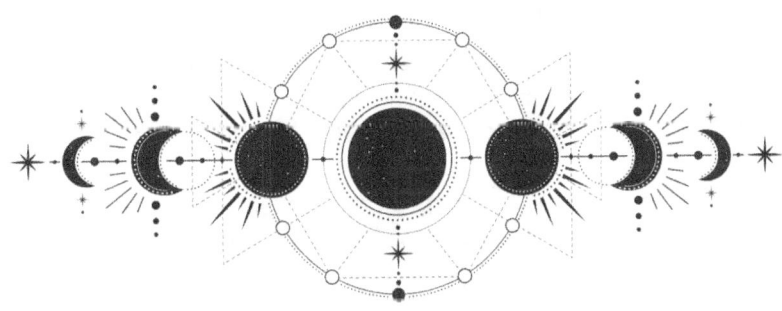

Gratitude Spell

Ingredients:
A white candle dressed with olive oil and rosemary
A few items to represent the things for which you are grateful
Optional: a sigil (mine is for "I am grateful for all that I receive")

Directions:
Light the candle and take a few moments to reflect upon your items and what they represent
Say aloud what you are thankful for. You can write it into a poem, a list that you seal by burning.

Gratitude Happiness Spell

Ingredients
small candle (yellow or orange)
a piece of paper, and a pen.

Directions
Find a quiet and comfortable space where you can focus without distractions.
Light the candle and sit in front of it.
Take a few deep breaths to center yourself and clear your mind.
On the piece of paper, write down three things you are grateful for in your life. These can be big or small, specific or general.
Hold the paper in your hands and close your eyes. Visualize each item on your list and feel the gratitude welling up inside you.
As you hold onto this feeling of gratitude, say aloud or silently:
"By the light of this flame, I call upon the power of gratitude. May it fill my heart with happiness and joy."
Place the paper near the candle so that it catches the light.
Sit quietly for a few moments, basking in the warmth of the candle and the feelings of gratitude and happiness.
When you feel ready, blow out or snuff out the candle and give thanks for the blessings in your life.
Keep the paper in a safe place as a reminder of the abundance and happiness that surrounds you.
Repeat this spell whenever you feel the need to cultivate gratitude and happiness in your life.

CHAPTER 10

Altar Ideas

Mercury in Retrograde
Altar Set Up

Many people feel wary when they hear we are moving into a Mercury Retrograde season.

While they are common and can be manageable, this is a suggested list of things you can arrange on your altar to assist in ensuring a smooth and easy-flowing Mercury Retrograde.

An image of the Magician tarot card:
The Magician is connected to Mercury energy, representing communication, learning, and action. The Magician can assist you with keeping your thoughts, words, and actions clear through Mercury Retro-grade.

A living plant that is associated with Mercury: Allow the energy of Mercury to thrive and grow on your altar with plants such as lavender, rosemary, peppermint, or thyme.

Incense associated with Mercury:
Burn incense with benzoin, gum mastic, frankincense, and/or rosemary to help purify your sacred space, stimulate mental agility, support concentration, and awaken spiritual awareness.

An image or statue of the god Mercury: If you feel like it, leave petitions for clarity, safe travels, speedy delivery, and smooth transactions with Mercury. Leave him offerings of almonds, hazelnuts, star anise, drawings of the Mercury glyph, lit yellow candles, images of the caduceus, or amulets shaped like wings.

Mercury-corresponding crystals: Dress your altar with crystals that are associated with the planet Mercury, such as hematite, mica, or muscovite. While the element known as mercury is poisonous and should never be used, you can still represent it with a jar of water mixed with silver glitter, ink, and/or dye.

Ostara Altar

Creating an altar for Ostara involves infusing it with symbols of fertility, balance, and the awakening of nature.

Altar Placement: Locate a space that receives ample natural light, symbolizing the increasing daylight of the season. East-facing or by a window is ideal for capturing the energy of the rising sun.

Altar Cloth: Drape the altar with a light-colored cloth, preferably in pastel shades, symbolizing the soft hues of spring. This represents the awakening and freshness associated with Ostara.

Symbols of the Season: Arrange items that symbolize fertility and rebirth, such as eggs (real or decorative), flowers, and seeds. Nestle eggs in nests or baskets to evoke a sense of nurturing and new beginnings.

Floral Arrangements: Decorate the altar with fresh flowers like daffodils, tulips, or lilies, reflecting the blossoming of nature. Floral arrangements can be placed in vases or scattered across the altar.

Candles: Place candles on the altar, preferably in colors associated with Ostara—pastels like light blue, pink, or yellow. These represent the balance of light and dark as the days lengthen.

Seasonal Crystals: Integrate crystals that resonate with the energy of spring, such as clear quartz, rose quartz, or amethyst. Arrange them creatively or use them as part of a crystal grid to amplify the altar's energy.

Symbols of Balance: Incorporate symbols that represent balance, such as the equal-armed cross or representations of the yin-yang. This aligns with the equilibrium of day and night during the equinox.

Greenery: Add potted plants or branches with fresh green leaves, signifying the renewal of life. This can include herbs like basil or mint, adding both aesthetic appeal and practical use.

Images or Statues: Include representations of spring deities or symbols, such as images of Eostre, the goddess of spring, or figures that embody the spirit of growth and fertility.

Offerings: Place offerings on the altar, like fruits, nuts, or honey, as a gesture of gratitude for the abundance of the season. These offerings can be consumed later or returned to nature.

Incense or Scents: Use floral or fresh scents through incense or essential oils. Scents like lavender, jasmine, or rose contribute to the sensory experience and enhance the atmosphere of the altar.

Divination Tools: If you practice divination, include tools like tarot cards, runes, or a scrying mirror. Ostara is a time for reflection and divination to gain insight into the coming season.

By carefully arranging these elements on your Ostara altar, you create a sacred space that resonates with the essence of the season—celebrating renewal, fertility, and the harmonious balance between light and dark.

CHAPTER 11

Introduction to Deities

Worshiping and dedicating to gods and goddesses is an important aspect of many pagan traditions, including those celebrating the Litha Sabbat. The honored and revered deities can vary greatly depending on the individual or group's beliefs and practices. Some may worship a pantheon of gods and goddesses, while others may focus their devotion on a single deity. Regardless of the approach, dedicating oneself to these powerful spiritual forces can be a significant and transformative experience.

Many pagans see their relationship with the divine as a two-way street. They believe they can receive blessings, guidance, and protection in return by offering devotion and reverence to the gods and goddesses. This energy exchange is often seen as a way to maintain balance in the world and one's life. Some also view the deities as archetypes or personifications of natural forces, such as the sun or the moon, and may seek to align themselves with these energies through worship.

There are many ways to worship and dedicate oneself to the gods and goddesses. Some may perform rituals or ceremonies, make food or drink offerings, or create sacred spaces in their homes or outdoor areas. Others may meditate, pray, or engage in personal acts of devotion. Whatever form it takes, this connection with the divine can be a source of inspiration, comfort, and spiritual growth for those who seek it.

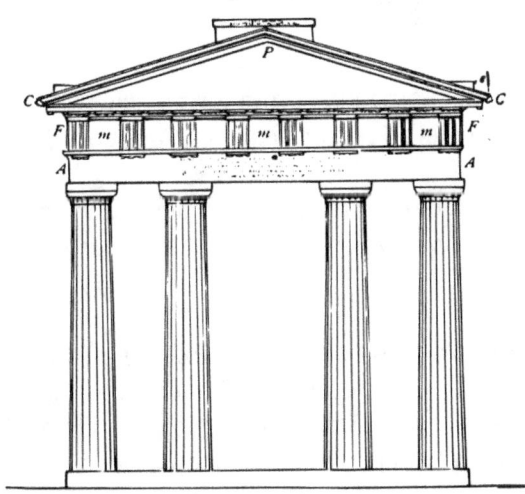

Amalthea (Greek)

Nymph or Goat: Amalthea is sometimes described as a nymph but more commonly as a divine goat in Greek mythology.

Nursemaid of Zeus: Amalthea is best known as the foster mother and nursemaid of Zeus, the king of the gods. In some versions, she is the daughter of Oceanus and the sister of the nymphs known as the Heliades.

Rhea's Strategy: To protect Zeus from his father Cronus, who had a habit of devouring his offspring, Rhea, Zeus' mother, gave him to Amalthea to be raised in secret.

The Goat's Horn: Legend has it that while Zeus was being cared for by Amalthea, he accidentally broke off one of her horns. The broken horn, often referred to as the "Cornucopia" or "Horn of Plenty," became a symbol of abundance and prosperity.

Symbol of Nourishment: Amalthea's horn, according to some traditions, had the magical ability to provide an endless supply of food and drink to those who possessed it. It is often depicted overflowing with fruits and grains.

Association with Fertility: Amalthea, as a nurturing figure and provider of sustenance, is sometimes associated with fertility and abundance.

Zeus' Youth: As Zeus grew stronger, he eventually overthrew Cronus and became the ruler of the Olympian gods. Amalthea played a crucial role in his early years, ensuring his well-being.

Constellation Capricornus: Some interpretations suggest that Amalthea was placed among the stars as the constellation Capricornus (Capricorn), the Sea Goat.

Milk of Amalthea: The milk of Amalthea is often described as a divine substance with healing properties. In some versions of the myth, Zeus was nourished by this special milk.

Other Nurturing Figures: While Amalthea is one of the most famous foster mothers of Zeus, other figures like the Curetes, Adrasteia, and even the bee-nymph Melisseus are also mentioned in various traditions as being involved in his care. Amalthea's role as the nurturing goat and provider of the Cornucopia contributed to her symbolic significance in Greek mythology. Her story emphasizes themes of protection, abundance, and the protective instincts of maternal figures.

Blodeuwedd (Welsh)

Creation by Math and Gwydion: Blodeuwedd is a woman created through magical means by the Welsh gods Math and Gwydion. She was formed from the blossoms of oak, broom, and meadowsweet.

Marriage to Lleu Llaw Gyffes: Blodeuwedd was created as a bride for Lleu Llaw Gyffes, the nephew of Math and Gwydion. Lleu was under a curse that he could not marry a human woman, so a wife had to be crafted for him.

Betrayal of Lleu: Despite her marital union with Lleu, Blodeuwedd falls in love with a hunter named Gronw Pebr. Together, they plot to kill Lleu.

Lleu's Invulnerability: Lleu possesses a unique vulnerability due to the manner of his creation. He cannot be killed indoors or outdoors, nor on horseback or on foot, and neither by day nor by night.

Conspiracy to Kill Lleu: Blodeuwedd tricks Lleu into revealing the specifics of his vulnerability. She then shares this information with Gronw, enabling him to plan an attack on Lleu.

Gronw's Attempted Murder: Gronw attempts to kill Lleu according to the specified conditions. Lleu, realizing the betrayal, transforms into an eagle and escapes.

Lleu's Healing: Gwydion, Lleu's uncle, searches for him and eventually finds the wounded eagle. With the help of magical incantations, Gwydion transforms Lleu back into human form and heals his wounds.

Punishment of Blodeuwedd: As punishment for her betrayal, Gwydion transforms Blodeuwedd into an owl, a symbol of both wisdom and exile. In Welsh, "blodeuwedd" means "flower face," and her transformation reflects her change from a beautiful woman into a bird.

Symbolic Associations: Blodeuwedd's story is often interpreted symbolically. Her creation from flowers represents the transient and fragile nature of beauty, while her betrayal and punishment embody themes of fidelity, consequences, and transformation.

Cultural Importance: The tale of Blodeuwedd is part of the Welsh collection of myths known as the Mabinogion. It explores complex themes of love, betrayal, and the consequences of defying divine arrangements. The story of Blodeuwedd is a significant narrative within Welsh mythology, illustrating the consequences of deceit and betrayal while exploring the transformative nature of divine punishment.

Eos (Greek)

Goddess of Dawn: Eos is the Greek goddess of dawn, symbolizing the morning light. She is associated with the daily rising of the sun, marking the beginning of a new day.

Parentage: Eos is one of the Titans, the ancient, primordial deities preceding the Olympian gods. She is the daughter of Hyperion (Titan of light) and Theia (Titaness of sight and brightness).

Siblings: Eos has two siblings who are also personifications of celestial bodies – Helios (the sun god) and Selene (the moon goddess).

Residence and Daily Journey: Eos is said to reside at the edge of the world, from where she rises each morning to announce the arrival of the sun. Her chariot is often described as drawn by two horses – Lampus and Phaeton.

Lovers: Eos is known for her romantic entanglements with various mortals and gods. One of her notable mortal lovers is Tithonus, a Trojan prince. Eos asked Zeus to grant Tithonus immortality but forgot to request eternal youth, resulting in Tithonus aging without end.

Children: Eos is the mother of several divine beings, including the Anemoi (Winds) and the Astra Planeta (Wandering Stars or Planets). Among her sons are Boreas (North Wind), Zephyrus (West Wind), and Notus (South Wind).

Association with Rosy Fingers: In poetic descriptions, Eos is often referred to as having "rosy fingers" or "rosy forearms," emphasizing the gentle and colorful transition of the sky at dawn.

Mythological Episodes: While Eos does not have a central mythology dedicated to her, she is mentioned in various myths, often playing a role in the background. Her interactions with other gods and mortals are intertwined with the broader stories of the Greek pantheon.

Cultural Depictions: Eos appears in various works of art, literature, and poetry. Her portrayal in Greek vase paintings often depicts her riding her chariot across the sky.

Roman Equivalent: In Roman mythology, Eos is equated with the goddess Aurora, who similarly personifies the dawn. Eos' role as the goddess of dawn underscores the significance of the daily cycle and the transition from night to day in Greek mythology. Her associations with light, beauty, and the celestial heavens contribute to her enduring

Eostre (Germanic)

Eostre, also spelled Ostara, is a Germanic goddess associated with spring and fertility. Here are the key facts about Eostre in Germanic mythology.

Spring Goddess: Eostre is a goddess of spring, symbolizing the renewal of life, fertility, and the arrival of warmer, sunnier days.

Germanic Origin: The worship of Eostre is rooted in Germanic pagan traditions, particularly among the Anglo-Saxons. She is considered part of the ancient Germanic pantheon.

Festival of Eostre: The celebration of Eostre was connected to a spring festival, likely involving feasting and various rituals to welcome the season of growth and abundance.

Easter Connection: Eostre's name is etymologically linked to the word "Easter." The Christian festival of Easter, celebrating the resurrection of Jesus Christ, coincides with the spring season and incorporates some elements associated with Eostre's festivities.

Symbolism of Hares and Eggs: Eostre is often associated with symbols of fertility, such as hares and eggs. The tradition of decorating eggs during Easter has its roots in pagan customs related to Eostre.

Legends and Myths: While specific myths about Eostre are not well-documented, her presence in Germanic folklore is connected to the broader themes of spring, growth, and the vitality of the natural world.

Cultural Adaptation: Eostre's worship declined with the spread of Christianity, but certain aspects of her symbolism were absorbed into Christian celebrations, particularly Easter. Eostre may have influenced the naming of the Christian holiday Easter.

Linguistic Origins: The name "Eostre" is derived from the Old English word "ēastre," which means spring. It is related to the Old High German word "ōstarūn," signifying the dawn or the east.

Modern Celebrations: In contemporary times, some modern pagan and neopagan traditions have revived celebrations associated with Eostre, marking the spring equinox with rituals and festivities.

Cultural Significance: Eostre's mythology is a testament to the importance of nature, cycles, and the changing seasons in ancient Germanic cultures. The symbols and traditions associated with Eostre continue to resonate in various forms today. While information about Eostre is limited, her significance in Germanic paganism has left an enduring legacy, primarily through the cultural connections between her festivities and the modern celebration of Easter.

Epona (Celtic)

Goddess of Horses: Epona is a Celtic goddess associated with horses, fertility, and the protection of equines. Her name is derived from the Gaulish word "epos," meaning horse.

Celtic Origin: Epona was worshipped primarily by the Celtic people, and her veneration spread across different regions, including Gaul (present-day France), Britain, and parts of the Roman Empire.

Symbolism of Horses: Horses held great significance in Celtic cultures, serving as both practical and symbolic animals. Epona's connection to horses made her a revered figure among those who relied on these animals for transportation, agriculture, and warfare.

Depictions: Epona is often depicted as a young woman riding or standing next to horses. In some representations, she is shown with a cornucopia, emphasizing her association with fertility and abundance.

Cult Centers: Temples and shrines dedicated to Epona have been found across Celtic territories. These places were centers of worship and likely served as focal points for equestrian rituals and offerings.

Guardian of Horses: Epona was believed to be a protective and nurturing figure for horses and their caretakers. She was invoked for the well-being of horses, safe journeys, and successful breeding.

Roman Influence: With the Roman conquests and interactions between Celtic and Roman cultures, Epona's worship extended into Roman territories. She was later incorporated into the Roman pantheon, and her popularity continued among Roman cavalry units.

Attributes of Sovereignty: In some interpretations, Epona is also associated with the concept of sovereignty, which symbolizes the sacred connection between the land, its rulers, and the prosperity of the people.

Mythological Narratives: There are limited surviving mythological narratives, specifically about Epona. Much of her worship and symbolism are understood through archaeological evidence, inscriptions, and depictions on artifacts.

Continued Reverence: While the ancient Celtic religion waned with the spread of Christianity, Epona's legacy endures in various forms. Some modern practitioners of Celtic-inspired or neopagan traditions honor Epona in their rituals, recognizing her as a symbol of horse magic, fertility, and the bond between humans and horses. Epona's significance lies in her role as a protector and benefactor of horses, reflecting the deep connection between Celtic cultures and these revered animals.

Flora (Roman)

Goddess of Flowers and Spring: Flora is the Roman goddess associated with flowers, vegetation, and the arrival of spring. She played a central role in the seasonal renewal of plant life.

Festival of Floralia: The Floralia, a festival dedicated to Flora, was celebrated annually from April 27 to May. It marked the beginning of the planting season and was characterized by lively festivities, including theatrical performances, games, and floral decorations.

Origins: Flora's worship in Rome is believed to have originated around the 4th century BCE. Her roots may have connections to earlier Sabine and Etruscan goddesses associated with flowering and fertility.

Parentage: Flora is sometimes mentioned as the daughter of Jupiter (Zeus in Greek mythology) and Terra (Gaea in Greek mythology), emphasizing her connection to the earth and its fertility.

Marriage to Zephyrus: Flora is often associated with Zephyrus, the West Wind. Their union symbolizes the gentle, warm breeze that heralds the arrival of spring and promotes the blossoming of flowers.

Cultural Symbolism: Flora's imagery is frequently associated with the beauty of nature and the blooming of flowers. She is depicted holding bouquets or standing in lush, blooming landscapes.

Protection of Gardens: Flora was believed to be a guardian of gardens and orchards. Her influence was thought to ensure the flourishing of crops and the beauty of cultivated plants.

Secular and Religious Importance: While Flora had a significant role in Roman religious practices, her influence extended into secular life. The celebration of Floralia, for example, involved various forms of entertainment, and her presence was invoked for agricultural prosperity.

Assimilation of Greek Counterpart: Flora's Greek counterpart is Chloris, a nymph associated with flowers. In Roman mythology, Flora absorbed the characteristics and functions of Chloris, becoming the primary deity of floral abundance.

Later Representations: Flora continued to be a popular figure in art and literature during the Renaissance and later periods. Her imagery often conveyed the beauty and fleeting nature of spring and blossoming flowers. Flora's mythology revolves around the celebration of spring, the flourishing of flowers, and the renewal of the natural world. The Floralia festival, dedicated to her, reflected the Roman appreciation for the vitality and beauty of the changing seasons.

Freya (Norse)

Goddess of Love, Fertility, and War: Freyja is a prominent goddess in Norse mythology, associated with love, beauty, fertility, and war. She is a member of the Vanir, a group of deities associated with fertility, prosperity, and nature.

Vanir and Aesir War: Freyja is often counted among both the Vanir and the Aesir, the two main groups of Norse gods. This is due to her close connection with both pantheons.

Parentage: Freyja is the daughter of Njord, the sea god, and sister to Freyr, the fertility god. In some accounts, she is also mentioned as the daughter of the giantess Skadi.

Symbols and Attributes: Freyja is commonly associated with several symbols, including the cat, which is often portrayed as her sacred animal. She possesses a magical cloak (feathered cloak or falcon skin) that allows her to transform into a bird. 5. **Valkyrie

Aspect: Freyja has a strong connection with the afterlife. She is often depicted as a leader of the Valkyries, warrior maidens who choose those who may die and those who may live in battles.

Search for Husband: Freyja's husband, named Od (or Ottar in some versions), is elusive, and her search for him is a recurring theme in Norse mythology. Od is associated with poetry and inspiration.

Brisingamen Necklace: Freyja is the owner of the Brisingamen, a beautiful and coveted necklace crafted by dwarves. In some tales, she acquires this necklace through a deal that involves spending a night with each of the four dwarves who created it.

Cultural Importance: Freyja held a significant place in Norse society, and she was often invoked in matters of love, fertility, and war. Her influence extended to matters of magic, divination, and seidr, a form of Norse sorcery.

Freyja's Tears and Golden Tears: Freyja is said to weep tears of gold whenever she misses her husband. Her tears are symbolic of longing and the emotional depth associated with her character.

Feasts and Celebrations: Freyja was honored with various feasts and celebrations, especially during important Norse festivals. Her role as a goddess of love and fertility made her a patron of weddings and celebrations.

Survival of Norse Mythology: Despite the decline of Norse mythology with the advent of Christianity, some aspects of Freyja's character endured in folklore and literature. In Scandinavian folklore, she is sometimes associated with the fairy queen or the Lady of Elfland. Freyja's multifaceted character, encompassing love, war, and magic, reflects the complex nature of Norse mythology. Her importance in both the Aesir and Vanir pantheons underscores her role as a significant and revered goddess in Norse cosmology.

Guinevere (Welsh / Arthurian)

Gwenhwyfar in Welsh: In Welsh mythology, Guinevere is known as Gwenhwyfar. Her character appears in early Welsh prose tales, particularly in the collection known as the Mabinogion.

Association with Arthur: Gwenhwyfar is often associated with Arthur, and her story is intertwined with the legends of the Welsh hero. She is presented as Arthur's queen, known for her beauty and tragic fate.

Kidnapping by Melwas: In the tale "Culhwch and Olwen," Gwenhwyfar is kidnapped by Melwas (Meleagant), leading to Arthur's pursuit to rescue her. This narrative theme of her abduction and rescue is a recurring motif in Arthurian legends. **Medieval Arthurian Tradition

Romance Literature: Guinevere gains prominence in later medieval Arthurian romances, particularly in works like Chrétien de Troyes' "Lancelot, the Knight of the Cart" and Sir Thomas Malory's "Le Morte d'Arthur."

Marriage to Arthur: In the Arthurian tradition, Guinevere is the queen and wife of King Arthur, the legendary king of the Britons.

Lancelot's Love: One of the most well-known aspects of Guinevere's story is her affair with Sir Lancelot. Their love affair becomes a central theme in later Arthurian literature and contributes to the downfall of the Round Table.

Damsel in Distress: Guinevere is sometimes portrayed as a damsel in distress, facing challenges and dangers that require the intervention of Arthur or the knights of the Round Table.

Conflict and Betrayal: The affair between Guinevere and Lancelot creates conflict within the Arthurian court, leading to the downfall of the Round Table. Guinevere's actions contribute to the weakening of Arthur's reign.

Imprisonment and Rescue: In some versions, Guinevere faces imprisonment, often accused of treason or adultery. Lancelot, along with other knights, attempts to rescue her.

Nunnery and Death: In some accounts, Guinevere retires to a nunnery as a form of penance. Her fate varies in different versions, including her eventual death.

Literary Adaptations: Guinevere's character has been adapted and reinterpreted in various literary works, plays, and films. Different authors emphasize various aspects of her character, creating nuanced and diverse portrayals. Guinevere's character is complex, reflecting themes of love, betrayal, and the moral challenges faced by the Arthurian court. Her role in the Arthurian legends has been influential, making her a figure of enduring fascination in literature and popular culture.

Libera (Roman)

Libera, also known as Liber Pater or simply Libera, is a Roman goddess associated with fertility, wine, and freedom.

Parentage: Libera is often identified with Persephone, the Greek goddess of the underworld, and is considered her Roman counterpart. She is the daughter of Ceres (Demeter in Greek mythology), the goddess of agriculture.

Fertility and Growth: Libera is primarily associated with fertility and the growth of plants, particularly grains and vines. She symbolizes the agricultural abundance and prosperity necessary for a successful harvest.

Connection to Liber: Libera is sometimes associated with Liber, a god of wine and fertility. Together, they represent the bountiful aspects of nature, with Liber often identified as a male counterpart to Libera.

Liber and Libera Festivals: The festival of Liberalia was celebrated in honor of Liber and Libera, typically observed on March 17. This festival marked the coming of age of young Roman boys and included rituals related to wine and fertility.

Worship and Cult Centers: Libera was venerated within the Roman religious context, particularly in association with agricultural and fertility rites. Temples and sanctuaries dedicated to her existed in various parts of the Roman Empire.

Mystery Cults: Libera, along with Ceres and Liber, were associated with mystery cults that involved secret rituals and initiation ceremonies. These cults were often centered around agricultural themes, reflecting the importance of fertility in Roman society.

Transformation of Persephone's Myth: The myth of Libera is closely linked to that of Persephone in Greek mythology. In Roman adaptations, the focus shifted towards the positive aspects of fertility and growth associated with Libera rather than the darker themes often associated with Persephone's abduction.

Cultural Influence: The worship of Libera and related deities was integral to Roman agricultural practices and religious traditions. These deities played a role in ensuring a successful harvest and the well-being of the Roman people.

Artistic Representations: Libera is depicted in various forms of Roman art, often shown holding a sheaf of wheat, a symbol of fertility and abundance. Her images were included in religious iconography and coins.

Roman Adaptation of Greek Myths: Roman mythology frequently adapted and incorporated elements from Greek mythology. The assimilation of Libera into the Roman pantheon reflects this cultural interchange and the Romans' tendency to integrate foreign deities into their own religious practices. Libera's role in Roman mythology highlights the importance of fertility and agricultural prosperity in the ancient Roman worldview. The festivals and rites dedicated to her, along with related deities like Liber and Ceres, were integral to Roman religious life.

Persephone (Greek)

Goddess of the Underworld: Persephone is a goddess in Greek mythology, primarily associated with the underworld. She is often referred to as the Queen of the Underworld.

Parentage: Persephone is the daughter of Zeus, the king of the gods, and Demeter, the goddess of agriculture and fertility.

Abduction by Hades: One of the most well-known myths about Persephone involves her abduction by Hades, the god of the underworld. Hades, smitten by Persephone's beauty, kidnaps her and takes her to the underworld to be his wife.

Search by Demeter: Demeter, devastated by her daughter's disappearance, wanders the earth in search of Persephone. During her grief, she caused a prolonged winter, resulting in the barrenness of the land.

Compromise with Zeus: Zeus, concerned about the impact of the eternal winter, intervened. A compromise was reached, allowing Persephone to spend part of the year with her mother on the surface (spring and summer) and the other part in the underworld with Hades (autumn and winter).

Role in the Seasons: The myth of Persephone is often linked to the changing seasons. Her time in the underworld corresponds to winter when Demeter mourns, and her return to the surface marks the arrival of spring and the blossoming of vegetation.

Epithets and Titles: Persephone is known by various nicknames and titles, including Kore (maiden), Despoina (mistress), and Chthonia (of the earth).

Associations with Rebirth: Persephone's cycle of descent and return is often seen as a symbol of rebirth and renewal. Her emergence from the underworld represents the rejuvenation of nature and the agricultural cycle.

Cult Worship: Persephone was worshipped in mystery cults, with Eleusis being a prominent center for her worship. The Eleusinian Mysteries, held in her honor, were secretive rites celebrating the cycles of life, death, and rebirth.

Artistic Representations: Persephone is depicted in various forms of Greek art. She is often shown as a young goddess, sometimes with Hades or accompanied by symbols like pomegranates associated with her time in the underworld.

Queen of the Dead: As the Queen of the Underworld, Persephone presides over the spirits of the dead. She is not considered a malevolent figure but a powerful deity associated with life and death. Persephone's myth is central to understanding the interconnectedness of life, death, and the changing seasons in Greek mythology. Her story reflects themes of fertility, transformation, and the cyclical nature of existence.

Rati (Hindu)

Rati is a Hindu goddess associated with love, passion, and desire.

Goddess of Love and Passion: Rati is the Hindu goddess of love, passion, and desire. She is considered the consort of Kamadeva, the god of love and desire.

Marriage to Kamadeva: Rati is married to Kamadeva, and their union symbolizes the essence of love and marital bliss in Hindu mythology.

Appearance: Rati is often depicted as a beautiful and alluring goddess, representing the enchanting aspects of love. Her appearance is described as captivating and charming.

Symbolism of Passion: Rati is associated with love's passionate and romantic aspects. She symbolizes the intense emotions that arise in romantic relationships.

Kamadeva's Companion: Rati is a devoted companion to Kamadeva and is often portrayed accompanying him. Together, they embody the divine forces that inspire love and desire.

References: Rati is mentioned in various Puranas (Hindu scriptures), including the Bhagavata Purana and the Vishnu Purana, where her story and attributes are described.

Legend of Kamadeva's Destruction: According to some versions of Hindu mythology, Rati played a role in the aftermath of Kamadeva's destruction by Lord Shiva's third eye. She mourned the loss of her husband and pleaded for his resurrection.

Prayers and Devotion: Devotees may invoke Rati through prayers and rituals, seeking her blessings for harmonious relationships, marital happiness, and the fulfillment of passionate desires.

Cultural Significance: The worship of Rati is not as widely documented or established in Hinduism as some other goddesses. However, her role as the goddess of love contributes to the diverse pantheon of deities representing different facets of existence.

Temple Worship: There are no widely known temples exclusively dedicated to Rati. Her worship is often integrated into rituals associated with Kamadeva or other deities related to love and relationships. Rati's mythology adds a nuanced dimension to the Hindu pantheon, emphasizing the divine aspects of love and passion. While less extensively explored than some other deities, Rati's presence highlights the multifaceted nature of Hindu goddesses and their roles in different aspects of life.

Renpet (Egyptian

Renpet is an ancient Egyptian goddess associated with the concept of time, specifically the annual flooding of the Nile and the agricultural season.

Goddess of Time: Renpet, also known as Renenutet or Ernutet, is a goddess in ancient Egyptian mythology who personifies the concept of time, particularly the cyclical nature of time related to the agricultural calendar.

Nile Flooding: Renpet is closely linked to the annual flooding of the Nile River, a crucial event in ancient Egypt that marked the beginning of the agricultural season. The flood deposited nutrient-rich silt, ensuring fertile soil for crops.

The symbolism of Harvest: The flooding of the Nile was essential for a successful harvest, and Renpet's association with this natural phenomenon made her a protective deity overseeing the agricultural cycle and the growth of crops.

Cobra Symbolism: Renpet is sometimes depicted as a cobra or a cobra-headed woman, emphasizing her protective and nurturing qualities. The cobra is a symbol of both danger and protection in Egyptian iconography.

Connection to Renenu: Renpet is often associated with Renenutet, a goddess of nourishment and the harvest. Together, they represent the cycle of agricultural productivity, from the flooding of the Nile to the ripening and harvesting of crops.

Role in Fertility Rituals: Renpet's influence extended to fertility rituals and ceremonies associated with ensuring a bountiful harvest. Worshipers sought her blessings for agricultural abundance and prosperity.

Offerings and Rituals: Devotees offered prayers and rituals to Renpet, particularly during times crucial to the agricultural cycle, such as the inundation of the Nile. Offerings were made to seek her favor for a fruitful and prosperous harvest.

Role in the Afterlife: In some contexts, Renpet was also associated with the afterlife. The cyclical nature of time represented by Renpet may have had symbolic connections to concepts of rebirth and eternity.

Cultural Significance: Renpet's significance was intertwined with the practical and spiritual aspects of ancient Egyptian life. Her role in overseeing the agricultural calendar emphasized the importance of the natural environment to Egyptian society.

Multiple Forms: Renpet could take various forms in Egyptian mythology, reflecting her multifaceted nature as a goddess associated with time, fertility, and protection. Renpet's mythology highlights the Egyptians' deep connection to the natural world and the significance they placed on the cyclical events, particularly the annual flooding of the Nile, which played a pivotal role in the agricultural success of the region.

Umai (Russian)

Umai is a goddess in Russia's mythology of the indigenous Turkic and Altai peoples.

Goddess of Fertility and Motherhood: Umai is primarily recognized as a goddess associated with fertility, motherhood, and the protection of women and children. She is revered as a nurturing and benevolent deity. Her benevolent influence is believed to ensure the health and prosperity of families.

Altai and Turkic Cultures: Umai is particularly venerated among the Altai and Turkic ethnic groups in Russia. Her worship is part of the traditional belief systems of these indigenous peoples.

Symbolic Representations: Umai is often represented as a maternal figure, emphasizing her role in fertility and the well-being of families. She may be depicted with symbols of abundance, such as sheaves of grain or a cornucopia.

Offerings and Rituals: Worshipers traditionally make offerings and perform rituals to Umai to seek her blessings for fertility, a successful harvest, and the protection of mothers and children. These rituals may involve prayers, dances, and offerings of food.

Connection to Nature: Umai's significance extends to the natural world, and she is associated with the well-being of the land. The health of the land and its fertility are linked to her protective influence.

Cultural Continuity: Umai's worship reflects the cultural continuity and resilience of indigenous beliefs among the Altai and Turkic peoples. Despite external influences, the reverence for Umai and related deities has persisted in these communities.

Relationship to Other Deities: In the broader Turkic and Altai pantheon, Umai is often associated with other deities related to fertility, agriculture, and the natural environment. Her interconnected role reflects these mythologies' holistic understanding of life and nature.

Ceremonies and Festivals: The Altai and Turkic communities observe ceremonies and festivals dedicated to Umai. These events celebrate fertility, family, and the interconnectedness of humanity with the natural world.

Oral Tradition: Much of the mythology surrounding Umai has been transmitted through oral tradition, with stories and rituals passed down from generation to generation. The oral nature of these traditions highlights their cultural significance. Umai's mythology underscores the importance of fertility, family, and the interconnectedness of human life with the natural world in the beliefs of the Altai and Turkic peoples in Russia.

Vila (Slavic)

Vila, also known as Rusalka or Samovila, is a supernatural being in Slavic mythology.

Nature Spirits: Vila is a type of nature spirit or fairy in Slavic folklore. These beings are often associated with specific natural elements, such as forests, rivers, and lakes.

Appearance: Vilas are usually depicted as beautiful, ethereal women with long, flowing hair. They are often described wearing white robes or dresses, emphasizing their otherworldly and enchanting nature.

Guardians of Nature: Vilas are considered guardians of the natural world. They are associated with forests, meadows, and bodies of water and are believed to have the power to protect or harm those who enter their domains.

Dancing in Circles: One characteristic associated with Vilas is their love for dancing in circles. These mystical dances are believed to occur in secluded forest areas or near bodies of water at night.

Nature's Wrath: While Vilas are generally benevolent, they can become vengeful if they feel their natural domains are threatened or disrespected. In such cases, they may inflict misfortune or harm upon intruders.

Connection to Water: In some Slavic traditions, Vilas are closely linked to bodies of water, especially rivers and lakes. They are sometimes considered water nymphs, and stories depict them residing near water sources.

Transformational Powers: Vilas are believed to possess magical and transformative powers. They can change their appearance at will and may sometimes appear as swans or other animals.

Relationship with Rusalkas: "Vila" is sometimes used interchangeably with "Rusalka" in Slavic folklore. Rusalkas are water nymphs or spirits associated with lakes and rivers and share similarities with Vilas.

Cultural Significance: Vila folklore is deeply rooted in Slavic cultural traditions. Stories about Vilas are often passed down through generations and have become integral to the rich tapestry of Slavic mythology.

Avoiding Vilas' Anger: Folk beliefs warn against angering Vilas. People were cautious about entering certain forest areas or swimming in specific lakes to avoid displeasing these nature spirits.

Influence on Art and Literature: Vila mythology has influenced various Slavic art, literature, and folk music forms. Vilas's enchanting and mysterious nature often serves as inspiration for creative works. Vila mythology reflects the Slavic people's deep connection to nature and belief in the supernatural beings that inhabit the natural world. Vilas embodies the allure and potential danger of Slavic regions' wild and untouched landscapes.

Aengus Macan Og (Irish)

Aengus Óg, or Aengus Mac Óg, is a prominent figure in Irish mythology.

God of Love and Youth: Aengus Óg is a god associated with love, youth, and beauty in Irish mythology. His name "Óg" means "young" or "youthful."

Parentage: Aengus is considered the son of Dagda, a powerful god associated with fertility and abundance. His mother is Boann, a goddess connected to the River Boyne.

Birth and Adoption: Legend states that Aengus was conceived and born on the same day. Due to circumstances surrounding his birth, Midir fostered and raised him as a member of the Tuatha Dé Danann, a supernatural race in Irish mythology.

Brugh na Bóinne (Newgrange): Aengus is associated with the famous prehistoric monument Brugh na Bóinne (Newgrange) in County Meath, Ireland. According to mythology, Aengus asked for the residence at Brugh na Bóinne, which was granted to him by the Dagda.

Caer Ibormeith: Aengus is renowned for his pursuit of love. The most famous tale involves his quest for Caer Ibormeith, a maiden transformed into a swan. Aengus eventually wins her love and breaks the enchantment.

Magical Birds: Aengus possesses two magical birds that can sing healing songs. These birds are associated with Aengus's character's healing and soothing aspects. His ability to transform into a swan is a recurring motif in his myths.

Role in the Second Battle of Magh Tuireadh: Aengus is mentioned in the Second Battle of Magh Tuireadh, an important event in Irish mythology where the Tuatha Dé Danann fought against the Fomorians. Aengus plays a role in these mythological battles.

Cultural Significance: Aengus Óg's stories contribute to the rich tapestry of Irish mythology, reflecting themes of love, youth, and the mystical landscape of ancient Ireland.

Survival in Folklore: Stories and references to Aengus Óg have endured in Irish folklore and storytelling, showcasing his lasting cultural significance in Ireland. Aengus Óg's tales highlight themes of love, pursuit, and the magical elements woven into Irish mythology. His association with Newgrange and his role in mythological battles contribute to his importance in the pantheon of Irish deities.

Cernunnos / Herne (Anglo-Celtic)

Cernunnos is a Celtic god associated with fertility, the wilderness, and the hunt. Herne is a figure with similar characteristics in English folklore, often identified with Cernunnos.

Celtic Deity: Cernunnos is a Celtic god worshipped in ancient Gaul and possibly other Celtic regions. His name is derived from a combination of "Cern," meaning horn, and "unnos," meaning one. Cernunnos is commonly depicted with antlers or horns on his head, symbolizing his connection to animals, nature, and fertility.

Fertility and Animals: Cernunnos is associated with fertility, the abundance of nature, and the animal kingdom. He is often depicted sitting cross-legged and surrounded by various animals, emphasizing his role as a wildlife guardian.

Torcs and Jewelry: Artistic representations often depict Cernunnos wearing torcs, a metal neck-ring, highlighting his status and connection to wealth and prosperity.

Gallo-Roman Artifacts: Images and depictions of Cernunnos are found on various Gallo-Roman artifacts, including sculptures and carvings. These artifacts suggest his importance in the religious practices of the ancient Celts.

English Folklore: Herne the Hunter is a figure in English folklore, often associated with Windsor Forest. He is a ghostly, supernatural hunter, sometimes depicted as a horned figure, and is linked to the hunting grounds of Windsor Great Park.

Horned Appearance: Like Cernunnos, Herne is sometimes depicted with antlers or horns on his head. This imagery connects him to the wild and the natural world.

Royal Connections: One legend suggests that Herne was a huntsman in the service of King Richard II. After a tragic incident, Herne's spirit becomes tied to the forest, and he appears as a ghostly figure.

Guardian of the Forest: Herne is often portrayed as a guardian or spirit of the forest, embodying nature's untamed and wild aspects.

Shakespeare's "The Merry Wives of Windsor": Herne gained literary prominence in Shakespeare's play "The Merry Wives of Windsor," where he is mentioned as a figure associated with the supernatural and the forest.

Cultural Adaptations: Herne's character has been adapted and incorporated into various cultural works, including literature, art, and modern Pagan and Neopagan practices.

Commonalities: Wilderness and Wildlife: Both Cernunnos and Herne share a connection to the wilderness, the hunt, and the animal kingdom, embodying untamed and primal forces.

Horned Imagery: The horned or antlered imagery associated with Cernunnos and Herne emphasizes their nature-related attributes and possibly points to shared symbolic significance. While Cernunnos is rooted in ancient Celtic mythology, Herne's figure is more localized to English folklore. Their similarities suggest a cultural continuity in the reverence for nature and the symbolism of the wild, especially in the context of the hunt.

The Green Man EU/North American

The Green Man is a mythological figure often depicted as a face surrounded by or made from leaves, vines, or other foliage. The concept has roots in European and North American folklore.

Symbol of Nature: The Green Man is a symbol associated with nature, fertility, and the cycle of growth and rebirth. His imagery is intertwined with the flourishing of vegetation during spring and summer.

Foliage Head: The Green Man is typically portrayed with a face surrounded by or emerging from foliage, leaves, or vines. This visual representation emphasizes his connection to the plant world.

Historical Roots: The Green Man motif has ancient roots and can be found in various cultures and religious traditions. It has appeared in medieval European churches, cathedrals, and art.

Pagan Origins: Some interpretations suggest that the Green Man has Pagan origins and may represent a nature deity or spirit associated with the vitality and renewal of the natural world.

Cultural Adaptations: The Green Man has been adapted into various artistic expressions, including literature, art, and contemporary pagan and neopagan practices. He continues to be a symbol embraced by those who value nature-based spirituality.

Wild Man Motif: The Green Man is sometimes associated with folklore's "Wild Man" motif. This archetype represents nature's untamed, primal forces and is often depicted as a figure covered in foliage or fur.

Seasonal Symbolism: The Green Man is often linked to seasonal changes, particularly the emergence of new growth in spring and the abundance of life during the warmer months.

Celtic and Druidic Connections: In Celtic mythology, the Green Man may be connected to deities associated with nature and vegetation. Some see a link between the Green Man and Celtic practices related to the reverence of the natural world.

Guardian of the Forest: The Green Man is sometimes considered a guardian spirit of the forest or the wilderness. His presence symbolizes the vital energy and life force inherent in the natural environment.

Modern Interpretations: In modern times, the Green Man has become a popular and recognizable symbol used in various contexts, including eco-spirituality and environmentalism, and as a decorative motif in architecture and art. The Green Man embodies the enduring human connection to nature and life cycles. Whether seen as a guardian spirit, a symbol of fertility, or an archetype of the wild forces of the earth, the Green Man remains a powerful and versatile figure in myth and culture.

Modron (Anglo-Welsh)

In Anglo-Welsh mythology, Mabon ap Modron is a figure associated with the Welsh mythological cycle.

Divine Child: Mabon ap Modron is a divine child figure in Welsh mythology. "Mabon" translates to "son" in Welsh, and "Modron" is a maternal figure often identified with the Celtic goddess Matrona.

Imprisonment and Rescue: In the Welsh myth of "Culhwch and Olwen," Mabon is mentioned as having been abducted by his mother, Modron, when he was three nights old. His whereabouts become a mystery, and he is eventually sought after for his wisdom and abilities.

Search for Mabon: In the tale, Culhwch, a hero, embarks on a quest to find Mabon ap Modron. The search involves enlisting the help of various mythological beings and heroes. The retrieval of Mabon becomes a central part of the narrative.

Connection to Seasonal Cycles: The story of Mabon ap Modron is often associated with the changing seasons. Some interpretations suggest that his abduction and subsequent rescue may symbolize the waxing and waning of light, reflecting the solar and agricultural cycles.

Link to the Otherworld: Mabon's imprisonment is said to occur in an Otherworldly realm, emphasizing Welsh mythology's magical and supernatural aspects. The Otherworld is a realm often associated with mystical beings and divine entities.

Role in the Mabinogion: The Mabinogion, a collection of Welsh medieval tales, references Mabon ap Modron. These tales provide insights into the mythological and heroic traditions of medieval Wales.

Symbol of Renewal: Mabon's release from imprisonment may symbolize renewal and the restoration of balance in the natural world. His return is sometimes associated with the vitality and fertility of the land.

Cultural Significance: Mabon ap Modron is one of the lesser-known figures in Welsh mythology, but his tale contributes to the rich tapestry of Welsh folklore and the Mabinogion. Mabon ap Modron's myth reflects themes of loss, quest, and restoration, contributing to the broader Welsh mythological cycle. The tale serves as a narrative thread connecting the divine and natural elements within Welsh cultural traditions.

Osiris (Egyptian)

Osiris is a prominent figure in ancient Egyptian mythology, associated with kingship, death, and rebirth.

God of the Afterlife: Osiris is primarily known as the god of the afterlife and the underworld in ancient Egyptian mythology. He holds a central role in the concept of resurrection and eternal life.

Kingship and Civilization: Osiris is also linked to kingship and the establishment of civilization. As a god-king, he brings order, agriculture, and the arts to the people.

Family Connections: Osiris is the son of the sky goddess Nut and the earth god Geb. He is the brother and husband of Isis, a powerful goddess in Egyptian mythology. They have a son named Horus.

Myth of Osiris and Set: The most well-known tale about Osiris involves his brother Set (Seth). Set becomes jealous of Osiris's rule and murders him. Osiris is then dismembered, and his body parts are scattered. With the help of her sister Nephthys and the god Anubis, Isis gathered the body parts and restored Osiris to life temporarily.

Resurrection and Afterlife: After his resurrection, Osiris becomes the ruler of the underworld. He judges the souls of the deceased, determining their fate in the afterlife. Osiris offers the promise of eternal life to those deemed worthy.

Symbolic Elements: Osiris is often depicted as a mummified pharaoh wearing the Atef white crown with two ostrich feathers. His green or black skin symbolizes rebirth and fertility.

Role in the Osirian Mysteries: The worship of Osiris was associated with mystery cults and rituals known as the Osirian Mysteries. These rites focused on death, resurrection, and the hope for an afterlife.

Horus and Osiris Connection: Osiris's son, Horus, is a significant figure in Egyptian mythology. The conflict between Horus and Set, representing order and chaos, reflects the perpetual struggle for cosmic balance.

Cultural Importance: Osiris is one of ancient Egypt's most widely worshiped and revered deities. His myth influenced religious beliefs, funerary practices, and the concept of an afterlife.

Festival of Osiris: The Osiris festival, known as the "Feast of Khoiak," was an annual celebration honoring Osiris. It involved processions, rituals, and performances depicting the mythological events of Osiris's life and death.

Judgment of the Dead: In the afterlife, Osiris presides over the Hall of Ma'at, where the hearts of the deceased are weighed against the feather of truth. Those with a pure heart are granted entry into the eternal paradise, while the wicked face punishment. Osiris's myth represents fundamental aspects of Egyptian religious beliefs, including the cycle of life, death, rebirth, and the enduring hope for an afterlife. His worship and symbolism had a profound impact on Egyptian culture and spirituality.

Pan (Greek)

Pan is a Greek god associated with nature, shepherds, and rustic music.

God of Nature: Pan is a deity in ancient Greek mythology and is often considered a nature god. He is associated with the wild, forests, mountains, and rustic landscapes. Appearance: Pan is typically depicted as a half-human, half-goat figure, a satyr. He has the upper body of a man and the lower body and horns of a goat.

Son of Hermes: According to some accounts, Pan is the son of the messenger god Hermes and a nymph named Dryope. His birth is associated with various myths and is depicted in different ways.

Pan's Lament: Pan is credited with creating a musical instrument called the pan flute or panpipes. The instrument is associated with his lament over the unrequited love for the nymph Syrinx, who was transformed into a reed to escape him.

Faunus in Roman Mythology: The Roman equivalent of Pan is Faunus. While they share many characteristics, Pan is often portrayed as more mischievous and carefree, while Faunus is associated with prophetic abilities.

God of Shepherds: Pan is considered the god of shepherds and flocks. His presence was believed to inspire awe and panic in the wilderness, leading to the word "panic" derived from his name.

Pan and Dionysus: Pan is sometimes associated with the god of wine and revelry, Dionysus. Together, they represent the untamed, joyful aspects of nature and celebrations.

Role in Panathenaic Festival: Pan had a role in the Panathenaic Festival in Athens, a celebration dedicated to the goddess Athena. His image was carried in a procession, and he was honored as a god of nature.

Cultural Significance: Pan was a popular deity in Greek folklore, representing the untamed forces of the natural world. His presence was thought to invoke both the beauty and the potentially chaotic aspects of the wilderness.

Legacy in Literature and Art: Pan's character has left a lasting impact on literature and art. He is often featured in poems, plays, and artistic representations, showcasing his dual nature as a playful and sometimes mischievous deity.

Pan as a Symbol: Pan has become a symbol of nature's untamed and primal aspects. His image and symbolism have persisted in various cultural references, including literature, music, and art. Pan's character embodies the spirit of nature and the untamed wilderness in Greek mythology. His dual nature as a playful, music-loving deity and a force of wild panic highlights the multifaceted relationship between humanity and the natural world.

Thor (Norse)

Thor is a prominent Norse mythology god associated with thunder, lightning, storms, strength, and protection.

God of Thunder: Thor is the Norse god of thunder, lightning, and storms. He is a mighty deity, often depicted wielding a magical hammer named Mjölnir.

Son of Odin: Thor is the son of Odin, the chief god in Norse mythology. His mother is Jord (or Fjörgyn), representing the earth.

Protector of Mankind: Thor is seen as a protector of both gods and humans. His role extends to defending Midgard (the world of humans) from various threats, including giants and other supernatural beings.

Appearance: Thor is typically described as a strong and robust figure with red hair and a beard. He is known for his distinctive hammer and often wears a magical belt called Megingjörð and iron gloves named Járngreipr.

Mjölnir: Thor's most iconic possession is Mjölnir, a mighty hammer crafted by the dwarves. Mjölnir is associated with thunder and lightning and can return to Thor after being thrown.

Protection Symbol: Mjölnir is also a symbol of protection, and miniature representations of the hammer were commonly worn as amulets by the Norse people.

Thor's Chariot: Thor is sometimes associated with a chariot pulled by two massive goats, Tanngrisnir and Tanngnjóstr. These goats could be sacrificed and brought back to life, providing sustenance for Thor during his travels.

Role in Norse Mythology: Thor plays a significant role in various Norse myths and sagas. He is often portrayed as a heroic and honorable figure, known for his feats in battles against giants and other mythological creatures.

Thunor in Anglo-Saxon Tradition: Thor's counterpart in Anglo-Saxon mythology is Thunor (or Þunor), reflecting the continuity of worship and mythology across different Germanic cultures.

Cultural Significance: Thor was a widely venerated deity in Norse society. His cult persisted even after the Christianization of Scandinavia, with some elements of Thor's mythology influencing medieval Scandinavian literature and folklore.

Thor's Day (Thursday): The English word "Thursday" is derived from Thor's name, emphasizing his enduring influence on language and cultural traditions.

Marvel Comics Adaptation: Thor has been adapted into popular culture, most notably in Marvel Comics. The comic book character and subsequent movie adaptations depict Thor as a superhero based on Norse mythology. Thor's mythology is deeply ingrained in Norse legend, and his character reflects the Norse understanding of natural forces, strength, and protection. His enduring popularity highlights Thor's significance in historical and contemporary contexts.

CHAPTER 12

Quicky
Duties

The Olympian Gods

Zeus / Jupiter
God of the Sky
King of weather, judgment, gods
Patron of: Rulers, judges
About: Husband and brother to Hera, he was king of the gods after overthrowing his father, Cronus.

Poseidon / Neptune
God of the Sea
Lord of water, horses, earthquakes
Patron of: Sailors, fishers
About: Easily angered, he lost the patronage of Athens to Athena, so he sent a monster to attack it.

Ares / Mars
God of War
Lord of warriors
Patron of: Warnors, athletes, Sparta
Related to: Worshipped for war, but sometimes considered too bloodthirsty and extreme.

Apollo
God of the Sun
Lord of Light, music, arts
Patron of: Musicians
About: Twins with Artemis, he is associated with the arts, knowledge, and the oracle of prophecy.

Hermes / Mercury
God of Messengers
Lord of messages, oratory, commence
Patron of: Messengers, merchants, thieves
About: Messenger of the gods, he was always on the move and loved playing tricks on others.

Dionysus / Bacchus
God of Wine
Lord of parties, wine
Patron of: Partiers
About: A popular god whose status as an Olympian is in question with Hestia. He loved festivities.

The Olympian Goddesses

Hera / Juno
Goddess of Motherhood
Queen of gods, marriage
Patron of: Marriages
About: Zeus's wife constantly punishes his lovers, for his infidelity while she remained pure.

Aphrodite / Venus
Goddess of Love
Lady of love, beauty, sex
Patron of: Lovers
About: Born from Uranus in the sea, she was given Hephaestus as her husband. But cheats on him with Ares.

Artemis / Diana
Goddess of the Moon
Lady of the hunt, right, virginity
Patron of: Hunters, young women
About: Twin with Apollo, she is a sworn virgin and protects young women's virtue.

Athena / Minerva
Goddess of Wisdom
Lady of wisdom, handicrafts, warfare
Patron of: Philosophers, Athens
About: Springing from Zeus' head after he ate her mother, she is the patron of Athens, and her wisdom rivals her fathers.

Demeter / Ceres
Goddess of the Harvest
Lady of plants, growth
Patron of: Gardeners, farmers
About: Hades took her daughter Persephone as a wife for part of the year, winter, during which Demeter refused to produce food.

Hestia / Vesta
Goddess of the Hearth
Lady of home, domesticity, family
Patron of: Servants, mothers
About: One of Cronus's daughters, her status as one of the 12 Olympians, is sometimes replaced by Dionysus.

CHAPTER 13

Omnism

Omniest - A person who does not claim any one religion, practice or belief, butfinds truth in them all.

Yoruba Traditions
"One who does evil to another does so to himself." - proverb

Atheism
"Treat others as you would want them to treat you and can reasonably expect them to want to be treated. Think about their perspective."
-The 10 Non-Commandments

Christianity
"Do unto others as you would have them do unto you."
-Matthew 7:12

Zoroastrianism
"Whatever is disagreeable to yourself, do not do unto others.
-Shayast-na-Shayast 13:29

Humanism
"Before performing an action which might harm another person, try to imagine yourself in their position, and consider whether you would want to be the recipient of that action. If you would not want to be in such a position, the other person probably would not either, and so you should not do it."
-Adam Lee

Bahá'í Faith
"And if thine eyes be turned towards justice, choose thou for thy neighbour that which thou choosest for thyself."
-Tablets of Bahá'u'lláh

First Peoples

"Even though you and I are in diferent boats, you in your boat and we our canoe, we share the same river of life. What befalls me befalls you." -Oren Lyons, Turtle Clan, Seneca Nation

Jainism

"A man should wander about treating all creatures as he himself would be treated."
-Sutrakritanga 1.11.33

Islam

"By no means shall you attain righteousness unless you give freely to others of that which you love; and whatever you give, of a truth Allah knows it well."
-Qur'an 3:92

Wicca

"And it harm none, do
what thou wilt." - Wiccan Rede

Judaism

"What is hateful to you, do not do to your fellow: this is the whole Torah; the rest is commentary; go and learn."
-Babylonian Talmud

Sikhism

"As you see yourself, see others as well; only then will you become a partner in heaven."
-Sri Guru Granth Sahib Ji, 480

Hinduism
"This is the sum of Dharma
-duty: Do nothing unto others which would cause
you pain if done to you."
-Mahabharata 5:1517

Shinto
The heart of the person before you is a mirror. See there your
own form."

Confucianism
"Tse-kung asked, 'Is there one word that can serve as a
principle of conduct for life?' Confucius
-Doctrine of the Mean 13.3

Taoism
"Regard your neighbor's gain as your gain, and
your neighbor's loss as your own loss."

Buddhism
"All are afraid of the stick, all
fear death. Putting oneself in another's place, one should not hurt or
kill others."
-Dhammapada, verse 129

Unitarianism
"We affirm and promote respect for the interdependent web of all
existence of which we are a part."
-7th Principle

CHAPTER 14

Magical
Creatures
and Beings

Banshee

The Banshee is a mythical creature from Irish folklore, often associated with a female spirit or fairy who wails as an omen of death.

Name and Meaning: The term "Banshee" is derived from the Irish bean sí, which translates to "woman of the fairy mound" or "woman of the sidhe."

Appearance: The Banshee is often described as a woman with long, flowing hair wearing a hooded cloak or shroud. Her appearance may vary, but she is commonly depicted as a pale, ethereal figure.

Cry or Wail: The most distinctive characteristic of the Banshee is her mournful cry or wail. This eerie sound is believed to foretell the death of a family member.

Death Omen: In Irish folklore, the Banshee is considered a harbinger of death. Her lament is said to be heard before the passing of a family member, acting as a forewarning to those who hear it.

Families and Lineages: The Banshee is often linked to specific Irish families or lineages, serving as a guardian spirit or protector. Her appearance is associated with the impending death of a member of these families.

Variations in Folklore: Different regions in Ireland have various interpretations of the Banshee. In some stories, she may appear as a young woman; in others, she may take on a more haggard or ghostly appearance.

Keening Tradition: The act of keening, a traditional form of vocal lamentation, is associated with the Banshee's cry. Keening was historically performed at funerals to express grief and mourning.

Association with Sidhe and Fairies: The Banshee is often linked to the Aos Sí, a supernatural race in Irish mythology that includes fairies and other magical beings. The belief is that she is a fairy woman fulfilling a specific role.

Celtic Folklore Influence: The Banshee has roots in Celtic folklore, where various supernatural beings were believed to interact with the mortal world. The concept of death omens and otherworldly messengers is common in Celtic mythology.

Female Spirits in Other Cultures: Similar motifs of female spirits or entities associated with death and mourning are found in various cultures worldwide. The Banshee, however, is distinctly tied to Irish folklore.

Evolution in Modern Stories: In contemporary literature and media, the Banshee's character has evolved beyond her traditional role. She is sometimes portrayed as a sympathetic figure or creature with complex motivations.

The Banshee's haunting cry and association with death contribute to her enduring presence in Irish folklore and impact on the cultural imagination.

Basilisk

The Basilisk is a legendary creature with origins in various mythologies, known for its serpentine or dragon-like appearance and its deadly gaze.

Cultural Origins: The Basilisk's origins can be traced to ancient Greek and Roman mythology, where it was described as a serpent or dragon. It later became a prominent figure in medieval European folklore.

Appearance: The Basilisk is typically depicted as a serpent or dragon, often with a crest or crown on its head. It may have wings, and its eyes are said to be particularly deadly.

Deadly Gaze: One of the most infamous characteristics of the Basilisk is its deadly gaze. According to legend, making eye contact with a Basilisk could cause death or turn the observer to stone.

Medieval Bestiaries: The Basilisk is frequently mentioned in medieval bestiaries, books describing various animals and mythical creatures. These texts often attributed fantastic and symbolic qualities to the Basilisk.

Mythological Roots: In Greek mythology, the Basilisk was associated with the serpent slain by Apollo, known as the Python. The Roman author Pliny the Elder contributed to the Basilisk's lore in his work "Naturalis Historia."

Egg-Hatching Legend: According to legend, a Basilisk could be born from a serpent's egg incubated by a toad. This mythical process was thought to occur in certain dark, hidden places.

Slayer of the Basilisk: The Basilisk was said to have a natural enemy - the weasel. It was believed that the odor of a weasel could kill a Basilisk or neutralize its deadly gaze.

Historical and Scientific Context: In historical writings, the term "Basilisk" was sometimes used to describe various venomous snakes. In modern taxonomy, it refers to a genus of small, venomous snakes found in tropical regions.

Symbolism: The Basilisk is often seen as a symbol of danger, fear, and the destructive power of serpents. Its mythical attributes contribute to its representation as a formidable and lethal creature.

Artistic Representations: The Basilisk has been depicted in various forms, including illuminated manuscripts, paintings, and sculptures. Artists often took creative liberties in portraying this mythical creature.

Literary References: The Basilisk has appeared in numerous works of literature, both ancient and modern, contributing to its enduring presence in cultural storytelling.

The Basilisk's legend has evolved, drawing from various cultural influences and weaving a tapestry of myth and folklore that continues to capture the imagination of people worldwide.

Centaur

A centaur is a mythological creature with a human's upper body and a horse's lower body. In Greek mythology, centaurs are often depicted as wild and unruly beings, embodying human and animal characteristics.

Origin: Centaurs trace their origin to Greek mythology and are often associated with the god Apollo or born from the union of Ixion and Nephele.

Appearance: The upper part of a centaur resembles that of a human, including the torso, arms, and head. The lower part is that of a horse, featuring four legs.

Behavior: Centaurs are frequently portrayed as a complex mix of civilized and wild traits. While some are wise and skilled in various arts, others are depicted as rowdy, aggressive, and prone to excessive drinking.

Chiron: Chiron is a notable exception among centaurs. Described as wise and knowledgeable in medicine, music, and the arts, Chiron is often depicted as a mentor to heroes like Hercules and Achilles.

Mythological Stories: Centaurs appear in various myths and legends. Notably, they played a role in the battle between the Lapiths and the centaurs at the wedding of Pirithous and Hippodamia.

Symbolism: Centaurs symbolize the duality of human nature, representing the struggle between civilization and primal instincts. They are a metaphor for individuals' challenges in balancing reason and emotion.

Literary and Artistic Representations: Centaurs have been a popular subject in literature, art, and popular culture. Their dual nature makes them intriguing characters, often used to explore identity and inner conflict themes.

Role in Modern Culture: Centaurs continue to be featured in various forms of media, including literature, films, and fantasy art. Their enduring presence highlights their significance in mythological storytelling and exploring humanity's complexities.

Chimera

The Chimera is a mythical creature originating in Greek mythology, known for its composite and fearsome nature.

Origin: The Chimera's roots are in Greek mythology, associated explicitly with stories from ancient sources like Homer's "Iliad" and Hesiod's "Theogony."

Composition: The Chimera is a hybrid creature, typically described as having the body and head of a lion, the tail of a serpent or dragon, and a goat's head protruding from its back. Some versions also include wings.

Parentage: The Chimera is often considered the offspring of Typhon and Echidna, making it a sibling to various other monsters in Greek mythology.

Location: The Chimera was said to dwell in Lycia, a region in Asia Minor. It terrorized the local population, breathing fire and causing destruction.

Heroic Confrontation: The hero Bellerophon, often aided by the winged horse Pegasus, is famous for slaying the Chimera. He accomplished this feat by using a combination of a spear and lead-tipped arrows.

Symbolic Meaning: The Chimera is interpreted symbolically, representing a monstrous and unbeatable adversary. Its composite nature is a metaphor for the diverse challenges one might face in life.

Fire-Breathing Ability: One of the distinctive features of the Chimera is its ability to breathe fire, a trait that adds to its formidable and terrifying nature.

Cultural Influence: The concept of the Chimera has had a lasting impact on literature, art, and popular culture. It continues to be referenced in various forms, symbolizing mythical creatures and hybrid beings.

Scientific Usage: The term "chimera" has been adopted in biology to describe an organism with cells or tissues from different genetic sources, reflecting the creature's composite nature in mythology.

Mythological Legacy: The Chimera's tale contributes to the rich tapestry of Greek mythology, showcasing the hero's triumph over a monstrous adversary and the enduring fascination with creatures that embody both danger and mystery.

Dragon

The dragon is a mythical creature with serpent or reptilian characteristics in various cultures worldwide.

Cross-Cultural Origins: Dragons have diverse origins, appearing in the mythology of numerous cultures, including Chinese, European, Middle Eastern, and Mesoamerican.

European Dragons: European dragons are commonly portrayed as large, fire-breathing creatures with wings and scales. They are often associated with medieval folklore, guarding treasure and terrorizing villages.

Guardians and Protectors: In some cultures, dragons are revered as protective entities. Chinese dragons, for example, are considered symbols of imperial power and guardians of sacred spaces.

Water Dragons: Some cultures, particularly in East Asia, depict dragons as water creatures associated with rivers, lakes, and oceans. These dragons are often benevolent and bringers of rain.

Dragon Slayers: Myths often feature heroic figures, such as Saint George or Siegfried, who slay dragons as part of their quests. This theme is prevalent in European medieval literature.

Symbolism of Power: Dragons often symbolize power, strength, and wisdom. In Chinese culture, they represent the Emperor and are associated with the five elements.

Cultural Impact: Dragons have significantly impacted art, literature, and popular culture. They appear in works like J.R.R. Tolkien's "The Hobbit" and in the heraldry of many European families.

Dragon Dance: The dragon dance is a traditional Chinese performance during festivals and celebrations. It involves a long dragon puppet manipulated by dancers, symbolizing good luck and prosperity.

Dragon Boat Festival: Celebrated in many Asian countries, this festival involves dragon boat races, where elaborately decorated boats resembling dragons race in rivers.

Modern Pop Culture: Dragons are popular in fantasy literature, movies, and games. They are iconic figures in franchises like "Game of Thrones" and "The Elder Scrolls."

Dragons' enduring presence in global mythology and adaptation in contemporary storytelling highlight their universal appeal as symbols of power, mystery, and the fantastical.

Gargoyles

Gargoyles are architectural sculptures often depicted as grotesque, winged creatures commonly found on buildings, especially Gothic cathedrals.

Origin of the Term: The word "gargoyle" is derived from the Old French "gargouille," which means throat or gullet. It is associated with the gurgling sound of water passing through the mouth of these sculptures.

Architectural Purpose: Gargoyles serve a functional purpose in architecture. They are designed as water spouts to redirect rainwater away from the sides of buildings, preventing erosion and damage.

Gothic Architecture: Gargoyles are most commonly associated with Gothic architecture, which was prevalent in medieval Europe from the 12th to the 16th centuries. They are often found on cathedrals, churches, and other stone structures.

Grotesque and Mythical Forms: Gargoyles come in various forms, often depicting grotesque or mythical creatures such as demons, dragons, animals, and human-animal hybrids. Their designs reflect the creativity and symbolism of the time.

Religious Symbolism: In medieval Christian architecture, gargoyles served a symbolic role. They were often crafted to represent evil or demonic forces, acting as protective guardians by warding off evil spirits from the sacred space.

Protection Against Evil: Gargoyles were believed to have apotropaic qualities, which could avert or deflect evil. Their intimidating and fierce appearance was thought to deter malevolent spirits or creatures.

Materials: Gargoyles are typically made of stone, such as limestone or granite, due to the durability of these materials. The stone carvings withstand weathering and provide a lasting decorative element.

Historical Examples: Notable examples of gargoyles can be found in cathedrals like Notre-Dame de Paris, Chartres Cathedral, and Westminster Abbey. Each gargoyle may have unique features, contributing to the artistic richness of the structure.

Gargoyles in Popular Culture: Gargoyles have become popular in modern culture, appearing in literature, movies, and television. The animated TV series "Gargoyles," created by Greg Weisman, features a group of gargoyles who come to life at night.

Gargoyles remain iconic symbols of medieval architecture, blending both functional and symbolic elements. Their intricate designs and enduring presence contribute to Gothic structures' rich history and aesthetics.

Harpy

The harpy is a mythical creature from Greek mythology, often depicted as a bird with a woman's face.

Greek Mythology: Harpies are best known from Greek mythology, where they are described as winged spirits with the faces of women and the bodies of birds.

Names: The most famous harpies are Aello, Celaeno, and Ocypete, each associated with specific characteristics or behaviors.

Characteristics: Harpies are typically portrayed with sharp claws, wings, and sometimes feathered bodies. Their faces are human, and they often exhibit a blend of avian and human features.

Wind Spirits: The name "harpy" is derived from the Greek word "harpēia," meaning "snatcher" or "swift robber." They were considered stormy winds, often associated with sudden gusts and tempests.

Punishment of Phineas: In Greek mythology, the harpies play a role in the story of Phineas. As punishment for revealing the secrets of the gods, Phineas was tormented by the harpies, who would swoop down, snatch his food, and befoul what remained.

Aeneas and the Harpies: In Virgil's "Aeneid," the Trojan hero Aeneas and his crew encounter the harpies on the Strophades islands. The harpies curse them, predicting hunger and hardship, but the Trojans eventually drive the harpies away.

Symbolism: Harpies symbolize stormy winds, chaos, and swift retribution. Their association with punishment and the disruption of order reflects their role in mythology.

Role in Popular Culture: Harpies continue to be a source of inspiration in popular culture, appearing in various fantasy books, movies, and games. They are often portrayed as fierce and menacing creatures.

Transformation in Modern Storytelling: In some modern interpretations, harpies are depicted with more sympathetic or complex traits, exploring their characters beyond their traditional roles as avian tormentors.

The harpy's presence in Greek mythology and its subsequent influence on art and literature highlights its role as a mythical creature representing swift retribution and the tumultuous forces of nature.

Kitsune

The Kitsune is a mythical creature from Japanese folklore, often depicted as a fox with magical abilities and intelligence.

Name and Meaning: The term "Kitsune" is Japanese for fox. In folklore, Kitsune is associated with intelligence and magical qualities.

Shape-Shifting Abilities: Kitsune is renowned for its shape-shifting abilities. They can transform into various forms, including that of a human. Older and more powerful Kitsune are said to be able to shape-shift into more complex forms.

Appearance: Kitsune are typically depicted as foxes with multiple tails, and the number of tails often indicates their age, wisdom, and power. The more tails a Kitsune has, the more powerful and wise it is believed to be.

Mischief and Trickery: Kitsune is known for mischievous and sometimes malicious behavior. They may play tricks on humans, possess them, or manipulate events to their advantage.

Guardians and Benefactors: While Kitsune is often associated with trickery, some stories depict them as benevolent beings acting as guardians or benefactors. They may offer guidance, protection, or even fall in love with humans.

Divine Messengers: In Shinto belief, Kitsune are considered divine messengers of the rice deity Inari. Inari shrines often have fox statues, and Kitsune are revered as messengers and protectors.

Transformation Tests: Folklore includes stories where Kitsune are challenged to prove their identity by transforming into different shapes or objects. Their skill in these tests is a measure of their magical prowess.

Gender and Seduction: Kitsune are often portrayed as female, and stories sometimes involve them using their shape-shifting abilities to seduce men. This seduction may be a test or may lead to various consequences.

Folktales and Literature: Kitsune has been featured in numerous Japanese folktales, poems, and literary works. Their presence in storytelling reflects their enduring significance in Japanese cultural imagination.

The Kitsune's multifaceted nature and its role in Japanese folklore contribute to its enduring appeal and cultural significance.

Leprechaun

The Leprechaun is a mythical creature from Irish folklore, often depicted as a small, mischievous fairy with a penchant for shoemaking and a pot of gold.

Appearance: Leprechauns are typically portrayed as small, old men about 2-3 feet tall. They are often dressed in green or red clothing, wear buckled shoes and sometimes don a hat.

Occupation - Shoemaker: One of the primary attributes associated with leprechauns is their skill as shoemakers. In folklore, they are often found mending or making shoes. The sound of a leprechaun's hammering alerts people to their presence.

Wealth and Gold: Leprechauns are often linked to possessing a pot of gold, usually hidden at the end of a rainbow. Capturing a leprechaun is believed to grant the captor access to the creature's treasure.

Mischief and Trickery: Leprechauns are known for their mischievous and trickster nature. They may play pranks on humans or lead them on chases in folklore, ultimately avoiding capture.

Elusiveness: Leprechauns are considered elusive and difficult to catch. Folklore often describes them as disappearing or using magical means to escape from those attempting to capture them.

Rainbow Connection: The association between leprechauns and rainbows, leading to pots of gold, is a relatively modern addition to the mythology. This idea likely originated from the vivid imagery of rainbows and the elusive nature of leprechauns.

Leprechaun Traps: In modern times, especially around St. Patrick's Day, children may create "leprechaun traps" hoping to catch one and obtain a wish or find the Leprechaun's gold.

Leprechauns in Folklore: Leprechauns are featured in various Irish folktales, often as supporting characters in larger narratives or as central figures in stories focusing on their trickery and treasure.

Cultural Symbolism: Leprechauns have become symbolic figures associated with Irish culture and are often linked to St. Patrick's Day celebrations. They are popularized in various forms of media, including literature, film, and advertising.

Leprechauns remain iconic figures in Irish folklore, representing a blend of mischief, craftsmanship, and the allure of hidden treasures. Their presence adds a whimsical and magical element to the rich tapestry of Irish myth and legend.

Phoenix

The phoenix is a mythical bird associated with rebirth and immortality, found in various mythologies around the world.

Cultural Origins: The phoenix has roots in ancient Egyptian, Greek, Roman, Chinese, and Persian mythologies, among others. The specifics of its characteristics and symbolism vary across cultures.

Rebirth and Immortality: The central theme of the phoenix is its ability to regenerate or be reborn from its ashes cyclically. This symbolism represents renewal, resurrection, and immortality.

Appearance: Descriptions of the phoenix's appearance vary, but common features include vibrant plumage, often in shades of red and gold, and a majestic, bird-like form. It is typically larger than other birds.

Greek and Roman Mythology: In Greek mythology, the phoenix is associated with the sun and was said to burst into flames upon death, only to be reborn from its ashes. The Roman poet Ovid's work "Metamorphoses" popularized this imagery.

Egyptian Bennu Bird: The phoenix has similarities to the ancient Egyptian Bennu bird, a symbol of creation and associated with the sun god Ra. The Bennu bird is often depicted as a heron or crane.

Chinese Fenghuang: The phoenix is known as Fenghuang in Chinese mythology. Unlike the Western phoenix, Fenghuang is often depicted as a composite of several birds and represents harmony, balance, and the union of opposites.

Persian Simurgh: The Simurgh shares similarities with the phoenix in Persian mythology. It is a benevolent, mythical bird associated with healing, and its feathers are said to possess medicinal properties.

Symbolism in Christianity: The phoenix has been linked to Christian symbolism, representing resurrection and eternal life. It is a metaphor for Christ's victory over death and the promise of life after death.

Literary References: The phoenix appears in various works of literature, including classical texts, medieval manuscripts, and modern fantasy. Notable examples include Dante's "Divine Comedy" and J.K. Rowling's "Harry Potter" series.

Scientific and Popular Culture References: The phoenix has inspired names for various astronomical phenomena and fictional characters in science fiction and fantasy.

Set

The Set Animal is a mythical creature from ancient Egyptian mythology, associated with the god Set (also spelled Seth).

Name: The Set Animal is also known as Sha or Typhonic Beast.

Origin: The Set Animal is deeply rooted in ancient Egyptian mythology, specifically associated with the god Set, considered both a deity of chaos and a protector of the desert.

Description: The Set Animal is often described as a mysterious and composite creature featuring traits of different animals. It is commonly depicted with a canine's body, perhaps resembling a jackal or aardvark, and sometimes has a long, forked tail.

Symbolism: In ancient Egyptian mythology, Set was a complex deity associated with chaos, storms, and the desert. The Set Animal symbolized the untamed forces of the wilderness and the unpredictable nature of Set himself.

Role in Mythology: Set was a deity known for rivalry with his brother Osiris, the god of life, death, and fertility. Set's actions, including the murder of Osiris, led to a struggle between chaos and order in Egyptian mythology.

Set Animal as a Protective Symbol: Despite its association with chaos, it was also considered a protective symbol. It was believed to guard against evil forces and protect the deceased in the afterlife.

Depictions in Art and Hieroglyphs: The Set Animal is commonly represented in ancient Egyptian art, hieroglyphs, and temple reliefs. Its distinctive form is recognizable in various contexts, emphasizing its significance in religious iconography.

Symbolic Representations: The Set Animal is often found on protective amulets, tomb decorations, and other religious artifacts. It was intended to provide spiritual protection and safeguard individuals in life and death.

Modern Interest: The Set Animal and its associated mythology continue to captivate the interest of scholars, historians, and enthusiasts of ancient Egyptian culture. Its symbolism adds to the intricate tapestry of ancient Egyptian religious beliefs and practices.

The Set Animal remains an intriguing and symbolic figure in ancient Egyptian mythology, representing both the chaotic and protective aspects associated with the god Set.

Sphinx

The Sphinx is a mythical creature with origins in ancient Egyptian and Greek mythology, known for its enigmatic and majestic appearance.

Origin: The Sphinx has roots in Egyptian and Greek mythology, with distinct cultural interpretations and symbolism.

Egyptian Sphinx: In ancient Egypt, the Sphinx was often depicted as a creature with the body of a lion and the head of a pharaoh or a deity, symbolizing the strength and wisdom of the rulers.

Great Sphinx of Giza: The most famous depiction of the Sphinx is the Great Sphinx of Giza, located on the Giza Plateau near the pyramids. It has a lion's body and a pharaoh's head, commonly believed to represent Pharaoh Khafre.

Greek Sphinx: In Greek mythology, the Sphinx is portrayed as a female creature with the body of a lion, the wings of a bird, and the head of a human. She is associated with mystery, riddles, and tragedy.

Riddle of the Sphinx: The Greek Sphinx is renowned for posing a riddle to travelers. According to the myth, she asked passersby the famous riddle, "What creature has one voice and yet becomes four-footed and two-footed and three-footed?" Oedipus successfully answered, revealing the answer as "Man," and the Sphinx perished.

Symbolism: The Sphinx symbolizes the intersection of human intelligence and animalistic strength. In Egypt, it represents royal power and protection, while in Greece, it embodies mystery and life's challenges.

Hybrid Nature: The Sphinx's combination of human and animal features underscores themes of duality and the merging of divine and mortal qualities.

Ancient Art and Sculpture: Sphinxes were commonly used as architectural and artistic elements in ancient civilizations. They appeared in sculptures, tombs, and temple entrances.

Cultural Influence: The Sphinx has left a lasting impact on various cultures and continues to symbolize mystery, wisdom, and the timeless allure of ancient civilizations.

Modern References: The Sphinx is frequently referenced in literature, art, and popular culture. Its iconic presence and association with riddles contribute to its enduring fascination and significance in storytelling.

Tengu

The Tengu is a mythical creature from Japanese folklore, often depicted as a supernatural being with both human and bird-like characteristics.

Name and Meaning: The term "Tengu" is derived from the Chinese tian-gou, meaning heavenly dog. However, in Japanese folklore, Tengu is more commonly associated with bird-like attributes.

Appearance: Tengu are typically portrayed with both human and avian features. They have human-like bodies but possess long noses resembling beaks. They are often depicted with wings, although some variations show them with crow-like or bird-like faces.

Mythological Origin: Tengu has roots in Japanese Shinto and Buddhist mythology. They are considered supernatural creatures associated with the spirit world and are sometimes seen as protectors of the mountains.

Shugendō Connection: Tengu are often associated with practitioners of Shugendō, a form of asceticism that combines elements of Buddhism, Shinto, and Taoism. In some beliefs, Tengu are both adversaries and protectors of those seeking enlightenment through mountain ascetic practices.

Mischievous Nature: Tengu are known for their mischievous and sometimes malevolent behavior. They may play tricks on humans, disrupt travelers, or create chaos. However, they are not purely evil, and some stories depict them as more benevolent beings.

Karasu Tengu: A subtype of Tengu, known as Karasu Tengu, has a crow-like appearance with wings and bird-like features. They are associated with crows and ravens, and their behavior is often more malevolent.

Leaf Fans: Tengu are often depicted carrying feathered fans called "tengu-ōgi" or "tengu tessen." These fans are said to have magical properties, and legends suggest they can create strong winds or manipulate fire.

Cultural Impact: Tengu have made their way into various aspects of Japanese culture, including literature, art, and theater. They are featured in Noh and Kabuki plays, where actors wear tengu masks to portray these mythical beings.

The Tengu's complex character, blending mischief and wisdom, adds to the richness of Japanese folklore and cultural traditions. Their association with mountains and spiritual practices reflects the diverse and dynamic nature of mythical creatures in Japanese mythology.

Unicorn

The unicorn is a legendary creature known for its single, spiraled horn protruding from its forehead. Although originating in various mythologies, it has become a symbol of purity and enchantment.

Mythological Origins: Unicorns have roots in diverse mythologies, including ancient Mesopotamian, Chinese, and European cultures. They are often associated with purity, grace, and elusive beauty.

Appearance: The unicorn is typically depicted as a horse-like creature with a single horn projecting from its forehead. It may have various colors, with white being the most common in Western depictions.

Symbolism: Unicorns are symbols of purity, innocence, and magic. In many cultures, their horns were believed to have healing properties and could neutralize poisons.

Ancient References: The earliest known references to unicorns come from ancient Mesopotamian texts. They are also mentioned in the Bible, further contributing to their mystical aura.

Medieval Europe: Unicorns gained prominence in medieval European folklore and heraldry. They were often considered untamable creatures, embodying purity and grace.

Hunting the Unicorn: In medieval and Renaissance art, hunting scenes featuring unicorns were a popular theme. These artworks depicted unicorns as elusive and noble creatures.

Allegorical Meaning: The unicorn became an allegorical figure, representing Christ in Christian symbolism. In this context, the horn symbolizes the unity of Christ's divine and human nature.

National Animal: Scotland adopted the unicorn as its national animal, representing nobility and purity.

Scientific Term: In biology, a "unicorn" can refer to a genetic chimera, an organism containing genetically distinct cells. This usage reflects the mythical creature's theme of rarity and uniqueness.

The unicorn's enduring presence in mythology and popular culture highlights its timeless appeal as a symbol of magic, purity, and the fantastical.

Valkyries

Valkyries are mythical figures from Norse mythology, often depicted as powerful and divine female warriors who serve the god Odin.

Name and Origin: "Valkyrie" is derived from Old Norse, where "valkyrja" describes these warrior maidens. In Old Norse, "Val" means "chooser of the slain."

Role in Norse Mythology: Valkyries are divine beings associated with battle, fate, and death in Norse mythology. They serve Odin, the Allfather, and are tasked with selecting those who may die in battle and those who may live.

Choosers of the Slain: One of the primary roles of Valkyries is to choose which warriors will die in battle and be taken to the afterlife in Odin's hall, Valhalla. Those selected by Valkyries are known as the Einherjar and are honored as heroes.

Odin's Companions: Valkyries are considered Odin's companions and are often depicted as his daughters or servants. They are associated with the realm of Asgard, the home of the Aesir gods.

Swooping Down to Battlefields: Valkyries are believed to descend onto battlefields to witness and choose the bravest warriors. They may also assist in the fighting, guiding the souls of the fallen to the afterlife.

Freyja's Connection: While Valkyries primarily serve Odin, there is a connection between Valkyries and the goddess Freyja. Some myths suggest that Freyja has her own group of warrior maidens, similar to Valkyries, called the "Valkyrjur."

Sisterhood: Valkyries are often described as a sisterhood, working together to fulfill their divine duties. They share a bond and camaraderie, reflecting their collective role in guiding souls.

Epic Poems: Valkyries are prominently featured in Old Norse epic poems, particularly in the Poetic Edda and the Prose Edda. These sources describe their role, appearance, and interactions with mortal heroes.

Ragnarök: Valkyries play a role in the apocalyptic event known as Ragnarök. During this event, they are said to ride into battle alongside the gods, participating in the cosmic conflict that leads to the end and rebirth of the world.

Valkyries are powerful and iconic figures in Norse mythology, embodying the ferocity of battle and the solemn duty of guiding fallen warriors to the afterlife.

Yeti

The Yeti, also known as the "Abominable Snowman," is a legendary ape-like creature said to inhabit the Himalayan mountains.

Cultural Origins: The Yeti is part of the folklore and mythology of the Himalayan region, including Nepal, Tibet, and Bhutan.

Physical Description: The Yeti is commonly described as a large, ape-like creature standing upright on two legs. It is covered in fur, often said to be brown or reddish-brown, with a mix of human and ape features.

Sightings and Reports: Local and trekkers in the Himalayas have reported Yeti sightings. However, evidence is often anecdotal, and no conclusive proof of the creature's existence has been presented.

Mythological Context: In local mythology, the Yeti is sometimes considered a guardian of the mountains and is integrated into the cultural beliefs of the indigenous peoples

First Western Exposure: The Western world learned about the Yeti through accounts of early 20th-century Western explorers and mountaineers in the Himalayas.

Mount Everest Expeditions: Interest in the Yeti heightened with the numerous expeditions to Mount Everest. Some climbers claimed to have seen large footprints, leading to speculation about the existence of a large unknown primate.

Famous Yeti Footprint: The most famous piece of evidence associated with the Yeti is the "Pangboche Hand." In the 1950s, a supposed Yeti hand was found in a monastery in Pangboche, Nepal. However, subsequent analysis suggested it belonged to a human.

Scientific Skepticism: The scientific community generally remains skeptical about the existence of the Yeti due to the lack of conclusive evidence, such as photographs, DNA samples, or specimens

Cultural Impact: The Yeti has become a cultural icon, featured in literature, films, and popular media. It is often portrayed as a mysterious and elusive creature in these depictions.

The Yeti remains an intriguing cultural and cryptozoological phenomenon, blending local mythology with Western exploration and continuing to capture the imagination of people around the world.

CHAPTER 15

The Moon

The Phases of the Moon

New

Sometimes called the Crescent Moon, when you can see the very first sliver of light in the sky. This phase promotes new beginnings, new endeavors, and new relationships. It is the time to make positive changes and plant seeds of ideas that will be harvested later.

Waxing

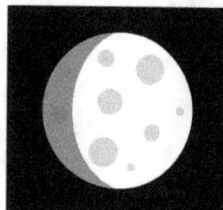

In this phase, the Moon appears to be growing in size, shifting from new to full as though it's gaining strength. It makes sense, then, that this is an excellent time to focus on increasing your knowledge, bank accounts, and relationships. This phase promotes healing.

Full

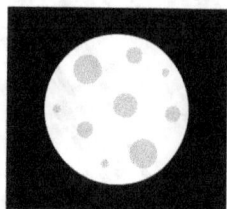

The Moon's most potent phase is when we see her entire illuminated face. This is a time of fulfillment, activity, and increased psychic ability for perfecting ideas, in other words, "getting your act together," celebrations, or renewing commitments to people or projects—the best time for spells of any kind.

Waning

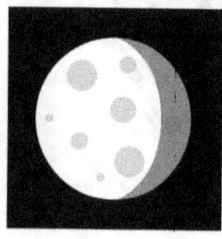

The Moon is decreasing in size as it journeys from full to dark. The waning Moon is a time of decrease, release, letting go, and completion. It is an excellent time to begin dieting, breaking bad habits, breaking off relationships, or dealing with legal matters.

March Moon

In this month's cosmic forecast, the March moon magic brings forth powerful energies for all signs. As the celestial bodies align, the universe encourages us to embrace the intentions of spring cleaning, clearing away stagnant energy to make room for new growth. The light and dark forces find a harmonious balance, guiding us to tap into the transformative powers of water magic. With the waxing phase, it's time to set intentions for new growth, illuminated by the radiant light of the moon. During the waning phase, we release clutter and negativity, restoring balance and paving the way for our dreams to blossom. So, dear readers, embrace the magic of March and allow the cosmic currents to guide you towards a path of renewed vitality and equilibrium.

April Moon

In the cosmic forecast for April, the stars align to usher in a wave of transformative energy with the arrival of April moon magic. This celestial phenomenon signals a time of rebirth and discovery, urging us to embrace the fertile energies of the universe. As we set our sights on new goals and aspirations, the cosmos invites us to harness the power of plant and flower magic, planting seeds of intention and watching them bloom with the rhythm of nature. Amidst this period of growth and flow, prepare to embark on a journey of change and self-discovery, guided by the ever-changing tides of the universe. So, dear readers, embrace the magic of April and allow the cosmic currents to lead you towards newfound vitality and abundance.

Moons of the Year

A rare second Full Moon in a single month is called a "Blue Moon." A rare second New Moon in a month is called a "Black Moon."

Different cultures gave the Moon different titles to express what the Moon means to them in a given month. As a result, some of the moon names make sense, while others may not make any sense.

Full Moon – January
Native American Tribes: Old Moon, Wolf Moon, Ice Moon, Moon after Yule, and Winter Moon
Siouan (Assiniboines) Tribe: Hard Time Moon
Inuit People of Northern Canada: Dwarf Seal Moon
Celtic: Wolf Moon, Stay Home Moon, Moon after Yule
Chinese: Holiday Moon
Fairy: Icicle Moon

Full Moon – February
Native American Tribes: Hunger or Starvation Moon, Storm Moon, Trapper's Moon, Moon of Ice, and Tree Moon
Siouan (Assiniboines) Tribe: Long Day Moon
Inuit People of Northern Canada: Seal Pup Moon
Celtic: Storm Moon, Ice Moon, and Snow moon
Chinese: Budding Moon
Fairy: Snowdrop Moon

Full Moon – March
Native American Tribes: Worm Moon, Crow Moon, Moon of Winds, Sap Moon, Fish Moon, Chaste Moon, and Death Moon
Siouan (Assiniboines) Tribe: Sore Eye Moon
Inuit People of Northern Canada: Snow Bird Moon
Celtic: Plough Moon, Wind Moon, Lenten (lengthening) Moon
Chinese: Sleeping Moon
Fairy: Waking Wood Moon

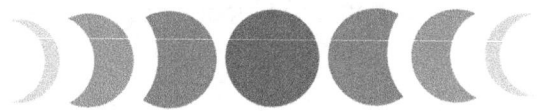

Moons of the Year

Full Moon – April
Native American Tribes: Pink Moon, Seed Moon, Frog Moon, Egg Moon, and Awakening Moon
Siouan (Assiniboines) Tribe: Frog's Moon
Inuit People of Northern Canada: Snow Melt Moon
Celtic: Budding Moon, New Shoots Moon, and Seed Moon
Chinese: Peony Moon
Fairy: Birthing Moon

Full Moon – May
Native American Tribes: Flower Moon, Hare Moon, Milk Moon, and Grass Moon
Siouan (Assiniboines) Tribe: Idle Moon
Inuit People of Northern Canada: Goose Moon
Celtic: Mother's Moon and Bright Moon
Chinese: Dragon Moon
Fairy: Moon of White Petals

Full Moon – June
Native American Tribes: Strawberry Moon, Planting Moon, and Green Corn Moon
Siouan (Assiniboines) Tribe: Full Leaf Moon
Inuit People of Northern Canada: Hunting Moon
Celtic: Mead Moon, Horse Moon, Dyan Moon, and Rose Moon
Chinese: Lotus Moon
Fairy: Wild Cherry Moon

Full Moon – July
Native American Tribes: Hay Moon, Summer Moon, Thunder Moon, and Buck Moon
Siouan (Assiniboines) Tribe: Red Berries Moon
Inuit People of Northern Canada: Dry Moon
Celtic: Claiming Moon, Wyrt or Herb Moon, and Mead Moon
Chinese: Hungry Ghost Moon
Fairy: Dancing Delight Moon

Full Moon – August
Native American Tribes: Sturgeon Moon, Corn Moon, Green Corn Moon, Dog Days Moon, and Lightening Moon
Siouan (Assiniboines) Tribe: Black Cherries Moon
Inuit People of Northern Canada: Swan Flight Moon
Celtic: Dispute Moon, Lynx Moon, and Grain Moon
Chinese: Harvest Moon
Fairy: Blackberry Harvest Moon

Moons of the Year

Full Moon – September
Native American Tribes: Singing Moon and Barley Moon
Siouan (Assiniboines) Tribe: Yellow Leaf Moon
Inuit People of Northern Canada: Harpoon Moon
Celtic: Wine Moon, Song Moon, Harvest Moon, and Barley Moon
Chinese: Chrysanthemum Moon
Fairy: Chestnut Moon

Full Moon – October
Native American Tribes: Traveller's Moon and Blackberry Moon
Siouan (Assiniboines) Tribe: Gophur Looks Back Moon
Inuit People of Northern Canada: Ice Moon
Celtic: Hunter's Moon, Blood Moon, and Seed Fall Moon
Chinese: Kindly Moon
Fairy: Moon of the Wild Hunt

Full Moon - November
Native American Tribes: Frosty Moon, Beaver Moon, Dark Moon, Tree Moon, Snow Moon, Freezing Moon, Ice Moon, and Migrating Moon
Siouan (Assiniboines) Tribe: Frost Moon
Inuit People of Northern Canada: Freezing Mist Moon
Celtic: Mourning Moon and Darkest Depths Moon
Chinese: White Moon
Fairy: Moon of the Wild Hunt

Full Moon – December
Native American Tribes: Cold Moon, Long Night Moon,
Siouan (Assiniboines) Tribe: Younger Hard Time Moon
Inuit People of Northern Canada: Dark Night Moon
Celtic: Oak Moon, Full Cold Moon
Chinese: Bitter Moon
Fairy: Mistletoe Moon

CHAPTER 16

Days of the
Week
for Spells

Days of the Week for Spells and Rituals

Monday
Best for psychic endeavors, invoking power, creative ideas, divine/inspirational messages, and healing.

Tuesday
Best for protection and building the strength of mind, body, and confidence.

Wednesday
Best for career/job issues, intellectual pursuits, travel planning and research.

Thursday
Best for finances, legal matters, spirituality, and development.

Friday
Best for romantic attraction, all relationships, reconciliation, physical makeovers, and beautifying your environment.

Saturday
Best for home-related issues, brainstorming future projects, committing to personal goals, weight loss, releasing bad habits, ending relationships, etc.

Sunday
Best for healing (body, mind, soul), management/decision-making, insights into problem-solving, divine intervention/miracles, and unique friendships.

Do what makes you comfortable waiting for the "right" day to perform rituals or divination is unnecessary. So you do you, Boo!

Monday

Zodiac: Cancer
Solar System: Moon
Rune: Lagu
Numbers: 2, 9
Colors: Blue (pale), Gray, Silver, White
Tarot: High Priestess, Moon
Trees: Birch, Elder, Myrtle, Willow
Misc. Plants: Moonwort, Wormwood
Herb and Garden: Bluebell, Chamomile, Gardenia, Jasmine, Poppy, Rose (white), Violet
Gemstones and Minerals: Emerald, Moonstone, Quartz (clear, white), Sapphire
Metal: Silver
From the Sea: Pearl
Goddesses: Hecate, Selene
Gods: Aegir, Thoth
Angel or Magical Beings: Gabriel
Issues, Intentions, and Powers: astral realm, clairvoyance, creativity, dream work, emotions, family, fertility, healing, the home, illumination, inspiration, intuition, love, magic (general, moon), prophecy, protection, psychic ability, travel, truth

Tuesday

Zodiac: Aries, Scorpio
Solar System: Mars
Rune: Tyr
Number: 5
Colors: Black, Orange, Red, Scarlet
Tarot: Strength, Wands (5, 6)
Trees: Cedar, Elm, Holly, Palm (dragon's blood)
Misc. Plants: Allspice, Ginger, Patchouli, Thistle
Herb and Garden: Basil, Garlic, Snapdragon
Gemstones and Minerals: Bloodstone, Emerald, Garnet, Ruby, Sapphire (star), Topaz
Metal: Iron
From the Sea:
Goddess:
God: Mars
Angel or Magical Beings: Elves
Issues, Intentions, and Powers: action, aggression, assertiveness, battle/war, challenges, courage, discipline, energy, healing, honor, integrity, justice, passion, purification, strength, truth

Wednesday

Zodiac: Gemini
Solar System: Mercury
Rune: Odal
Number: 3
Colors: Orange, Purple, Silver, Violet, Yellow
Tarot: The Magician, Wheel of Fortune, Pentacles (8)
Trees: Aspen, Hazel, Rowan
Misc. Plant: Fern
Herb and Garden: Dill, Jasmine, Lavender, Lily of the Valley
Gemstones and Minerals: Agate, Amethyst, Aventurine, Lodestone, Opal, Ruby (star), Turquoise
Metal: Mercury
From the Sea:
Goddess: Athena
Gods: Hermes, Mercury, Odin
Angel or Magical Beings: Raphael
Issues, Intentions, and Powers: business, cleverness, communication, creativity, crossroads, divination, fear, improvement (self), insight, intelligence, introspection, knowledge, loss, money, problems, skills, travel, wisdom

Thursday

Zodiac: Capricorn, Pisces
Solar System: Jupiter
Rune: Thorn
Numbers: 4, 8
Colors: Blue (royal), Green, Indigo, Purple
Tarot: Pentacles (ace, 9, 10)
Trees: Laurel, Maple, Oak, Pine
Misc. Plants: Cinnamon, Cinquefoil, Grain (wheat), Nutmeg
Herb and Garden: Honeysuckle, Sage
Gems and Minerals: Amethyst, Carnelian, Cat's Eye, Chrysoberyl, Sapphire, Turquoise
Metal: Tin
From the Sea:
Goddess: Juno
Gods: Jupiter, Thor, Zeus
Angel or Magical Beings:
Issues, Intentions, and Powers: abundance, business, desire, endurance, fidelity, honor, justice (legal matters), leadership, loyalty, luck, money, prosperity, relationships, success, well-being

Friday

Zodiac: Taurus
Solar System: Venus
Rune: Peorth
Numbers: 6, 9
Colors: Aqua, Blue, Green, Indigo, Pink
Tarot: Empress, Lovers, Cups (2)
Trees: Apple, Birch, Myrtle
Misc. Plants: Saffron, Sandalwood
Herb and Garden: Feverfew, Raspberry, Rose, Strawberry, Thyme, Violet
Gemstones and Minerals: Alexandrite, Amber, Cat's Eye, Chrysoberyl, Emerald, Rose Quartz, Ruby
Metal: Copper
From the Sea:
Goddesses: Aphrodite, Freya, Frigg, Lakshmi, Venus
God: Eros
Angel or Magical Beings: Auriel
Issues, Intentions, and Powers: beauty, emotions, fertility, friend/ ship, happiness, love, magic, passion, pleasure, romance, sex/uality, wisdom

Saturday

Zodiac: Aquarius
Solar System: Saturn
Rune: Dag
Number: 7
Colors: Black, Gray (dark), Indigo, Purple (dark)
Tarot: Temperance, Swords (knight, 2)
Trees: Alder, Cypress, Hawthorn, Pomegranate
Misc. Plants: Mullein, Myrrh
Herb and Garden: Morning Glory, Thyme
Gems and Minerals: Amethyst, Apache Tears, Diamond, Hematite, Jet, Labradorite, Turquoise
From the Sea:
Goddess: Hecate
God: Saturn
Angel or Magical Beings: Fairies
Issues, Intentions, and Powers: banish, bind, business, death, discipline (self), freedom, justice, karma, life, limitations/ boundaries, money, motivation, negativity, obstacles, peace, problems, protection, willpower, wisdom

Sunday

Zodiac: Leo
Solar System: Sun
Rune: Sigel
Number: 1
Colors: Gold, Gray, Orange, Pink, White, Yellow
Tarot: Chariot, Sun, Wands (ace)
Trees: Ash, Birch, Laurel
Misc. Plants: Cinnamon, Frankincense
Herb and Garden: Carnation, Marigold, St. John's Wort, Sunflower
Gemstones and Minerals: Amber, Carnelian, Diamond, Quartz (clear), Sunstone, Tiger's Eye, Topaz
Metal: Gold
From the Sea: Pearl
Goddess: Brigid
God: Helios
Angel or Magical Beings: Elves
Issues, Intentions, and Powers: accomplishment, action, ambition, attraction, authority, beauty, confidence, creativity, energy (solar), fame, freedom, friend/ship, goals, growth (personal), healing, hope, illumination, justice, leadership, light, money power (personal), pride, prosperity, protection, spirituality, strength, success, visions, warmth, well-being

Time of the Day for Spells and Rituals

Dawn - At dawn, the sun's fragile rays spread like a blanket of hope over an awakening world. At this time, choices are made, and paths unfold before us, full of life-giving potentiality.

Midday/Noon - Midday is when sunlight shines the strongest - a reminder of our strength and courage to tackle whatever lies ahead. It provides the motivation we need to persevere, no matter what obstacle stands in our way.

Dusk/Twilight - As dusk approaches, the sun bids a wistful farewell to the sky. Its goodbye is made of change and final goodbyes, an invitation to new beginnings if we're brave enough to open our hearts.

Midnight - At midnight, we come to the precipice of a journey into uncertainty; here is where paths diverge, and endings have no choice but to be accepted. It's an inevitable transition from one day to another, filled with promise yet also cloaked in sadness.

Do what makes you feel comfortable. There's no need to wait for the "right" time to perform rituals or divination. You do you, Boo!

Dawn

Zodiac:
Solar System: Venus
Runes: Beorc, Hagal, Thorn
Number:
Color:
Tarot: Swords
Trees:
Misc. Plants:
Herb and Garden:
Gemstones and Minerals:
Metal:
From the Sea:
Goddess: Brigid
Gods: Byelobog, Janus, Njord, Surya
Angel or Magical Beings: Raphael
Issues, Intentions, and Powers: activate/awaken, beginnings, crossroads, fertility, hope, life (vitality), light, nurture, purpose, romance, youth

Midday/Noon

Zodiac: Leo
Solar System: Sun
Runes: Dag, Rad, Sigel
Number:
Color:
Tarot: Wands
Trees:
Misc. Plants:
Herb and Garden:
Gemstones and Minerals:
Metal:
From the Sea:
Goddess:
God: Byelobog
Angel or Magical Beings: Michael
Issues, Intentions, and Powers: determination, obstacles, strength, willpower

Dusk/Twilight

Zodiac: Cancer
Solar System: Venus
Runes: Feoh, Jer, Peorth
Numbers:
Colors:
Tarot: Cups
Trees:
Misc. Plants:
Herb and Garden:
Gemstones and Minerals:
Metal:
From the Sea:
Goddess:
God: Gabriel
Issues, Intentions, and Powers: banish, change/s, endings, the otherworld/underworld, sorrow

Midnight

Zodiac: Taurus
Solar System: Earth, Venus
Runes: Is, Tyr, Ur
Number:
Color:
Tarot: Pentacles
Trees:
Misc. Plants:
Herb and Garden:
Gemstones and Minerals:
Metal:
From the Sea:
Goddess:
God:
Angel or Magical Beings: Auriel
Issues, Intentions, and Powers: crossroads, endings, release

CHAPTER 17

Astrology

March Energy Quicky

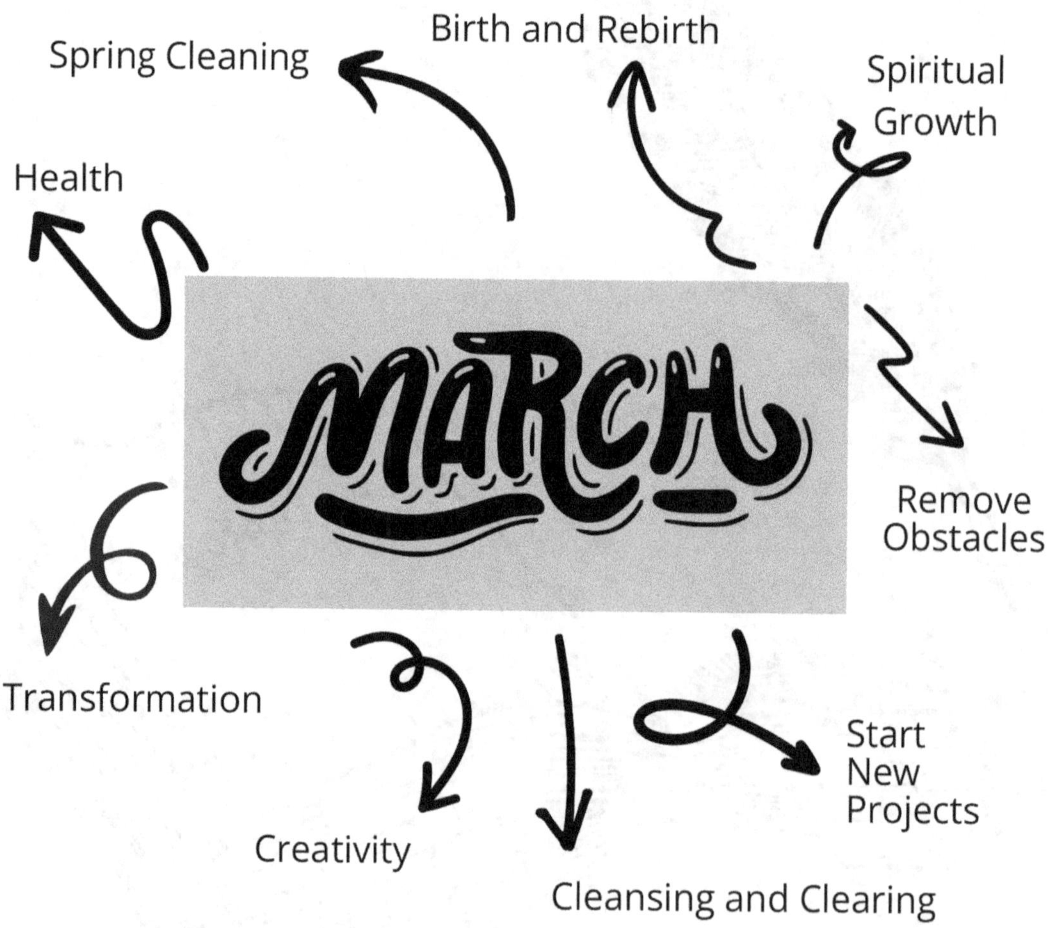

Spring Cleaning

Birth and Rebirth

Spiritual Growth

Health

MARCH

Remove Obstacles

Transformation

Creativity

Cleansing and Clearing

Start New Projects

March Focus

Harnessing the Energy of March for Growth, Prosperity, and Abundance

March presents the ideal environment for growth, prosperity, and fruitfulness. Start planting the physical and metaphysical seeds for what you desire to harvest later in the year. Additionally, engage in spring cleaning to eliminate negativity and blockages that could hinder the manifestation of your dreams. Remember to stay connected with the Earth and to focus on grounding yourself to attract prosperity and love. Be kind to yourself, expand your knowledge, and grow spiritually this March.

April Energy Quicky

Abundance

Prosperity

Gratitude

Love

Balance

APRIL

Rebirth

Renewal

Give Back

New Beginnings

Creativity

Kindness

HELLO SPRING

April Focus

April's Focus: Prosperity and Abundance, New Beginnings, Rebirth, Renewal, Gratitude, Blessings, Creativity, Balance, Fertility, Compassion, and Change

April unfolds as a fertile ground for growth, prosperity, and abundance. It beckons us to sow the seeds, both in the tangible and spiritual realms, that will burgeon into a bountiful harvest later in the year. Just as nature awakens, we are encouraged to engage in a metaphorical spring cleaning, clearing away negativity and blockages that might impede the manifestation of our dreams. Staying connected with the Earth and grounding ourselves become essential practices, inviting prosperity and love into our lives. In the spirit of self-kindness, let us expand our knowledge and embark on a spiritual growth journey throughout April.

Zodiac

Each zodiac sign is associated with specific flowers that are thought to resonate with the characteristics and traits of individuals born under that sign.

Flowers

Aries (March 21 - April 19): Honeysuckle - represents the energetic and dynamic nature of Aries individuals. Its vibrant and fragrant flowers mirror the enthusiasm and passion associated with this fire sign.

Taurus (April 20 - May 20): Rose - particularly in shades of pink, aligns with Taurus' appreciation for beauty and sensuality. This classic flower symbolizes love, stability, and the enduring nature of Taurus individuals.

Gemini (May 21 - June 20): Lavender - with its versatile uses and soothing scent, reflects the dual nature of Geminis. It embodies the communicative and adaptable qualities of individuals born under this sign.

Cancer (June 21 - July 22): White Lily - white lily, symbolizing purity and nurturing, resonates with the emotional and caring nature of Cancer individuals. It reflects their connection to home and family.

Leo (July 23 - August 22): Sunflower - vibrant and bold sunflower aligns with Leo's confident and sunny disposition. It represents strength, positivity, and the desire to shine, mirroring Leo's leadership qualities.

Virgo (August 23 - September 22): Chrysanthemum - known for their precision and order in petal arrangement, suits Virgo's detail-oriented and analytical nature. The flower reflects Virgo's appreciation for perfection.

Libra (September 23 - October 22): Rose (Blue) - although rare in nature, symbolizes the unique and artistic qualities of Libra individuals. They represent the harmonious and balanced nature of this sign.

Scorpio (October 23 - November 21): Geranium - with their intense colors and rich symbolism, align with Scorpio's passionate and transformative nature. The flower reflects Scorpio's depth and intensity.

Sagittarius (November 22 - December 21): Carnation - with their lively colors, represent the adventurous and optimistic spirit of Sagittarius individuals. The flower symbolizes joy and enthusiasm.

Capricorn (December 22 - January 19): Pansy - known for their resilience and enduring bloom, suit Capricorn's disciplined and determined nature. The flower reflects Capricorn's commitment to achieving goals.

Aquarius (January 20 - February 18): Orchid - with their unique and unconventional beauty, align with Aquarius' innovative and independent qualities. The flower symbolizes creativity and originality.

Pisces (February 19 - March 20): Water Lily - which thrives in watery environments, resonates with Pisces' intuitive and dreamy nature. The flower symbolizes deep emotions and spiritual connection.

While these associations between zodiac signs and flowers are symbolic and based on tradition, they add a unique and personalized touch to floral choices for gifts or decorations. Individuals often resonate with the flower that aligns with their zodiac sign's characteristics.

Crystals

Like flowers many crystals are believed to have energies that individuals born under each zodiac sign find useful. The following is a list of crystals that are associated with each zodiac sign:

Aries (March 21 - April 19): Bloodstone - with its energizing properties, it aligns with Aries' dynamic and courageous nature. It is believed to enhance vitality and boost motivation.

Taurus (April 20 - May 20): Rose Quartz - the crystal of love and harmony, resonates with Taurus' appreciation for beauty and sensuality. It is thought to bring emotional healing and promote self-love.

Gemini (May 21 - June 20): Citrine - known for its bright and positive energy, suits Gemini's communicative and adaptable nature. It is believed to enhance mental clarity and creativity.

Cancer (June 21 - July 22): Moonstone - with its connection to the moon and intuition, aligns with Cancer's emotional and nurturing qualities. It is believed to promote emotional balance and intuition.

Leo (July 23 - August 22): Tiger's Eye - a stone of confidence and courage, resonates with Leo's bold and ambitious nature. It is thought to enhance personal power and bring focus.

Virgo (August 23 - September 22): Amazonite - with its calming energy, suits Virgo's analytical and practical nature. It is believed to promote balance and harmony while reducing stress.

Libra (September 23 - October 22): Lepidolite - known for its calming and balancing properties, aligns with Libra's pursuit of harmony and justice. It is thought to ease anxiety and promote emotional well-being.

Scorpio (October 23 - November 21): Labradorite - a stone of transformation, resonates with Scorpio's intense and transformative nature. It is believed to enhance intuition and spiritual growth.

Sagittarius (November 22 - December 21): Sodalite - with its connection to wisdom and truth, suits Sagittarius' adventurous and philosophical nature. It is believed to enhance communication and insight.

Capricorn (December 22 - January 19): Garnet - a stone of strength and grounding, aligns with Capricorn's disciplined and determined nature. It is thought to enhance focus and endurance.

Aquarius (January 20 - February 18): Amethyst - known for its spiritual and calming properties, resonates with Aquarius' innovative and humanitarian nature. It is believed to enhance intuition and clarity.

Pisces (February 19 - March 20): Aquamarine - a stone of serenity and connection to water, suits Pisces' dreamy and intuitive nature. It is thought to enhance communication and spiritual awareness.

The use of crystals that correspond to specific zodiac signs is based on metaphysical beliefs and traditions. People often choose crystals that resonate with their individual energies and preferences. Whether for healing, meditation, or decoration, selecting zodiac-specific crystals is a personal and symbolic choice.

Gemstones

The association between gemstones and zodiac signs is rooted in historical traditions and beliefs about the metaphysical properties of stones and is undoubtably the most popular of these.

Aries (March 21 - April 19): Diamond - symbolizing strength and clarity, aligns with Aries' bold and dynamic nature. It is believed to enhance courage and promote inner strength.

Taurus (April 20 - May 20): Emerald - a gem associated with love and prosperity, resonates with Taurus' appreciation for beauty and stability. It is thought to bring harmony and abundance.

Gemini (May 21 - June 20): Agate - known for its balancing properties, suits Gemini's dual nature. It is believed to enhance mental clarity, balance emotions, and promote communication.

Cancer (June 21 - July 22): Moonstone - symbolizing intuition and emotional balance, aligns with Cancer's nurturing and intuitive qualities. It is believed to enhance emotional well-being.

Leo (July 23 - August 22): Ruby - a gem associated with passion and vitality, resonates with Leo's bold and charismatic nature. It is thought to bring energy and enhance creativity.

Virgo (August 23 - September 22): Sapphire - a stone of wisdom and focus, suits Virgo's analytical and practical nature. It is believed to enhance mental clarity and promote spiritual insight.

Libra (September 23 - October 22): Opal - Opal, symbolizing harmony and balance, aligns with Libra's pursuit of equilibrium. It is thought to enhance love, creativity, and positive energy.

Scorpio (October 23 - November 21): Topaz - Topaz, a gem associated with strength and transformation, resonates with Scorpio's intense and transformative nature. It is believed to bring emotional balance and courage.

Sagittarius (November 22 - December 21): Turquoise - Turquoise, a stone of protection and healing, suits Sagittarius' adventurous and philosophical nature. It is thought to bring positive energy and enhance intuition.

Capricorn (December 22 - January 19): Garnet - Garnet, symbolizing strength and grounding, aligns with Capricorn's disciplined and determined nature. It is believed to enhance focus and promote success.

Aquarius (January 20 - February 18): Amethyst - Amethyst, a gem associated with spiritual insight and calmness, resonates with Aquarius' innovative and humanitarian nature. It is believed to enhance intuition and clarity.

Pisces (February 19 - March 20): Aquamarine - Aquamarine, symbolizing serenity and connection to water, aligns with Pisces' dreamy and intuitive nature. It is thought to enhance communication and spiritual awareness.

The use of gemstones based on zodiac signs is rooted in symbolism and belief systems. Individuals often choose stones that resonate with their personal energies and preferences. Whether worn as jewelry, used for meditation, or placed in the living environment, these gems are embraced for their perceived metaphysical qualities.

Numerology

Numerology is a belief system that ascribes significance to numbers and their purported influence on human life and events. It is based on the idea that numbers have inherent symbolic meanings and vibrations that can influence various aspects of our lives, including personality traits, relationships, career paths, and even the timing of events.

Basic Principles: Numerology is based on the principle that every number has a unique vibration and energy that can influence a person's life and destiny. By analyzing the numbers associated with a person's birth date, name, or other significant events, practitioners believe they can gain insights into that person's character and life path.

Core Numbers: In numerology, specific numbers are considered particularly significant and are often referred to as core numbers. These include the Life Path Number, Destiny Number, Soul Urge Number, and Personality Number, among others. Each core number is calculated using specific methods based on a person's birth date or name.

Life Path Number: One of the most important numbers in numerology is the Life Path Number. This number is derived from a person's date of birth and represents their life's purpose, challenges, and opportunities. It is calculated by adding together the digits of the birth date until you get a single-digit number unless the result is 11, 22, or 33, which are considered master numbers and are not reduced further.

Destiny Number: The Destiny Number is calculated from a person's full birth name and represents their innate talents, abilities, and potential future opportunities. It is determined by assigning numerical values to each alphabet letter and then adding them together to get a single-digit or master number.

Soul Urge Number: Also known as the Heart's Desire Number, the Soul Urge Number is derived from the vowels in a person's name and represents their innermost desires, motivations, and emotional needs.

Personality Number: The Personality Number is calculated from the consonants in a person's name and reflects how others perceive them and the persona they project to the world.

Compatibility and Timing: Numerology is also used to assess compatibility between individuals, predict the outcome of relationships, and determine auspicious times for important life events, such as marriage or starting a new business.

History and Cultural Significance: Numerology has ancient roots and can be found in various cultures and traditions worldwide, including ancient Babylonian, Egyptian, Chinese, and Indian civilizations. It has been practiced for centuries and continues to be popular today, with many people consulting numerologists for guidance and insights into their lives.

Criticism and Skepticism: While numerology has many adherents who believe in its accuracy and efficacy, it is also met with skepticism and criticism from skeptics and scientists who view it as a pseudoscience lacking empirical evidence. Numerology ascribes specific meanings to each number and some number sequences.

Here's a brief overview of the meanings associated with each number:
Number 1: Represents independence, leadership, ambition, innovation, and individuality. It Is related to new beginnings and taking the initiative.
Number 2: Symbolizes balance, harmony, cooperation, diplomacy, and partnership. It highlights the importance of relationships and working together with others.
Number 3: Represents creativity, communication, self-expression, and optimism. It is associated with joy, enthusiasm, and a sense of playfulness.
Number 4: Symbolizes stability, organization, hard work, and practicality. It emphasizes building a solid foundation and being disciplined in pursuit of goals
Number 5: Represents freedom, adaptability, versatility, and adventure. It signifies change, unpredictability, and embracing new experiences.
Number 6: Symbolizes harmony, nurturing, responsibility, and family. It is associated with domestic life, service to others, and compassion.
Number 7: Represents introspection, spirituality, wisdom, and intuition. It symbolizes seeking knowledge, Inner growth, and a deeper understanding of life's mysteries.
Number 8: Symbolizes success, abundance, power, and material wealth. It emphasizes financial prosperity, achievement, and the rewards of hard work.
Number 9: Represents humanitarianism, compassion, universal love, and endings. It symbolizes completion, fulfillment, and the culmination of a cycle.

Master Numbers:

Number 11: Considered a master number, it represents spiritual enlightenment, intuition, and psychic abilities. It symbolizes spiritual awakening and a higher purpose.
Number 22: Another master number symbolizes mastery, vision, and the ability to manifest dreams into reality. It represents the potential for great achievements and building something substantial.
Number 33: The highest master number, it symbolizes compassion, selflessness, and the embodiment of spiritual principles. It represents the highest level or spiritual awareness and service to humanity.

Number Sequences

111: Often associated with manifestation and alignment with one's desires. It can indicate a strong connection to the universe and the power of positive thinking.

222: Symbolizes balance and harmony in relationships and partnerships. It suggests you are on the right path and should trust the process.

333: Represents spiritual growth, guidance, and divine protection. It signifies that your angels and spirit guides are nearby, offering support and encouragement.

444: Symbolizes stability, security, and divine protection. It suggests that your angels surround you with love and guidance, and you are supported in your endeavors.

555: Signifies major life changes and transformations. It suggests that you are in a period of transition and should embrace new opportunities and possibilities.

These interpretations are just a starting point; individuals may interpret numbers differently based on their beliefs and experiences.

Birth Chart Meanings

Your **Sun** is about yourself.

Your **Moon** is your heart.

Your **Rising** is how you look.

Your **Mercury** is the way you think.

Your **Venus** is how you love.

Your **Mars** is how you deal with life.

Your **Jupiter** is your luck.

Your **Saturn** is how you discipline yourself and your responsibilities.

Your **Uranus** is how unique you are.

Your **Neptune** is your imagination.

Your **Pluto** is your transformation.

Your **Chiron** is how you heal.

Your **Ceres** is how you take care of yourself.

Your **Pallas** is your relationship.

Your **Juno** is beauty and influence.

Your **Vesta** is your potential and your organization.

Your **North Node** is how you develop in your current life.

Your **South Node** is how you developed in your past life.

Your **Midheaven** is your career; how others view you.

Your **Lilith** is your hidden emotions.

For help with your birth chart try:
https://astro.cafeastrology.com/natal.php

Astrological Signs

Aries
March 21 - April 19
for those born under the sign of
The Ram

Taurus
April 20 - May 20
for those born under the sign of
The Bull

Gemini
May 21 - June 20
for those born under the sign of
The Twins

Cancer
June 21 - July 22
for those born under the sign of
The Crab

Leo
July 23 - August 22
for those born under the sign of
The Lion

Virgo
August 23 - September 22
for those born under the sign of
The Virgin

Libra
September 23 - October 22
for those born under the sign of
The Scales

Scorpio
October 23 - November 21
for those born under the sign of
The Scorpion

Sagittarius
November 22 - December 21
for those born under the sign of
The Archer

Capricorn
December 22 - January 19
for those born under the sign of
The Goat

Aquarius
January 20 - February 18
for those born under the sign of
The Water Bearer

Pisces
February 19 - March 20
for those born under the sign of
The Fishes

CHAPTER 18

Solar
System

Solar System

The boundless expanse of the universe holds a captivating realm known as the solar system, a complex web of celestial bodies that has fascinated humanity for generations. At the heart of this cosmic spectacle is the radiant and mighty Sun, a colossal star that provides the life-giving energy that fuels our world. Orbiting Earth, our loyal companion, the Moon, enchants us with its shimmering phases and mysterious allure. Together, these elements paint a mesmerizing portrait of the grandeur and diversity present in our cosmic neighborhood. In this journey of exploration, we'll delve into the wondrous dynamics that define the solar system, bask in the brilliance of the Sun, and unravel the enigma of the Moon's influence on our planet.

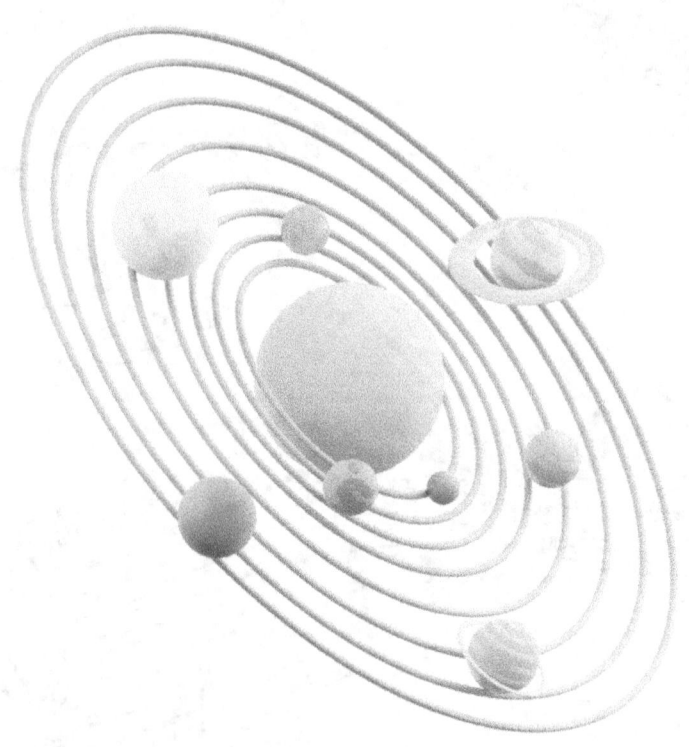

Solar System: Earth
Zodiac: Capricorn, Taurus, and Virgo
Chakra: Root
Celebrations: Earth Day and Walpurgis
Season: Winter
Day:
Time of Day: Midnight
Rune:
Number: 4
Colors: Black, Brown, Green, and White
Tarot:
Trees: Acacia and Oak
Misc. Plant: Grain
Herb and Garden:
Gemstones and Minerals: Agate (brown), Ametrine, Andalusite, Bloodstone, Carnelian, Chrysoprase, Citrine, Diopside, and Moss Agate
Metal:
From the Sea:
Goddesses: Anat, Ceres, Coatlicue, Cybele, Demeter, Gaia, Inanna, Isis, Maia, and Nanna
Gods: Adonis, Attis, Dionysus, Dumuzi, Ea, Enki, Faunus, Geb, and Vertimnus
Angel: Auriel
Issues, Intentions, and Powers: agriculture, creativity, grounding, healing, the home, magic (animal), nurture, peace, protection, purpose, revenge, and spirits

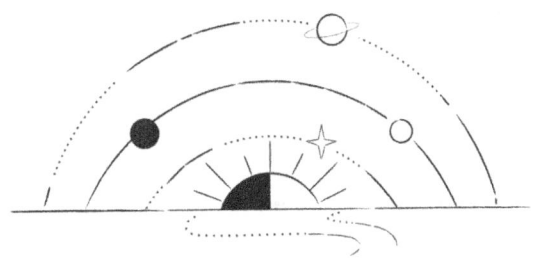

$$2\!\!\!\downarrow$$

Solar System: Jupiter
Zodiac: Pisces and Sagittarius
Chakras: 3rd Eye, Heart, and Solar Plexus
Celebrations:
Season:
Day: Thursday
Time of Day:
Rune: Man
Numbers: 3, 4, and 5
Colors: Blue, Green (light, sea), Indigo, Purple, Turquoise, and Violet
Tarot: Wheel of Fortune
Trees: Birch, Cedar, Chestnut, Fir, Horse Chestnut, Linden, Magnolia, Maple, Oak, Olive, Palm (coconut), Pine, Sycamore, Walnut, and Yew
Misc. Plant: Aloe, Anise, Betony, Cinquefoil, Meadowsweet, Myrrh, Nutmeg, and Star Anise
Herb and Garden: Agrimony, Borage, Clove, Dandelion, Honeysuckle, Lemon Balm, and Sage
Gemstones and Minerals: Amethyst, Ametrine, Diopside, Emerald, Lepidolite, Sapphire, Sugilite, Turquoise, and Zircon (red)
Metal: Tin
From the Sea:
Goddesses: Devi, Hera, Justitia, and Nut
Gods: Baal, Indra, Jupiter, Marduk, and Zeus
Mythical Being: Unicorn
Issues, Intentions, and Powers: abundance, astral realm, authority, business, control, dignity, discipline, favors, generosity, honor, influence, intuition, justice, kindness, leadership, luck, the mind, money, opportunities, optimism, power, pride, problems, prosperity, responsibility, spirituality, success, wealth, well-being, and wisdom

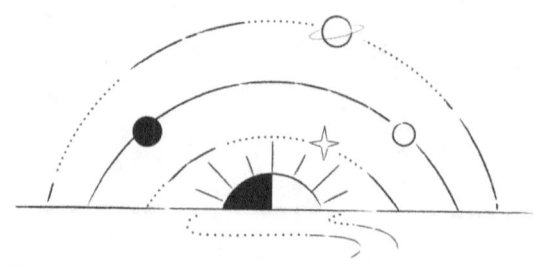

Solar System: Mars
Zodiac: Aries and Scorpio
Chakras: Root, Sacral, Solar Plexus, and Throat
Celebrations:
Season:
Day: Tuesday
Time of Day:
Rune: Man
Numbers: 2, 3, 5, and 9
Colors: Crimson, Maroon, Orange, Pink, and Red
Tarot: Devil, Emperor, and Tower
Trees: Alder, Blackthorn, Fir, Hawthorn, Holly, Juniper, Palm (dragon's blood), Pine, and Yew
Misc. Plant: Allspice, Anise, Asafoetida, Black Cohosh, Blessed Thistle, Bloodroot, Coriander, Cumin, Deer's Tongue, Galangal, Ginger, High John, Mustard, Nettle, Pepper, Reed, Thistle, and Wormwood
Herb and Garden: Anemone, Basil, Broom, Garlic, Gorse, Honeysuckle, Pennyroyal, Rue, Snapdragon, and Sweet Woodruff
Gemstones and Minerals: Beryl, Bloodstone, Citrine, Diamond, Garnet, Hematite, Jasper (red), Onyx, Pyrite, Rhodochrosite, Rhodonite, Ruby, Sard, Sardonyx, Tourmaline (red, watermelon), Tsavorite, and Zircon (red)
Metals: Iron and Steel
From the Sea: Coral (red)
Goddesses: Anat, Astarte, Badb, Durga, Macha, Maeve, Minerva, and Nanna
Gods: Ares, Indra, Mars, Nergal, Odin, Set, and Thor
Mythical Being: Unicorn
Issues, Intentions, and Powers: action, aggression, anger, assertiveness, battle/war, beginnings, courage, death, defense, desire, determination, emotions, endurance, energy (sexual), enmity, growth, justice, life, lust, magic (general, defensive, dragon, sex), passion, power, sexuality (male), skills, strength, and willpower

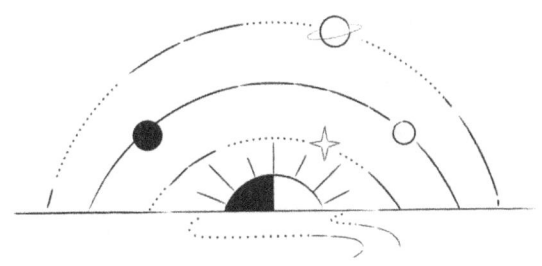

Solar System: Mercury
Zodiac: Gemini and Virgo
Chakras: 3rd Eye, Root, Sacral, Solar Plexus, and Throat
Celebrations:
Season:
Day: Wednesday
Time of Day:
Rune:
Numbers: 1, 4, 5, and 8
Colors: Blue (navy), Gray, Green, Orange, Purple, Silver, Violet, and Yellow
Tarot: Hermit, Lovers, and Magician
Trees: Ash, Aspen, Cedar, Cherry, Elder, Hazel, Juniper, Linden, Olive, Pomegranate, and Acacia
Misc. Plants: Anise, Betony, Bittersweet, Cinquefoil, Flax, Horehound, Mandrake, Mistletoe, and Sandalwood
Herb and Garden: Agrimony, Bergamot, Clover, Dandelion, Dill, Fennel, Fern, Honeysuckle, Jasmine, Lavender, Lilac, Lily of the Valley, Marjoram, Peppermint, Periwinkle, Rosemary, Sage, and Valerian
Gemstones and Minerals: Agate (fire, green, red, snakeskin, tree), Amber, Aventurine, Blue Lace Agate, Carnelian, Cat's Eye, Citrine, Fluorite, Hematite, Jasper, Moss Agate, Onyx, Opal, Peridot, Rhodochrosite, Sardonyx, Sodalite, Sphene, and Topaz
Metals: Aluminum and Mercury
From the Sea: Coral (red)
Goddesses: Athena, Maat, Maia, Minerva, and Seshat
Gods: Anubis, Arawn, Coyote, Hermes, Loki, Lugh, Mercury, Odin, Ogma, Thor, and Thoth
Angels: Michael and Raphael
Issues, Intentions, and Powers: adaptability, balance, business, change(s), cleverness, communication, creativity, crossroads, deceit, divination, fear, improvement, inspiration, intelligence, justice, learning, love, magic, memory/memories, messages/ omens, the mind, money, moods, power, rebirth, renewal, skills, travel, wealth, and wisdom

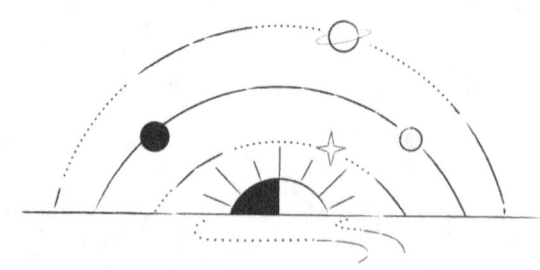

Solar System: Moon
Zodiac: Cancer
Chakra: Sacral
Celebrations: Beltane, Imbolc, Lughnasadh, and Samhain
Season:
Day: Monday
Time of Day:
Runes: Is and Lagu
Numbers: 2, 3, 0, and 13
Colors: Blue, Gray Green (sea), Orange, Silver, and White
Tarot: Chariot, High Priestess, and Moon
Trees: Birch, Mesquite, Olive, Palm, Rowan, and Willow
Misc. Plants: Aloe, Lotus, Moonwort, Myrrh, Nutmeg, Saffron, and Sandalwood
Herb and Garden: Bergamot, Blackberry/Bramble, Gardenia, Grape, Iris, Jasmine, Lemon Balm Lily, Poppy, and Rosemary
Gemstones and Minerals: Agate, Angelite, Aquamarine, Beryl, Calcite (clear), Herkimer Diamond, Moonstone, Morganite, Opal, Quartz, Sapphire, Selenite, and Turquoise
Metal: Silver
From the Sea: Coral (white), Moon Snail, Mother-of-Pearl, Mussel, and Pearl
Goddesses: Aine, Aphrodite, Ariadne, Arianrhod, Artemis, Cerridwen, Diana, Freya, Hecate, Ishtar, Isis, Juno, Luna, Nanna, Persephone, Rhiannon, Sedna, Selene, and Spiderwoman
Gods: Aegir, Hermes, Horus, Janus, Jupiter, Khensu, Shiva, and Thoth
Angel: Gabriel
Magical Beings: Fairies, Mermaids and Dragons
Issues, Intentions, and Powers: action, agriculture, animals, balance (inner), beginnings, change(s), consciousness (and subconscious), creativity, cycles, darkness, death, divination, dream work, emotions, enchantment, endings, energy (general, receptive), family, fertility, growth, guidance, healing, hexes, the home, illumination, imagination, inspiration, intuition, jealousy, life (rhythms), light, loneliness, love, magic (general, crone, moon, night), manifestation, moods, negativity, night-mares, obstacles, peace, power, pregnancy/childbirth, protection, psychic ability, rebirth/renewal, secrets, self-work, sensitivity, sorrow, spirits, transformation, wisdom, and witches/ witchcraft

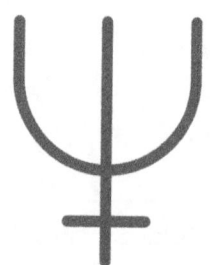

Solar System: Neptune
Zodiac: Aquarius and Pisces
Chakras: 3rd Eye and Crown
Celebrations:
Season:
Day:
Time of Day:
Rune:
Number: 7
Colors: Blue, Green (light, sea), Indigo, Lavender, Purple, and Turquoise
Tarot: Hanged Man
Trees: Ash
Misc. Plants:
Herb and Garden:
Gemstones and Minerals: Amethyst, Angelite, Aquamarine, Beryl, Celestite, Fluorite, Jade, Labradorite, Lapis Lazuli, Lepidolite, Sapphire, and Turquoise
Metal:
From the Sea: Coral and Mother-of-Pearl
Goddesses: Amphitrite, Brigid, Ran, Sedna and Tiamat
Gods: Aegir, Manannan, Neptune, and Poseidon
Angel:
Magical Beings: Fairies and Mermaids
Issues, Intentions, and Powers: awareness (expand), clairvoyance, community, consciousness (subconscious), creativity, dream work, enchantment, energy (psychic), guardian, guidance, inspiration, intuition, life, the otherworld/ underworld, power, protection, psychic ability, sensitivity, visions

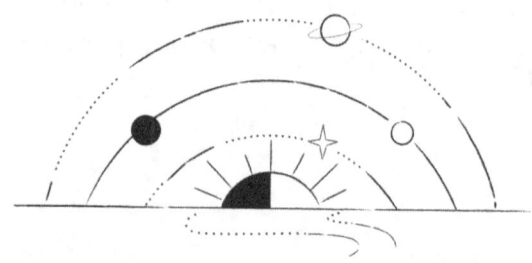

Solar System: Pluto
Zodiac: Cancer and Scorpio
Chakra: Sacral
Celebrations:
Season:
Day:
Time of Day:
Rune:
Number:
Colors: Blue, Green (light, sea), Indigo, Lavender, Purple, and Turquoise
Tarot: Hanged Man
Tree: Cypress
Misc. Plants: Belladonna, Bittersweet, Nettle, and Reed
Herb and Garden: Basil and Fern (bear paw)
Gemstones and Minerals: Amethyst, Garnet, Jet, Kunzite, Labradorite, Obsidian, Quartz (tourmalated), Spinel, Tourmaline, and Tsavorite
Metal:
From the Sea:
Goddesses: Ereshkigal, Hathor, Hecate, Hel, Hera, Kali, the Morrigan, and Persephone
Gods: Pluto and Osiris
Angel:
Magical Beings:
Issues, Intentions, and Powers: the afterlife, changes, danger, darkness (inner), death, dream work, justice, karma, memory/memories, the otherworld/underworld, rebirth/renewal, secrets, sexuality, spirituality, transformation, and wealth

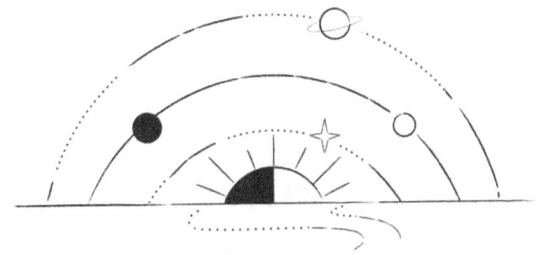

Solar System: Saturn
Zodiac: Aquarius, Capricorn, and Libra
Chakra: Crown, Heart, Root, and Throat
Celebrations:
Season:
Day: Saturday
Time of Day:
Rune: Peorth
Numbers: 3, 7, and 8
Colors: Black, Blue (navy), Brown, Gray (dark), Green (dark), Indigo, and Yellow (light)
Tarot: Death, Hanged Man, and World
Tree: Aspen, Beech, Blackthorn, Cypress, Elm, Fir, Holly, Magnolia, Mesquite, Mimosa, Pine, Poplar, Rowan, Witch Hazel, and Yew
Misc. Plants: Cinnamon, Clove, Bamboo, Eyebright, Frankincense, Galangal, Ginseng, Grain
Herb and Garden: Amaranth, Carnation, Comfrey, Ivy, Monkshood, Morning Glory, Rue, and Solomon's Seal
Gemstones and Minerals: Apache Tears, Azurite, Carnelian, Hematite, Jasper (brown), Jet, Obsidian, Onyx, Sapphire, Sardonyx, Serpentine, and Tourmaline (black)
Metal: Lead
From the Sea: Coral (black)
Goddesses: Ariadne, Ceres, Demeter, Dôn, Durga, Hecate, Hera, Juno, Kali, and Rhea
Gods: Amun, Khensu Saturn
Angel:
Magical Beings:
Issues, Intentions, and Powers: agriculture, ambition, astral realm, authority, banish, bind, business, concentration/ focus, darkness, death, discipline, endings, endurance, freedom, goals, grounding, justice, karma, knowledge, limitations/ boundaries, longevity, loyalty, lust, the mind, obstacles, peace, purification, relationships, stability, strength.

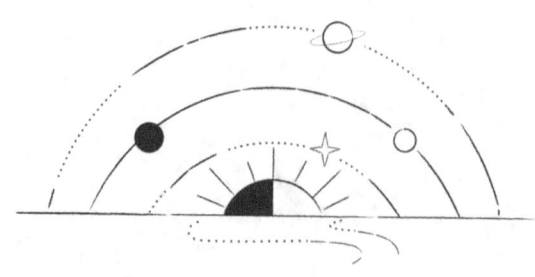

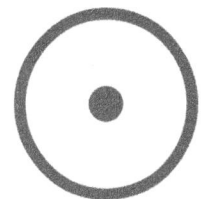

Solar System: Sun
Zodiac: Aries, Cancer, and Leo
Chakra: Solar Plexus
Celebrations: Litha, Mabon, Ostara, Walpurgis, and Yule
Season:
Day: Sunday
Time of Day: Noon
Rune: Jera and Sigel
Numbers: 1 and 6
Colors: Gold, Orange, and Yellow
Tarot: Death, Hanged Man, and World
Tree: Acacia, Ash, Birch, Cedar, Chestnut, Hazel, Horse Chestnut, Juniper, Laurel, Linden, Oak, Olive, Palm, Rowan, Walnut, and Witch Hazel
Misc. Plants: Belladonna, Bittersweet, Henbane, Lady's Slipper, Mandrake, Mullein, Patchouli, Skullcap, and Thornapple
Herb and Garden: Angelica, Broom, Carnation, Chamomile, Chrysanthemum, Daffodil, Daisy, Goldenseal, Gorse, Heliotrope, Lovage, Marigold, Peony, Rosemary, St. John's Wort, and Sunflower (com), Lotus, Mistletoe, and Saffron
Gemstones and Minerals: Amber, Ametrine, Beryl (golden), Calcite (orange, red), Carnelian, Chrysoberyl, Citrine, Diamond, Herkimer Diamond, Peridot, Quartz, Ruby, Sunstone, Tiger's Eye, Topaz, Tourmaline (black), and Zircon
From the Sea: Coral (black)
Goddesses: Aine, Amaterasu, Bast, Brigid, Hathor, Phoebe, Sekhmet, and Spider Woman
Gods: Adonis, Agni, Amun, Apollo, Baal, Belenus, Helios, Horus, Jupiter, Lugh, Marduk, Mithras, Ogma, Osiris, Pushan, Ra, Shiva, Surya, and Vishnu
Angel: Raphael
Magical Beings: Dragon, Griffin, Phoenix, Sphinx, Unicorn, Dragon, Griffin, Phoenix, Sphinx, and Unicorn
Issues, Intentions, and Powers:

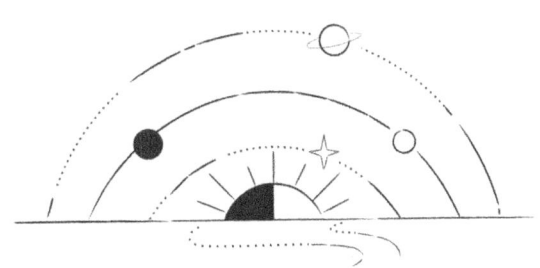

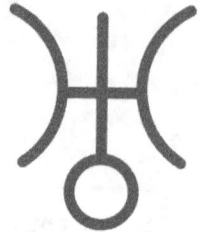

Solar System: Uranus
Zodiac: Aquarius and Gemini
Chakras: Brow, Crown, and Throat
Celebrations:
Season:
Day: Sunday
Time of Day:
Rune:
Number: 4
Colors: Indigo and Yellow (light)
Tarot: Fool, Star, and Tower
Tree: Ash and Rowan
Misc. Plants: Belladonna, Bittersweet, Henbane, Lady's Slipper, Mandrake, Mullein, Patchouli, Skullcap, and Thornapple
Herb and Garden: Angelica, Broom, Carnation, Chamomile, Chrysanthemum, Daffodil, Daisy, Goldenseal, Gorse, Heliotrope, Lovage, Marigold, Peony, Rosemary, St. John's Wort, and Sunflower (com), Lotus, Mistletoe, and Saffron
Gemstones and Minerals: Amazonite, Aventurine, Herkimer Diamond, Labradorite, and Quartz
From the Sea: Coral (black)
Goddesses: Anat, Aphrodite, Danu, Inanna, Ishtar, and Isis
Gods:
Angel:
Magical Beings:
Issues, Intentions, and Powers: ambition, anger, change(s), community, cooperation, freedom, goals, hope, illumination, improvement, intuition, motivation, power, and relationships

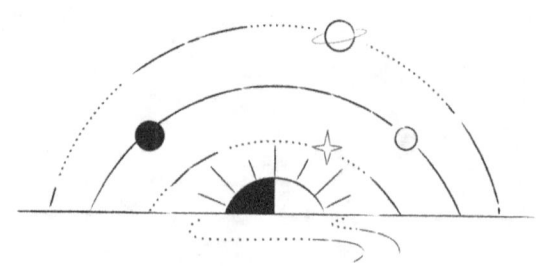

Solar System: Venus, Also known as the Morning and Evening Star
Zodiac: 3rd Eye, Heart, Sacral, and Throat
Chakras: Brow, Crown, and Throat
Celebrations:
Season:
Day: Friday
Time of Day: Dawn, Dusk, and Midnight
Rune: As and Ken
Numbers: 5, 6, and 7
Colors: Aqua, Blue (light), Green, Indigo, Lavender, Mauve, Pink, Rose, White, and Yellow (light)
Tarot: Empress, Justice, and Star
Tree: Alder, Apple, Aspen, Birch, Cherry, Elder, Magnolia, Myrtle, Sycamore, and Willow
Misc. Plants: Ioe, Burdock, Cardamom, Coltsfoot, Cowslip, Dittany, Orris Root, and Sandalwood
Gemstones and Minerals: Alexandrite, Aventurine, Azurite, Calcite, Carnelian, Cat's Eye, Celeste Chrysoberyl, Chrysocolla, Chrysoprase, Desert Rose, Diamond, Dioptase, Emerald, Jade, Jasper (green), Kunzite, Lapis Lazuli, Lodestone, Malachite, Peridot, Rhodochrosite, Rose Quart, Sapphire, Sodalite, Tourmaline (blue, green, pink, watermelon), Tsavorite, Turquoise
Metal: Copper
From the Sea:
Goddesses: Astarte, Ishtar, and Venus
Gods: Quetzalcoatl
Angel:
Magical Beings:
Issues, Intentions, and Powers: affection, agriculture, astral realm, attraction, beauty, beginnings, connections, creativity, desire, emotions, energy (receptive, sexual), fertility, friendship, gentleness, happiness, harmony: kindness, love, lust, magic (sex), needs, passion, pleasure rebirth/renewal, relationships, reversal, romance, sensuality, sexuality, stress, and unity

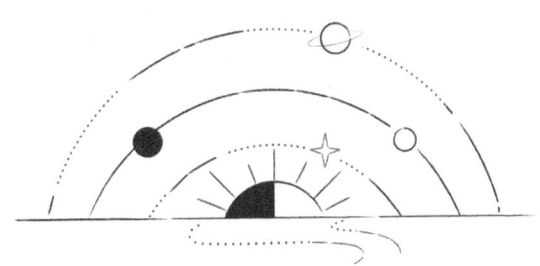

Retrogrades

What is retrograde?
A planet could be retrograde—meaning that it appears to be spinning backward from the vantage point of Earth. What's happening? Well, the Earth is completing its orbit around the Sun faster than other planets outside of its orbit. Periodically, it will outpace them—that's when retrograde mayhem breaks loose!

Much like a speeding car or train passing a slower one, the planet being passed will appear to stop and move backward—the apparent retrograde period.
Then, once the Earth completely passes this planet in its orbit, the motion appears normal again, and the planet is said to be "direct" or "prograde" (to use the short scientific term). Chances are, you've been in a vehicle before that felt like it was moving in reverse when it was passed, this is just like that!

What about the "shadow" period?
It isn't over 'til it's over! Each retrograde cycle has a "shadow period" — the awkward adjustment of the retrograde planet from apparent backward to forward motion...and vice-versa. For that reason, you may feel the stirrings of a retrograde cycle for several days, even weeks, before it officially begins.

Pluto
Saturn
Neptune
Chiron
Jupiter
Uranus
Mars
Venus

Planetary Retrogrades

Planetary retrograde is an astrological occurrence that happens when a planet seems to move backward in its orbit from the perspective of Earth. This occurs due to differences in the orbital speed of the planets relative to Earth's position. It's important to note that planets don't actually change their direction, but the apparent retrograde motion occurs due to how the Earth orbits around the Sun.

Astrologers believe that planetary retrogrades can influence the energy and vibration of the planet in question, which can affect us. During a retrograde, the planetary energy is said to turn inward, and its impact can be felt more strongly in our lives. Different planets are believed to affect us in different ways, and their retrogrades may also have other effects.

Mercury Retrograde: It occurs three to four times a year for around three weeks. It is known for causing communication issues, technology malfunction, and travel delays. It's essential to take extra care when making important decisions or signing contracts during this time.

Venus Retrograde: This happens every eighteen months for about 40-43 days. It's a time for re-evaluating relationships, romantic connections, and money matters. It's a good time for reflection and introspection on handling these areas.

Mars Retrograde: This happens every two years for two months
It brings up feelings of frustration, anger, and aggression. It is important to be patient and avoid impulsive actions during this time.

Jupiter Retrograde: This happens every thirteen months for around four months. It can be a time for introspection and personal growth, but it can also cause setbacks in areas of expansion and growth.

Saturn Retrograde: This occurs every year for around four months. It is time to take stock of responsibilities and make necessary changes. Obstacles and lead to personal growth and development.ItCanBringChallengesAnd

Uranus Retrograde: This happens every year for around five months. It can bring unexpected changes and upheavals, but it can also bring innovation and new ideas.

Neptune Retrograde: This occurs every year for around five months; it's time for spiritual growth and reflection but can also cause confusion and delusion.

Pluto Retrograde: This happens every year for around six months. It's a time for transformation and personal growth but can also bring power struggles and intense emotional experiences.

Retrogrades

Mercury Retrograde:

Mercury takes 88 days to make one complete revolution around the Sun. Mercury moves into retrograde three times per year for anywhere between 19 to 24 days. When Mercury retrogrades, mistakes, misunderstandings, and problems in communication and transportation are likely. Do not sign contracts, buy new items, or begin new projects. It is an excellent time to plan, research, and prepare for something that will happen later. Try to evaluate how you communicate and actively remain present.

Venus Retrograde:

Venus takes 225 days to make a complete revolution around the Sun and is stationary for between a few hours or 3 or 4 days. Venus moves into retrograde every 18 months and then stays that way for about 6 weeks. When Venus goes retrograde, money and love areas are reviewed, and old relations could return to resume or be completed. New love relationships may produce a change of heart when Venus goes direct. Investments done during the retrograde phase of Venus could lose value. Old relationship issues you thought were settled rear their ugly heads. Heal those issues.

Mars Retrograde:

Mars takes approximately 2 years or 687 days to complete a revolution around the Sun. Mars moves into retrograde every 2 years + 2 months and then stays that way for about 55 to 80 days. When Mars goes retrograde, any direct action becomes difficult. Traveling within, finishing incomplete tasks, redoing, renovating, and repairing will work better than pushing forwards with any new direct ventures. Look your issues in the eye and tackle them once and for all. Self-care is your best friend during these times.

Jupiter Retrograde:

Jupiter takes around 12 years to make a complete revolution around the Sun. After that, Jupiter goes retrograde every year for about 120 days. When Jupiter goes retrograde, reviewing our visions, ideals, and belief systems in life is good. This reminds us that we need to work to achieve our dreams and re-align with our authentic selves.

Saturn Retrograde:

Saturn takes around 29.5 years to make a complete revolution around the Sun. Saturn goes retrograde every year for about 140 days. When Saturn goes retrograde, it is an excellent time to revisit our relationship and work on long-term goals, responsibilities, and duties is a time to restructure how we manifest our reality and find a new attitude towards obstacles. A chance to revisit karmic lessons, which are gentler and more familiar than new ones. Focus on self-discipline.

Retrogrades

Uranus Retrograde:
Uranus takes about 84 years to make a complete revolution around the Sun, thus spending almost 7 years in each sign of the Zodiac. Uranus moves into retrograde approximately every year for around 148 days. When Uranus goes retrograde, our inner freedom is the focus. An excellent time for us to look for new paths toward accomplishing older intentions, using its energy to help us think creatively.

Neptune Retrograde:
Neptune takes about 164 years to make a complete revolution around the Sun, thus spending almost 14 years in each sign of the Zodiac. Neptune moves into retrograde approximately every year for around 150 days. When Neptune retrogrades, our spirituality, inner tranquility, and vision become the focus. Smashes illusion, giving us the sometimes-surprising opportunity to see ourselves more clearly, unlike the other retrogrades. It forces you out of your comfort zone.

Chiron Retrograde:
It is a comet between Saturn and Uranus; Chiron takes about four years to move from sign to sign, although it spends 7 to 8 years in Aries and Pisces and only one to two years in Virgo and Libra. It entered Aries on April 17, 2018, retrograded back into Pisces on September 25, 2018, and finally moved back into the cardinal fire sign on February 18, 2019, which will remain until June 19, 2026. Chiron retrograde can be valuable for paying attention to your dreams, journaling, or addressing past trauma alongside a therapist.

Pluto Retrograde:
Pluto takes 248 years to make a complete revolution around the Sun, thus spending, on average, about 21 years in each sign of the Zodiac. Pluto moves into retrograde approximately every year for around 5 or 6 months. When Pluto goes retrograde, reflecting on how we are doing with change and transformation is good. It urges us to evaluate our relationship with power. Embrace your inner strength and use it to empower others.

CHAPTER 19

Elemental Magic

The elements are another essential aspect of Witchcraft; we often call on them during spells and rituals. There are four primary elements, each of which has particular associations. Each element represents a different type of energy that you can harness.

Earth Magic - The element of Earth is the foundation of all life. The color green and the northern quarter align with the element of Earth. It is potent in spells that require wisdom and spells for fertility, prosperity, strength, and wealth.

Air Magic - The element of air is light fuel for all living things. It is represented by the color yellow and the eastern quarter when casting a circle. Spells for renewal, change, intuition, and knowledge call upon the air.

Fire Magic - The element of fire is a source of creation and destruction of life. It is represented by the color red and the southern quarter when casting a circle. Spells for passion, inspiration, intuition, creativity, and protection use fire.

Water Magic - Water represents the flow of life. It is represented by the color blue and the western quarter when casting a circle. It is powerful in spells for healing, peace, and compassion.

Air

Symbol: △
Number: 5
Solar System: Jupiter, Mercury, and Uranus
Zodiac: Aquarius, Gemini, and Libra
Celebration: Ostara
Season: Spring
Time of Day: Dawn
Runes: Beorc, Hagal, and Thorn
Ogham: Onn
Tarot: Fool, Swords, and Wands
Direction: East
Sense: Smell
Energy: Yang
Chakras: Crown, Heart, and Throat
Colors: Blue (light), Gray, Lavender, Pink, Red, Silver, White, and Yellow (bright, light)
Trees: Acacia, Alder, Apple, Ash, Aspen, Cedar, Chestnut, Elder, Elm Fir, Hawthorn, Hazel, Holly, Horse Chestnut, Laurel, Linden, Maple, Mesquite, Oak, Olive, Palm, Pine, Sycamore, Walnut, and Yew
Herbs and Flowers: Agrimony, Anemone, Bergamot, Borage, Broom, Clover, Comfrey, Dandelion, Fern, Ivy, Lavender, Lily of the Valley, Marjoram, Marigold, Mugwort, Peppermint, Primrose, Sage, Spearmint, Thyme, Vervain, Violet, and Yarrow
Misc. Plants: Anise, Bamboo, Bittersweet, Eyebright, Frankincense, Goldenrod, Horehound, Meadowsweet, Mistletoe, Myrrh, Nutmeg, Reed, Sandalwood, Star Anise, and Wormwood
Gemstones and Minerals: Agate (tree), Ametrine, Angelite, Aragonite, Aventurine, Blue Lace Agate, Celestite, Chrysoberyl, Desert Rose, Moldavite, Opal, Quartz (clear), Sodalite, Sphene, Staurolite, Topaz (blue), and Tourmaline (blue)
Metals: Aluminum, Mercury, and Tin
From the Sea: Angel Wing and Jingle

Air

Angels: Michael and Raphael
Goddesses: Amaterasu, Athena, Arianrhod, Hera, Nut, and Phoebe
Gods: Hermes, Khnum, Mimir, Mercury, Quetzalcoatl, Thoth, and Zeus
Magical Beings: Elves, Fairies, Pixies
Animal: Gazelle
Birds: Albatross, Condor, Eagle, Falcon, Hawk, and Seagull
Reptile:
Insect/Misc.: Firefly
Mythical: Dragon, Sphinx, and Thunderbird
Ritual Tools: Athame, Incense, and Sword
Principle: To Know
Issues, Intentions, and Powers: acceptance, action, Astral Realm, beginnings, business, clairvoyance, clarity, communication, concentration/ focus, consecrate/bless, creativity, divination, enchantment, energy, enlightenment, fairness, freedom, harmony, healing, imagination, inspiration, intelligence, intuition, justice, knowledge, learning, life, light, loss, magic (animal, dragon), memory/memories, the mind, money, motivation, order/ organize, power, protection, psychic ability, purification, relationships, release, the senses (hearing, smell, touch), shamanic work, spirits, spirituality, travel, visions, weather (general, lightning, storms), willpower, and wisdom

Earth

Symbol: ▽
Numbers: 4, 6, 8
Solar System: Earth, Saturn, and Venus
Zodiac: Capricorn, Taurus, and Virgo
Celebrations: Earth Day, Hunting of the Wren, and Yule
Season: Winter
Time of Day: Midnight
Runes: Is, Tyr, and Ur
Ogham: Ioho
Tarot: Pentacles
Direction: North
Sense: Touch
Energy: Yin
Chakra: Root
Colors: Black, Brown, Green, and White
Trees: Ash, Blackthorn, Cedar, Cypress, Elder, Elm, Holly, Juniper, Locust, Magnolia, Maple, Oak, Olive, Pine, Pomegranate, Rowan, Spruce, and Witch Hazel
Herbs and Flowers: Comfrey, Fern, Honeysuckle, Ivy, Jasmine, Mugwort, Primrose, Sage, and Vervain
Misc. Plants: Cinquefoil, Clove, Grains, Henbane, High John, Horehound, Mandrake, Patchouli, and Reed
Gemstones and Minerals: Agate, Alexandrite, Amazonite, Amber, Andalusite, Apophyllite, Calcite (green), Cat's Eye, Cerussite, Chrysocolla, Chrysoprase, Diopside, Emerald, Fluorite, Hematite, Jade, Jasper, Jet, Kunzite, Malachite, Moss Agate, Peridot, Petrified Wood, Quartz (rutilated), Salt, Smoky Quartz, Staurolite, Sugilite, Tourmaline (black, brown, green, watermelon), Turquoise, and Unakite
Metals: Lead and Mercury
From the Sea: Coral (black)

Earth

Angels: Gabriel and Auriel

Goddesses: Anat, Ariadne, Artemis, Asherah, Bertha, Ceres, Demeter, Gaia, Kore, Nephthys, Persephone, Rhea, and Rhiannon

Gods: Adonis, Arawn, Cernunnos, Dionysus, Geb, the Green Man, Khnum, Marduk, Mimir, Pan, Prometheus and Vishnu

Magical Beings: Brownies, Dryads, Elves, Fairies, Gnomes, Pixies

Animals: Antelope, Armadillo, Badger, Bear, Boar, Buffalo / Bison, Cattle, Deer (stag), Dog, Elephant, Goat, Groundhog, Hippopotamus, Jaguar, Mole, Otter, Pig, Prairie Dog, and Wolverine.

Birds: Blue Jay, Chicken, Crow, Goose, Sparrow, Swan, Turkey, and Woodpecker

Reptiles: Crocodile, Snake, Toad, Tortoise, and Turtle

Insect/Misc: Dragonfly

Mythical: Dragon and Selkies

Ritual Tool: Pentacle

Principle: To Be Silent

Issues, Intentions, and Powers: abundance, acceptance, agriculture, anxiety, balance, beginnings, business, comfort, communication, consecrate/bless, consciousness, creativity, cycles, death, endurance, energy (general, receptive), family, fertility, gentleness, grounding, growth, healing, hexes, the home, justice, life, magic (dragon), manifestation, money, nurture, the otherworld/underworld, patience, peace, pregnancy/childbirth, prosperity, protection, purpose, rebirth/renewal, relationships, the senses (smell, touch), sensuality, sexuality, spirits (nature spirits), stability, strength, success, support, travel, warmth, wealth, weather, well-being, willpower, and wisdom

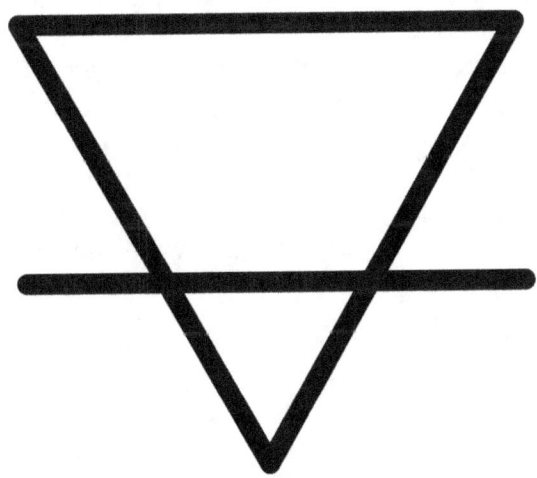

Fire

Symbol:
Numbers: 1, 3, 9
Solar System: Jupiter, Mars, and Sun
Zodiac: Aries, Leo, and Sagittarius
Celebrations: Beltane, Imbolc, and Litha
Season: Summer
Time of Day: Midday
Runes: Dag, Ken, Rad, and Sigel
Ogham: Ur
Tarot: Judgement, Swords, and Wands
Direction: South
Sense: Sight
Energy: Yang
Chakra: Solar Plexus
Colors: Crimson, Gold, Orange, Pink, Red, White, and Yellow
Trees: Alder, Ash, Beech, Blackthorn, Cedar, Cherry, Chestnut, Elder, Hawthorn, Holly, Horse Chestnut, Juniper, Laurel, Mesquite, Oak, Olive, Palm (dragon's blood), Pine, Pomegranate, Rowan, Walnut, Willow, Witch Hazel, and Yew
Herbs & Flowers: Amaranth, Anemone, Angelica, Basil, Carnation, Chrysanthemum, Dill, Fennel, Garlic, Goldenseal, Gorse, Heliotrope, Hibiscus, Holy Basil, Lovage, Marigold, Pennyroyal, Peony, Peppermint, Poppy, Primrose, Rosemary, Rue, St. John's Wort, Snapdragon, Sunflower, Sweet Woodruff, and Vervain
Misc. Plants: Allspice, Asafetida, Betony, Black Cohosh, Blessed Thistle, Bloodroot, Cinnamon, Cinquefoil, Clove, Coriander, Cumin, Deer's Tongue, Flax, Frankincense, Galangal, Ginger, Ginseng, High John, Mandrake, Mullein, Mustard, Nettle, Nutmeg, Pepper, Thistle, and Wormwood
Gemstones & Minerals: Agate (banded, black, brown, fire, red, red-banded, snakeskin), Amber, Amet-rine, Apache Tears, Beryl (golden), Bloodstone, Calcite (orange, red), Carnelian, Citrine, Diamond, Garnet, Hematite, Herkimer Diamond, Jasper (red), Obsidian, Onyx, Opal (fire), Peridot, Pyrite, Quartz, Rhodochrosite, Rhodonite, Ruby, Sard, Sardonyx, Serpentine, Smoky Quartz, Spinel, Staurolite, Sunstone, Tiger's Eye, Topaz, Tourmaline (red), Tsavorite, and Zircon (red)
Metals: Antimony, Brass, Gold, Iron, and Steel
From the Sea: Coral (red)

Fire

Angel: Michael

Goddesses: Aine, Amaterasu, Bertha, Brigid, Danu, Durga, Freya, Hestia, Kupala, Pele, Phoebe, Sekhmet, Spider-Woman, and Vesta

Gods: Agni, Belenus, Brahma, Dionysus, Hephaestus, Horus, Inari, Indra, Khnum, Mimir, Nergal, Nord, Perun, Prometheus, and Vulcan

Magical Beings: Mermaids and Salamanders

Animals: Goat, Hedgehog, Horse, Lion, Porcupine, Sheep (ram), and Tiger

Birds: Crane, Eagle, Falcon, Heron, Macaw, Peacock, Quail, Robin, Swallow, Woodpecker, and Wren

Reptiles: Lizard, Salamander, and Snake

Insects/Misc.: Bee, Cicada, Firefly, Ladybug, Praying Mantis, and Scorpion

Mythical: Dragon and Phoenix

Ritual Tools: Censer and Wand

Principle: To Will

Issues, Intentions, and Powers: action, activate/awaken, ambition, anger, authority, battle/war, cheerfulness, communication, concentration/ focus, confidence, consecrate/bless, courage, creativity, defense, desire, destruction, divination, energy, faith, freedom, healing, honor, illumination, influence, inspiration, intelligence, intuition, justice, leadership, life, light, love, lust, magic (general, defensive, dragon, sex), the mind, motivation, passion, power, protection, psychic ability, purification, purity, purpose, release, revenge, sexuality, stimulation, transformation, truth, warmth, weather (general, lightning), and willpower

Water

Symbol:
Numbers: 2, 7
Solar System: Mercury, Moon, Neptune, Pluto, and Saturn
Zodiac: Cancer, Pisces, and Scorpio
Celebrations: Mabon and Neptunalia
Season: Autumn
Time of Day: Dusk
Runes: Feoh, Jera, Lagu, and Peorth
Ogham: Eadha, and Eamhancholl
Tarot: Cups, Hanged Man, and Moon
Direction: West
Sense: Taste
Energy: Yin
Chakra: Sacral
Colors: Aqua, Black, Blue, Gray, Green (blue, sea), Indigo, Lilac, Purple, Silver, Turquoise, Violet, and White
Trees: Alder, Apple, Ash, Aspen, Beech, Birch, Cedar, Cherry, Chestnut, Cypress, Elder, Elm, Hazel, Horse Chestnut, Locust, Magnolia, Mesquite, Mimosa, Myrtle, Olive, Poplar, Spindle-tree, Spruce, Sycamore, Willow, Witch Hazel, and Yew
Herbs & Flowers: Aster, Blackberry / Bramble, Catnip, Chamomile, Columbine, Comfrey, Daffodil, Daisy, Feverfew, Foxglove, Gardenia, Geranium, Grape, Heather, Hibiscus, Hyacinth, Iris, Ivy, Jasmine, Lady's Mantle, Lemon Balm, Lilac, Lily, Monkshood, Morning Glory, Passionflower, Periwinkle, Poppy, Raspberry, Rose, Solomon's Seal, Spearmint, Strawberry, Thyme, Valerian, Violet, and Yarrow
Misc. Plants: Aloe, Belladonna, Burdock, Cardamom, Coltsfoot, Cowslip, Dittany, Henbane, Lady's Slipper, Lotus, Meadowsweet, Moonwort, Myrrh, Orris Root, Reed, Sandalwood, Skullcap, Spikenard, Star Anise, Thornapple, Vanilla, and Water Lily
Gemstones & Minerals: Alexandrite, Amethyst, Ametrine, Angelite, Aquamarine, Aragonite, Azurite, Beryl, Blue Lace Agate, Calcite, Charoite, Chrysocolla, Dioptase, Fluorite, Jade, Jasper (ocean), Jet, Kyanite, Labradorite, Lapis Lazuli, Larimar, Lepidolite, Lodestone, Moonstone, Morganite, Obsidian (gold sheen), Opal, Quartz, Rose Quartz, Sapphire, Selenite, Sodalite, Staurolite, Sugilite Topaz (blue), Tourmaline (black, blue, pink, watermelon), Tsavorite, Turquoise, and Zircon (blue)
Metals: Copper, Mercury, and Silver
From the Sea: Coral, Mother-of-Pearl, and Pearl

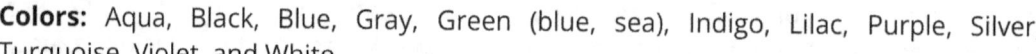

Water

Angels: Raphael

Goddesses: Amphitrite, Aphrodite, Bad, Boann, Brigantia, Chalchiuhtlicue, Coventina, Isis, Kupala, Ran, Sarasvati, Sedna, and Tiamat

Gods: Aegir, Belenus, Ea, Khnum, Mabon, Manannan, Mimir, Neptune, Njord, Osiris, Poseidon, and Prometheus

Magical Beings: Mermaids, Norns, and Undines

Animals: Bat, Beaver, Cattle (cow), Dog, Hare, Hippopotamus, Horse, Moose, Otter, Polar Bear, and Raccoon

Birds: Albatross, Blackbird, Cormorant, Crane, Dove, Duck, Heron, Kingfisher, Seagull, Stork, Swan, Swift, and Vulture

Reptiles: Crocodile, Frog, Salamander, Snake, and Toad

Insect/Misc.: Dragonfly

Mythical: Dragon and Selkies

Ritual Tools: Cauldron, Chalice, and Cup

Principle: To Dare

Issues, Intentions and Powers: adaptability, agriculture, balance, beginnings, change/s, clairvoyance, compassion, consecrate/bless, consciousness (subconscious), creativity, desire, divination, dream work, emotions, empathy, energy (general, psychic, receptive), fertility, friendship, grace, growth, healing, heartbreak, influence, introspection, intuition, life, magic (animal, dragon, moon), memory /memories, nurture, patience, power, pregnancy/childbirth, protection, psychic ability, purification, purity, rebirth/ renewal, reconciliation, reversal, secrets, sensitivity, sensuality, shamanic work, sleep, sorrow, spirituality, strength (inner), stress, transformation, weather (general, storms), well-being, and wisdom

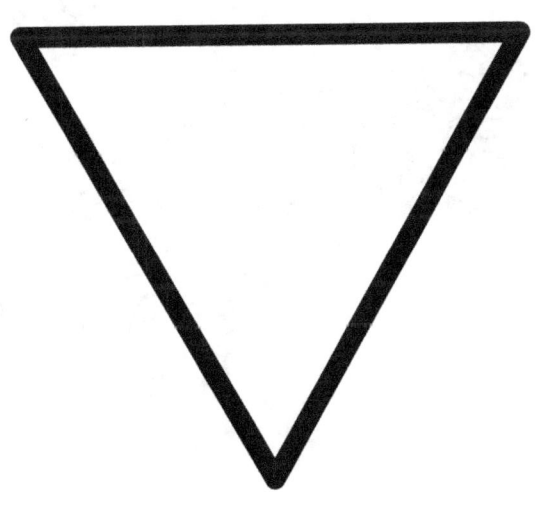

CHAPTER 20

Tarot & Oracle

Tarot Cards

Tarot is an intricate divination system consisting of 78 cards divided into major and minor arcana cards. Heavily relying on classical mythology and symbolism, tarot is thought to allow one to receive answers to the events in question by interpreting messages based on how the cards are dealt. This can be done utilizing card spreads like the classic Celtic cross, or a simple 3 card past, present, and future layout.

Oracle Cards

Less structured than tarot, oracle cards use a combination of artwork and written interpretations which can sometimes include exercises. Oracle cards can be based on nearly any subject matter and are open to various styles and formats. Perfect for guiding without the intricacies associated with tarot.

Ostara ~ Spring Equinox

Card 1 - Seeds and dreams to plant
Card 2 - What they need to grow
Card 3 - How to nurture them and yourself
Card 4 - How to prep for their arrival

Ostara

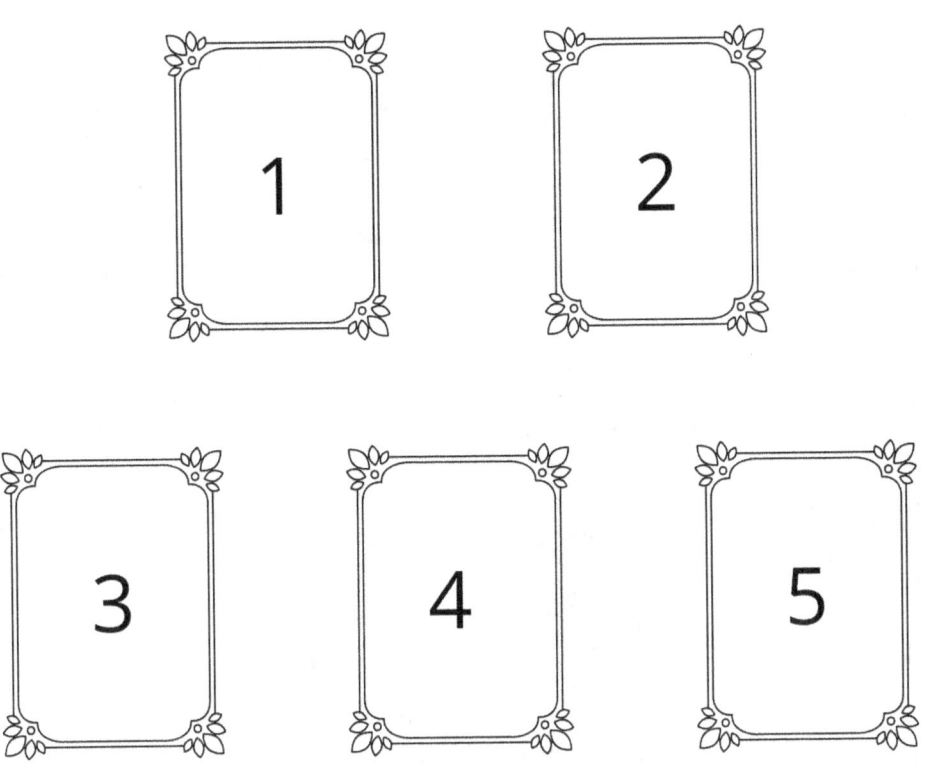

Card 1 - Where is there renewal
Card 2 - What form will this growth take
Card 3 - How can I nurture this growth
Card 4 - What must I spring clean out of my life
Card 5 - How can I let go of these things to allow growth

Ask Your Guides

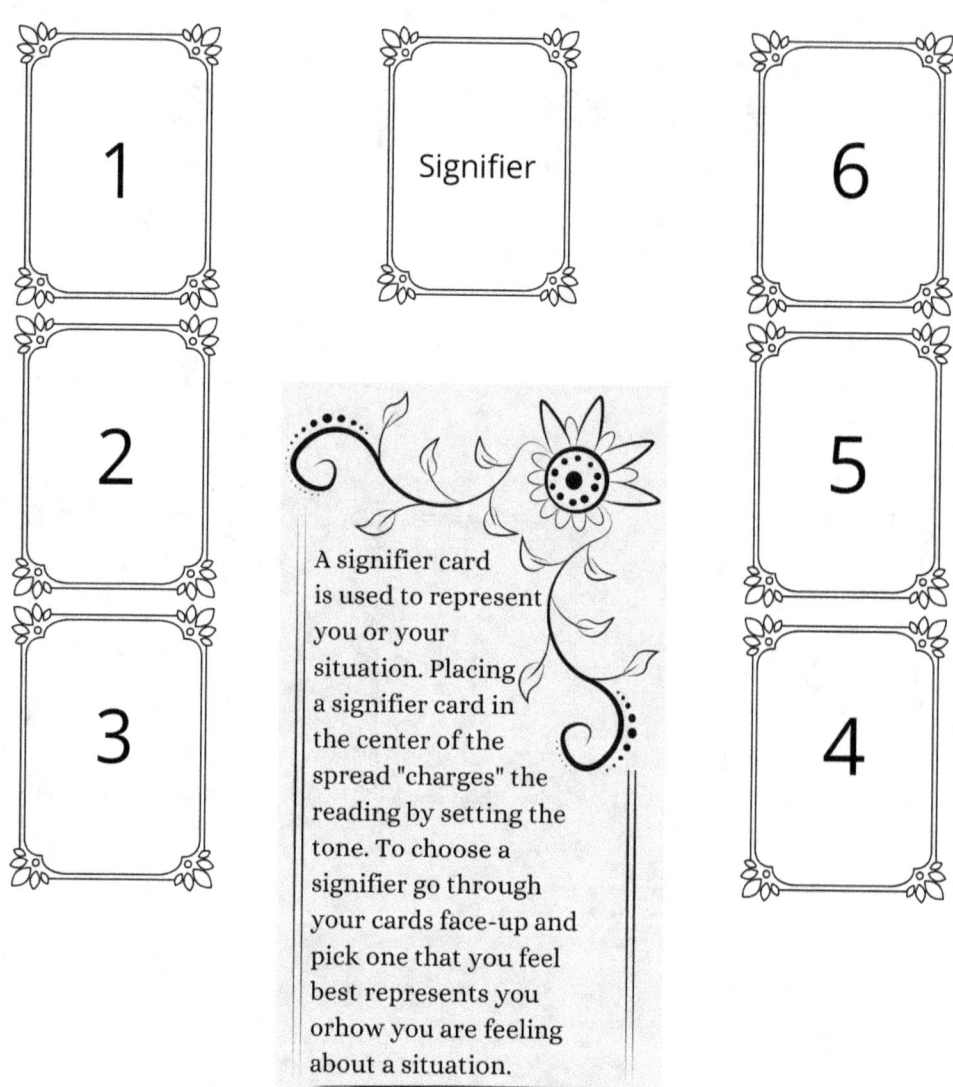

1

2

3

Signifier

6

5

4

A signifier card is used to represent you or your situation. Placing a signifier card in the center of the spread "charges" the reading by setting the tone. To choose a signifier go through your cards face-up and pick one that you feel best represents you orhow you are feeling about a situation.

Card 1 - What do I want for myself
Card 2 - What do I no longer need
Card 3 - What have I cared too much for
Card 4 - What have I cared too little for
Card 5 - What have I agreed to that is no longer true
Card 6 - What new belief would liberate me

Elemental Guidance

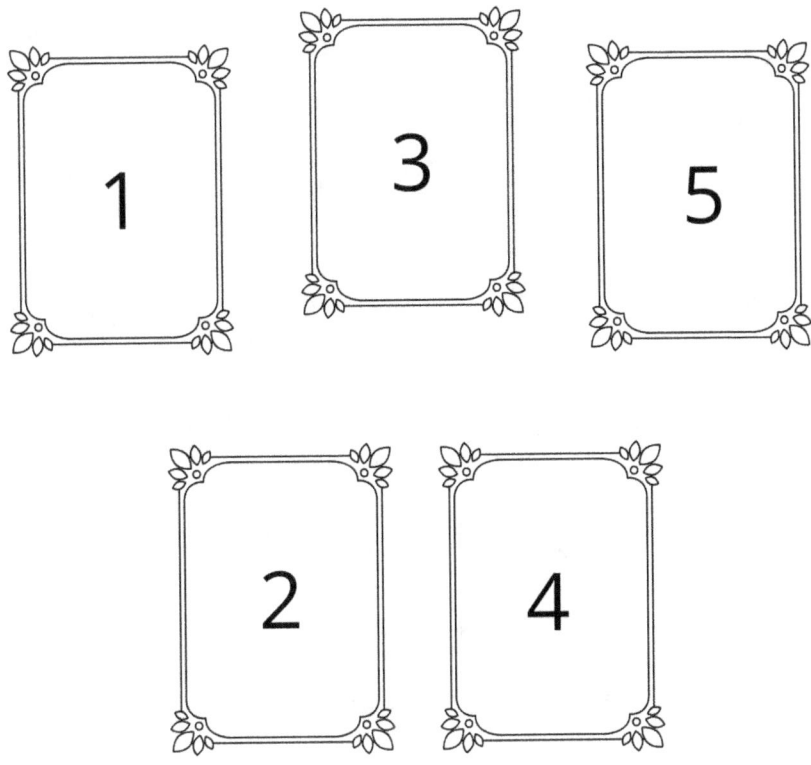

Card 1 - Earth How do I need to ground myself
Card 2 - Spirit How do I need to nourish my spirit
Card 3 - Air Where should I focus my attention right now
Card 4 - Water What is my intuition trying to tell me
Card 5 - Fire What goals and dreams should I pursue

Higher Self Messages

Card 1 - Where should I shift my focus
Card 2 - What truth am I hiding from myself
Card 3 - What is my spirit asking for right now
Card 4 - What needs to be released
Card 5 - Final message

Manifest My Desire

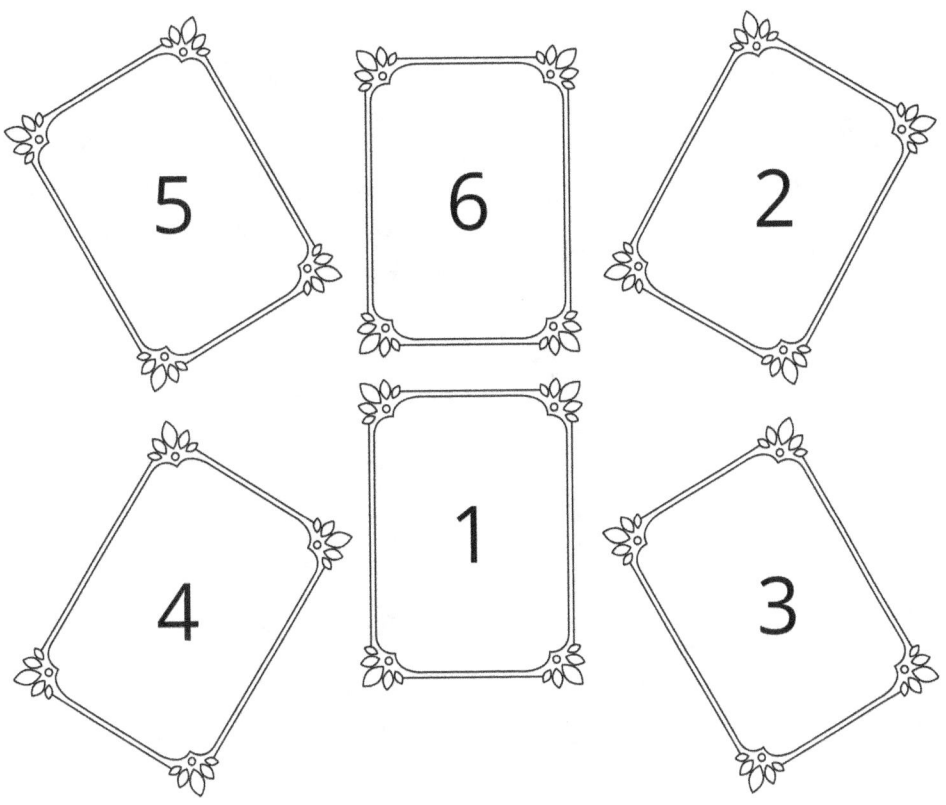

Card 1 - A card you pick to represent your desire(s)
Card 2 - What you can do right now to manifest your desires
Card 3 - Where in life do you need a little nudge
Card 4 - Where in life do you need to relax
Card 5 - Something you are missing that can help you
Card 6 - A resource you must tweak to help your desire come to fruition

Abundance and Prosperity

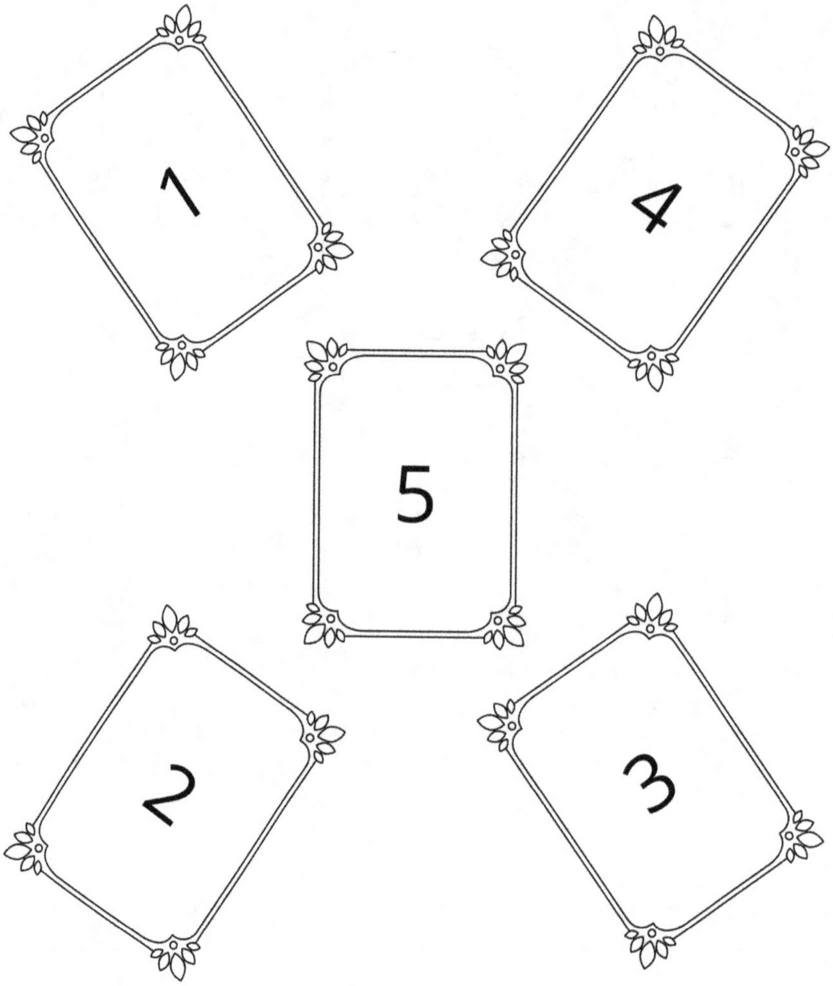

1

4

5

2

3

Card 1 - What past achievement am I grateful for
Card 2 - What inner traits of mine am I grateful for
Card 3 - What exterior things am I grateful for
Card 4 - What future prospects am I grateful for
Card 5 - Who am I grateful for

Soul Work

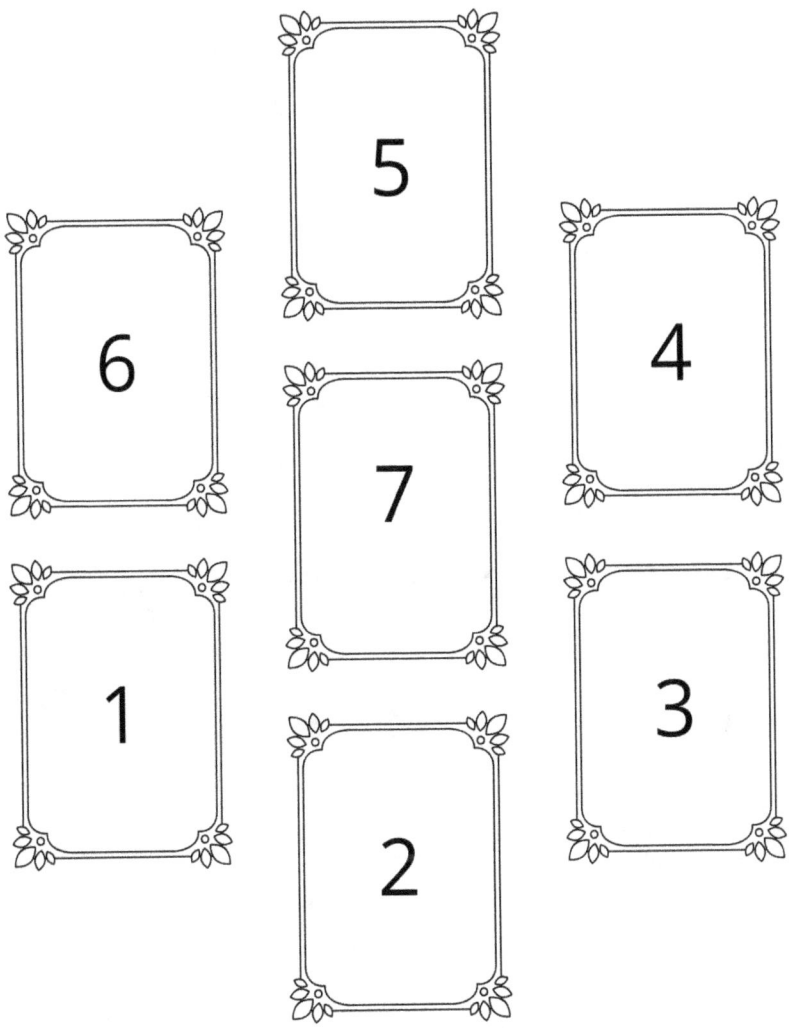

Card 1 - My soul's personality
Card 2 - My soul's purpose
Card 3 - My soul's gift
Card 4 - My soul's challenge
Card 5 - Advice for my soul's development
Card 6 - Advice for soul's progress
Card 7 - My soul's message for me

Racing Thoughts

Card 1 - What is triggering these thoughts
Card 2 - What am I not understanding
Card 3 - How can I change these thoughts

Stress Relief

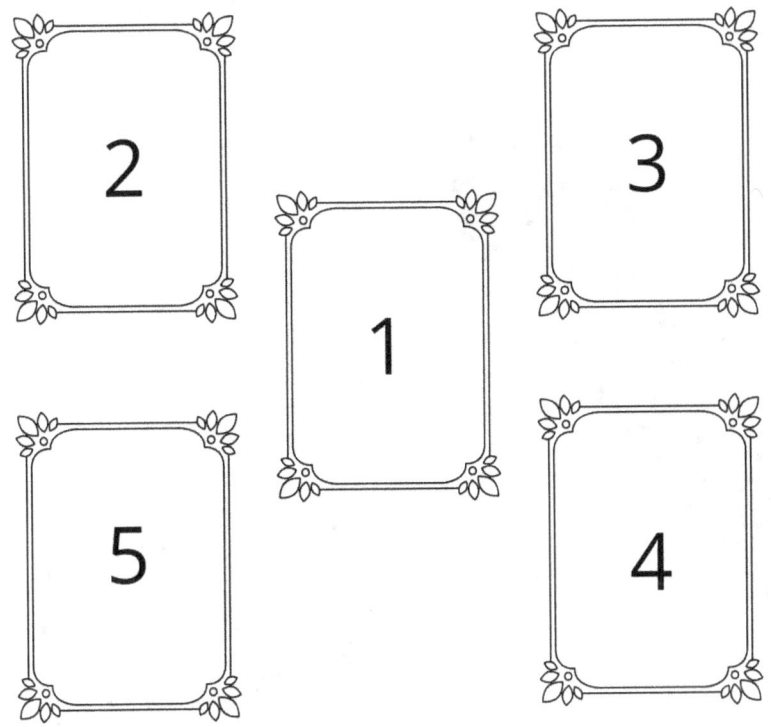

Card 1 - The root of my current stress
Card 2 - The healthiest way to cope with this stress
Card 3 - Important lesson I'm learning
Card 4 - Something I'm not seeing clearly
Card 5 - How to avoid this problem in the futur

CHAPTER 21

Nurturing Pollinators

Pollinators

Bees play a crucial role in the health and sustainability of our ecosystem, and their survival is paramount.

Pollination - Bees are primary pollinators of many flowering plants, including a significant portion of the crops that make up our global food supply. They facilitate the reproduction of plants by transferring pollen from the male parts (anthers) to the female parts (stigmas) of flowers.

Biodiversity - The pollination activities of bees contribute to the biodiversity of ecosystems. A diverse range of flowering plants depends on bees for pollination, which supports other wildlife species that rely on these plants for food and habitat.

Food Production - Bees are essential for producing fruits, vegetables, nuts, and seeds. Many crops that form the foundation of our diets, such as apples, berries, almonds, and coffee, depend on bee pollination. The economic value of bee-pollinated crops is immense.

Ecosystem Health - The presence of bees is indicative of a healthy ecosystem. Their activities contribute to the overall health and resilience of natural habitats. A decline in bee populations can signal broader ecological imbalances.

Honey Production - Bees are also essential for honey production. Honey has cultural, culinary, and medicinal significance in many societies, making bees important for both ecological balance and human well-being.

Seed Production - Bees are crucial in producing seeds for many plant species. This is vital for the regeneration and continuation of plant populations, ensuring the genetic diversity of plant life.

Economic Impact - Bees' agricultural and economic significance cannot be overstated. The value of crops pollinated by bees is estimated in the billions of dollars annually. Agriculture, as well as various industries, relies heavily on the ecosystem services provided by bees.

Environmental Stewardship - Bees contribute to sustainable agriculture by supporting natural pollination processes. Maintaining healthy bee populations is a form of ecological stewardship that helps reduce the need for artificial pollination methods.

Indicator Species - Bees can serve as indicators of environmental health. Their sensitivity to changes in habitat, pesticide use, and climate makes them a valuable species for monitoring broader ecological trends.

Global Interconnectedness - Bee populations are interconnected globally. Challenges faced by bees, such as habitat loss, pesticide exposure, and diseases, have widespread implications that transcend geographical boundaries.

The decline of bee populations, as observed in phenomena like colony collapse disorder, raises concerns about food security, ecological balance, and the overall health of our planet. Promoting bee conservation, habitat protection, and sustainable agricultural practices is critical to ensuring the continued well-being of both bees and the ecosystems they support.

Pollinators: Guardians of Ecosystems

Defining Pollinators
Pollinators, such as bees, beetles, ants, butterflies, and hummingbirds, are vital in the life cycle of flowering plants, ensuring the health of ecosystems. The globally celebrated Pollinator Week in late June highlights their importance and the challenges they encounter, emphasizing the year-round need to safeguard them.

The Issue: Decreasing Populations
Declining pollinator numbers significantly threaten ecosystems and human well-being, impacting the production of essential goods like foods, beverages, fibers, spices, and medicines. Taking steps like minimizing pesticide use, planting for pollinators, and raising awareness is crucial to address this issue.

Minimizing Environmental Impact
Reducing your impact is an immediate way to assist pollinators. Opt for organic alternatives to harmful pesticides or apply treatments when pollinators are less active. Increasing green spaces by planting more and paving less creates additional habitats for these essential creatures.

Creating Pollinator-Friendly Gardens
Establish a garden that supports pollinators by planting a variety of flowers that bloom from early spring to late fall, focusing on native and non-invasive species. Avoid hybrids that may lack essential nectar, pollen, and fragrance, and consider the needs of caterpillars to support butterflies' lifecycles.

Raising Awareness
Spread the word about pollinator conservation to empower others in enhancing habitats, rebuilding populations, and raising global awareness. Engage in discussions with friends, neighbors, and family, and share online to contribute to the collective effort of nurturing and preserving pollinators.

Nurturing Pollinators for Healthy Ecosystems
Home gardeners play a crucial role in promoting and maintaining pollinator populations, including honeybees, native bees, butterflies, and hummingbirds. Recognizing the decline in these populations due to habitat loss, diseases, and pesticide use highlights the urgency of collective conservation efforts.

Understanding Pollinators' Role
Recognizing the vital role of pollinators in transferring pollen between flowers for fertilization and seed and fruit development is essential. By supporting pollinator populations, we contribute to the health and sustainability of our local ecosystem.

Helping The Pollinators

One of the most effective ways to help bees, butterflies, and hummingbirds is by creating and preserving their habitats. Planting native flowering plants that provide nectar and host plants for butterfly larvae is essential for butterfly conservation. Similarly, choosing a diverse range of native wildflowers, shrubs, and trees that produce nectar-rich blooms throughout the year can attract bees and hummingbirds to your garden or outdoor space. By providing a continuous supply of food sources, individuals can ensure the survival and well-being of these important pollinators.

Reducing the use of pesticides and herbicides in your yard and garden is critical for conserving bees, butterflies, and hummingbirds. Pesticides can harm these pollinators directly through contact or ingestion and indirectly by reducing their food sources and disrupting their reproductive behaviors. Instead, practice integrated pest management techniques, such as hand-picking pests, using natural predators, and companion planting, to minimize the need for chemical interventions. Creating pesticide-free environments can provide safer foraging opportunities for bees, butterflies, and hummingbirds.

Additionally, advocating for policies and regulations that restrict the use of harmful pesticides in urban and agricultural settings can help protect these pollinators and their habitats on a larger scale. Supporting legislation aimed at habitat conservation, sustainable land management practices, and promoting biodiversity-friendly initiatives can also contribute to preserving bees, butterflies, and hummingbirds. Through these collective efforts, individuals can make a meaningful impact in safeguarding these vital pollinators and ensuring their continued presence in our ecosystems.

Bee Attractants

Lavender (Lavandula spp.)
Sunflowers (Helianthus spp.)
Bee balm (Monarda spp.)
Sage (Salvia spp.)
Coneflowers (Echinacea spp.)
Catmint (Nepeta spp.)
Borage (Borago officinalis)
Black-eyed Susan (Rudbeckia spp.)
Thyme (Thymus spp.)
Honeysuckle (Lonicera spp.)
Rosemary (Rosmarinus officinalis)
Purple coneflower (Echinacea purpurea)
Oregano (Origanum spp.)
Cosmos (Cosmos spp.)
Foxglove (Digitalis spp.)
Butterfly bush (Buddleja spp.)
Mint (Mentha spp.)
Yarrow (Achillea spp.)
Goldenrod (Solidago spp.)
Phacelia (Phacelia spp.)
Marjoram (Origanum majorana)
Lemon balm (Melissa officinalis)
Fennel (Foeniculum vulgare)
Crocus (Crocus spp.)
Penstemon (Penstemon spp.)
Zinnias (Zinnia spp.)
Bee plant (Scrophularia spp.)
Anise hyssop (Agastache spp.)
Russian sage (Perovskia spp.)
Globe thistle (Echinops spp.)
Columbine (Aquilegia spp.)
Snapdragon (Antirrhinum spp.)
Chives (Allium schoenoprasum)
Echinops (Echinops spp.)
Liatris (Liatris spp.)
Bluebell (Campanula spp.)
Aster (Aster spp.)
Hyssop (Hyssopus officinalis)
Primrose (Primula spp.)
Rose (Rosa spp.)
Bee orchid (Ophrys apifera)
Snapdragon (Antirrhinum majus)

Speedwell (Veronica spp.)
Baptisia (Baptisia spp.)
Gaillardia (Gaillardia spp.)
Helenium (Helenium spp.)
Sedum (Sedum spp.)
Lamb's ear (Stachys byzantina)
Bergamot (Monarda didyma)
Butterfly weed (Asclepias tuberosa)

These plants are known for their nectar-rich flowers, which attract bees and provide them with a valuable food source. When planning a bee-friendly garden, consider incorporating a variety of these plants to provide continuous blooms throughout the growing season.

Butterfly Attractants

Butterfly bush (Buddleia davidii)
Milkweed (Asclepias spp.)
Lantana (Lantana spp.)
Coneflowers (Echinacea spp.)
Zinnias (Zinnia spp.)
Black-eyed Susan (Rudbeckia spp.)
Pentas (Pentas lanceolata)
Verbena (Verbena spp.)
Aster (Aster spp.)
Salvia (Salvia spp.)
Phlox (Phlox spp.)
Coreopsis (Coreopsis spp.)
Butterfly weed (Asclepias tuberosa)
Blanket flower (Gaillardia spp.)
Marigold (Tagetes spp.)
Joe Pye weed (Eutrochium spp.)
Sweet Alyssum (Lobularia maritima)
Liatris (Liatris spp.)
Bee balm (Monarda spp.)
Honeysuckle (Lonicera spp.)
Purple coneflower (Echinacea purpurea)
Milk thistle (Silybum marianum)
Hollyhock (Alcea spp.)
Mint (Mentha spp.)
Dianthus (Dianthus spp.)
Red clover (Trifolium pratense)
Globe thistle (Echinops spp.)
Sedum (Sedum spp.)
Passionflower (Passiflora spp.)
Ironweed (Vernonia spp.)
Yarrow (Achillea spp.)
Lavender (Lavandula spp.)
Fennel (Foeniculum vulgare)
Swamp milkweed (Asclepias incarnata)
Goldenrod (Solidago spp.)
Ajuga (Ajuga spp.)
Columbine (Aquilegia spp.)
Lilac (Syringa spp.)
Red valerian (Centranthus ruber)
Helenium (Helenium spp.)

Dill (Anethum graveolens)
Thistle (Cirsium spp.)
Tithonia (Tithonia spp.)
Sweet William (Dianthus barbatus)
Blue mist shrub (Caryopteris x clandonensis)
Verbascum (Verbascum spp.)
Baptisia (Baptisia spp.)
Sweet peas (Lathyrus spp.)
Butterfly pea (Clitoria ternatea)
Coneflower (Rudbeckia spp.)

These plants are known for their colorful blooms and nectar-rich flowers, which attract butterflies of various species. Incorporating a diverse range of these plants into your garden or landscape can help create a butterfly-friendly environment and provide essential food sources for these beautiful insects throughout the seasons.

Hummingbird Attractants

Salvia (Salvia spp.)
Trumpet vine (Campsis spp.)
Bee balm (Monarda spp.)
Fuchsia (Fuchsia spp.)
Lantana (Lantana spp.)
Cardinal flower (Lobelia cardinalis)
Red hot poker (Kniphofia spp.)
Columbine (Aquilegia spp.)
Penstemon (Penstemon spp.)
Sage (Salvia spp.)
Butterfly bush (Buddleja spp.)
Honeysuckle (Lonicera spp.)
Coral bells (Heuchera spp.)
Yucca (Yucca spp.)
Hollyhock (Alcea spp.)
Bottlebrush (Callistemon spp.)
Firecracker plant (Russelia spp.)
Agastache (Agastache spp.)
Cape honeysuckle (Tecomaria capensis)
Lobelia (Lobelia spp.)
Trumpet creeper (Campsis radicans)
Hummingbird mint (Agastache spp.)
Morning glory (Ipomoea spp.)
Catmint (Nepeta spp.)
Scarlet runner bean (Phaseolus coccineus)
Coral bells (Heuchera spp.)
Gladiolus (Gladiolus spp.)
Larkspur (Delphinium spp.)
Hollyhock (Alcea spp.)
Crocosmia (Crocosmia spp.)
Bee balm (Monarda spp.)
Cardinal flower (Lobelia cardinalis)
Honeysuckle (Lonicera spp.)
Snapdragon (Antirrhinum spp.)
Foxglove (Digitalis spp.)
Petunia (Petunia spp.)
Zinnia (Zinnia spp.)
Bleeding heart (Dicentra spp.)
Red hot poker (Kniphofia spp.)
Verbena (Verbena spp.)

Angel's trumpet (Brugmansia spp.)
Hosta (Hosta spp.)
Morning glory (Ipomoea spp.)
Pincushion flower (Scabiosa spp.)
Shrimp plant (Justicia brandegeana)
Jasmine (Jasminum spp.)
Beard tongue (Penstemon spp.)
Mexican sunflower (Tithonia spp.)
Four o'clocks (Mirabilis jalapa)
Aloe (Aloe spp.)

These plants are known for their tubular-shaped flowers and nectar-producing blooms, which are attractive to hummingbirds. Incorporating a variety of these plants into your garden or landscape can create a hummingbird-friendly environment and provide essential food sources for these fascinating birds throughout the seasons.

Butterfly Puddler

Butterflies require salt and minerals in their diet, but most gardens lack a natural supply, making a Butterfly Puddler essential.

Puddler Sand and Salt Recipe
Combine ½ to ¾ cup of salt with 1 gallon of sand and pour the mixture into the puddler as needed.
Adjust the amount based on the puddler's size, ensuring it is covered in water.
After the water evaporates, a mineral-rich residue is left behind, serving as a butterfly salt lick.
If the puddler usage decreases, store the salted mixture for future use and refill the puddler with a fresh batch.

Supplies Needed:
Terracotta pot and saucer
Play sand
Compost
Decorative rocks and beach glass
Acrylic paint for outdoor use
Butterflies usually obtain water from nectar but visit the puddler for essential minerals.
Place the puddler in a sunny spot once completed.

Directions:
Mix 3 parts sand with 1 part compost and spread it in the saucer.
Create a "river" in the sand by adding decorative pebbles.
Place flat rocks or beach glass along the river for butterflies to perch.
Add water to form mud, then set the puddler in the garden.
Replenish the water every few days to a week based on the evaporation rate. Clean the puddler monthly with biodegradable soap, and refresh the sand and compost.

Bee Bath

Bee baths, simple water sources, can benefit bees in your garden by providing essential hydration. Just like they need nectar and pollen, bees rely on water for survival and to regulate their temperature on hot days. Offering water can enhance bee survival, health, and attraction for pollination. Especially valuable in hot, dry weather when water is scarce, bee baths support local bee populations critical for crop pollination and ecosystem diversity. Alongside bee baths, planting bee-friendly flora, avoiding pesticides, and providing nesting habitats can further support bees and foster a healthy ecosystem.

To aid bee populations, consider planting pollinator-friendly plants, avoiding pesticides and herbicides, and providing nesting habitats. These steps can help bee populations and encourage a thriving ecosystem.

Tips for Selecting Containers for Bee Baths:
Shallow and broad: Opt for a shallow container (around 2 inches deep) to prevent drowning and allow easy access for bees. Choose containers with smooth edges to avoid harming bees as they reach the water.
Material: Use bee-safe materials like ceramic, glass, or food-grade plastic to avoid harmful chemicals leaching into the water.
Color: Bees are attracted to bright colors, so select containers in vibrant hues like yellow, blue, or white to attract bees. Place the container within easy reach and provide a clear path to the water source for bees.

When filling your bee bath container with water, consider these key points to ensure bee safety.
Use clean, fresh water: Bees are sensitive to water quality, so opt for clean, fresh water to prevent bacteria growth. Keep the water depth around 1/2 inch to ensure bee safety. Bees prefer warm water, so use room temperature water to attract them.
Regularly refill the container: Bees need access to fresh water, so refill the container daily or every other day.
Maintain a consistent water level: Bees use landmarks to locate water sources, so keep the water level consistent for easy access.
Adding rocks or pebbles to your bee bath offers various benefits. Rocks or pebbles serve as stable landing pads for bees while they drink. Rocks create a shallow area for bees to drink safely. Rocks help filter out debris and pollutants to maintain clean water. When adding rocks or pebbles, clean rocks and ensure they are free from harmful chemicals.
Choose the right size: Select rocks that fit comfortably and offer a stable landing pad.
Arrange carefully: Place rocks on a portion of the bottom without overcrowding to allow bees access to the water.
Position the bee bath in a sunny location for maximum bee attraction.

Placing your bee bath in a sunny location is a critical aspect to consider when creating a water source for bees.

Aids in evaporation: Bees are drawn to warm water, so positioning the bee bath in a sunny spot attracts them. Sunlight helps evaporate excess water, preventing mosquito breeding and maintaining cleanliness.

Enhances visibility: Bees are more likely to spot a brightly colored bee bath in a sunny area, increasing visits to the water source.

Provides warmth: Bees need warmth to fly and regulate their body temperature. A sunny bee bath offers a warm spot for bees to rest and dry off after drinking.

Tips for placing your bee bath in a sunny spot:
Choose a secure location to avoid disturbance.
Provide shade during hot weather to prevent overheating.
Protect from wind to avoid water disturbance.
By situating your bee bath in a sunny spot, you create an attractive and effective water source for bees, supporting their well-being and survival.

Don't forget to change the water regularly.

Regular water changes are essential for a healthy bee bath.

Prevents harmful bacteria growth by avoiding standing water.
Maintains fresh water to attract bees.
Helps prevent mosquito breeding by avoiding stagnant water.
Tips for changing the water in your bee bath:

Change the water at least once a week.
Rinse the container thoroughly before refilling.
Refill with clean water to the appropriate level and add rocks or pebbles if desired.

DIY Bucket Bath

Like the bowl fountain, this bath gives you more water without needing daily refills. By using a bucket as the water reservoir and a straightforward top piece as the fountain, you can go a week without having to refill.

Supplies:

5-gallon bucket for the reservoir. Or any 3-5 gallon or above sized container (such as a large planter pot with NO drain holes).

For the top piece, use a plastic chip and dip tray for a fountain effect, or just use the bucket lid for a more "splash pad" effect.

Submersible pump – either solar-powered or electric (plug).

Enough tubing to run from the top to the bottom of your bucket/container. You can find this at hardware or aquarium stores. Bring your pump with you for sizing, and make sure the tubing fits snugly on the pump outflow and any nozzle attachments you will be using—something to make holes in the plastic. If you have drill bits, that could work.

Here are the basic steps. Once you catch on to the basic idea, you can let your creativity run wild with your designs!

Directions:

Cut your tube to size (to reach from the top of the bucket to the bottom. It doesn't have to be exact; leave a little slack for "wiggle room."

Place the tube facedown on your lid/topper piece in the center. Using a marker, trace around the tube. This is the size of the hole you need to cut to thread the tube through.

At various points in your top piece, drill small holes. These holes will allow the water to drain back into the bucket. Small holes are best to avoid getting debris and bugs in your bucket. You will probably need 5-8 holes, but you can start low and adjust later. Just make sure to place them where they will drain into the bucket.

Place the pump inside the bucket, attach the tubing, and thread the tubing up through the lid hole, and voila!

Decorate as you see fit! You can paint the bucket (non-toxic paint). Add some stones (don't cover your drain holes) for the birds to stand on—group stones around the water nozzle for more cascading.

DIY Hummingbird Fountain

Ensure the water is shallow, barely a centimeter deep, as hummingbirds do not bathe in deep water.
Use a fountain to keep the water moving, as hummingbirds prefer flowing water over stagnant water.
The water can either shower and spray or be gentle and bubbling.
Hummingbirds enjoy wet rocks for gripping and grooming.

DIY Rock Fountain

Creating this is simple - just a bowl with a pump. You can customize it to your liking, whether simple or elaborate and place it in your garden or a tabletop.

Supplies:
A shallow bowl, preferably not more than 5 inches deep, to accommodate the pump and fist-sized rocks. A wide-rim soup bowl shape works well, but any bowl with a rim will do.
Submersible pump: solar-powered or electric.
Fist-sized rocks.

Directions:
Place the pump in the center of your bowl
Arrange the rocks in a circle around the pump.
Add water, enough to cover the pump except for the top of the nozzle, and make sure the tops of the rocks are above the waterline.
Place the bowl wherever you want. If you use a solar pump, ensure the solar panel is in a spot with direct sun, and you're done.

Magical Water

Water is a revered element with transformative and purifying properties, making it sacred to life. In the realm of spirituality and magic, different types of magical water hold immense power and are utilized for various purposes. Each enchanted kind of water has unique qualities, making it a versatile tool for spellwork, rituals, and energetic practices. Moon water offers soothing and healing properties, while holy water is potent and protective. These enchanted waters serve as conduits for intention and manifestation.

When combined with intention, visualization, and focused energy, the power of water is amplified in magic and spirituality. These different types of magical water serve as potent tools that allow practitioners to connect with the natural forces and energies around us. Whether seeking healing, protection, purification, or manifestation, the versatile uses of magical water offer a profound connection to the mystical realms.

Magical Water Properties

Rain Water: Growth and rebirth spells, cleansing, scrying, altar water, and ritual baths.

Storm Water: Vitality, self-esteem, courage, mental strength, strengthening spells, and protection.

Dew Water: Healing, beauty, eyesight, love, fertility, working with the fae, and cleansing.

Snow Water: Unthaw a situation, transformation, balance, peace, consecrating, and endings.

Moon Water: Charging, blessing or cleanse, bath rituals, powering spells, healing magic, curses, and hexes.

Sun Water: Protection, healing, clairvoyance, happiness, fertility, and creativity.

River Water: Moving on, focusing energy, warding, breakthrough, power, and charging.

Sea Water: Cleansing, banishing, protection, emotional balance, healing rituals, and manifestation.

Spring Water: Growth, holy water, cleansing, abundance, potions, and beauty.

Lake Water: Peace, joy, contentment, relaxation, self-reflection, and self-discovery.

Wellwater: Healing, wishes, intuition, manifestation, connection to otherworldly beings.

Swamp Water: Banishing, binding, hexing, cursing, and reversing.

Use clean, filtered water like distilled or spring water to add more magic to your recipes.

Rain Water

Catch the rainwater any time of day and bottle it up for your craft usage. Good for rebirth, cycles, transformation, cleansings, protection, altar water, ritual baths, peace, tranquility, purification, scrying, divination, and asperging.

Lake Water

Good for peace, happiness, contentment, joy, relaxation, reflection, personal journey, and growth.

Swamp Water

Good for revenge magic, binding, hexing, curses, and banishing

Dew Water

Collect dew water during the morning from windows, leaves, or flowers. Good for healing, cleansing, beauty, love, passion, fertility, and fae magic

Well Water

Good for connecting with elemental spirits, sprites, and the fae healing, intuition, scrying, manifestation, and wishes.

Spring Water

Good for growth, cleansing, abundance, fae work, love, fertility, healing, positivity, strength, purify altars, divination tools, endurance and grounding

I Got a Jar of Dirt!

Types of Dirt and Their Magical Uses

Graveyard
Traditionally used in divination, cursing, love, and protection spells.
Avoid collecting from an unclean spirit's grave for most workings.
Leave an offering in exchange for the dirt.
Try to collect from an ancestor's grave to ensure the energy you are collecting is safe.

Churchyard
Traditionally used for many intentions and spells:
Healing
Prosperity
Purification
Protection
Mending relationships
Justice workings

Crossroad
They are traditionally used in road-opening spells.
Used in journeying to the underworld, as it helps open the gate to the other realms.
They are used as offerings to guardians and gods of the crossroads: Hecate, Hermes, Papa Legba, etc.

Backyard
Traditionally used in workings for the family, home, and property:
Purification
Protection
Peace
Collect from the 4 corners of the property if possible.

Graveyard

Working with Graveyard Dirt: Traditional Use in Healing, Protection and Prosperity Spells.

Graveyard dirt has long been used for its mystical properties, particularly in healing, protection, and prosperity spells. However, following specific guidelines when collecting graveyard dirt is essential to avoid negative energies. Here are some tips:

Avoid collecting dirt from the grave of an unwell spirit. Always leave an offering in exchange for the dirt gathered. Collecting dirt from ancestors' graves rather than from unknown ones is recommended. By following these guidelines, you can safely and effectively work with graveyard dirt in your practice.

Churchyard

Churchyard dirt is a versatile substance that can be utilized in magic and witchcraft for various purposes. Some of the most popular intentions and spells include:

Healing
Prosperity
Purification
Protection
Mending relationships
Justice workings

Crossroads

The Power of Crossroads Dirt in Road Opening Spells. Crossroads dirt has been used in road-opening spells for years and is particularly helpful in journeying to the underworld. This is because it helps to open the gate to other realms. Additionally, it's a great offering to guardians of the crossroads, such as Hecate and Papa Legba.

Leave

Things to leave at the crossroads for power or ritual.

Offerings
Spiritual offerings and prayers can be left at the crossroads to show thanks or strengthen your relationships with spirits. Be sure to leave appropriate offerings for the particular spirits you are working with or for the specific prayer/work.

Active Spells
The crossroads is a perfect place to anchor spells related to the power of that crossroads. Burying a spell designed to work long term here will allow the work to stay strong and progress without being actively worked at home.

Spell Remains
Most spellwork remains can be buried, burned, or left at the crossroads. This brings their energy to full completion. It lets any leftover prayer or intent in the work's plants, petitions, or other remains be fully and safely released. Use mindfully.

Take

Things to take from the crossroads for spells or charms.

Dirt
Crossroads dirt brings the power of manifestation from the crossroads. Dirt from male crossroads is excellent to manifest customers to a business. Dirt from a divine crossroads mixed into a garden or field attracts good spirits and increases harvest.

Stones
Crossroads stones carry the power of the crossroads itself with them. Pregnant women can carry stones from a female crossroads to protect the baby.
Stones from damned crossroads may be left in a house, yard, or field to curse it and make it barren.

Coins
Coins found at the crossroads are especially powerful. Silver coins found here protect from haunting nightmares and evil spirits. Copper coins protect one who carries them from love spells and binding. You may leave coins on purpose to pick up later, but found is always best.

Spiritual Water Properties

Fast Luck - Brings fast luck, money luck, quick outcomes, and aids manifestation.

Love Water - It brings love and resonates with love, harmony, and compassion.

7 African Powers - Draws strength from the 7 African Orishas.

Protection - Protects you, your space, your place, and your things.

Road Opener - Removes obstacles, brings new opportunities, and opens pathways.

Peruvian FL Water- Help with spiritual work, purification, rituals, and cleansing.

Destroy Everything - Destroys all conditions, jinxes, and curses and removes all things that do not serve you.

Attraction or Come To Me - Attracts the things you want, need, or desire in your life.

Tobacco Water - Draws spirits of nature, helps communication between worlds, and honors ancestors.

Success & Prosperity - Attracts success, abundance, money, and positivity.

Florida Water - It brings protection, spiritual cleansing, and positive vibes.

Florida Water Recipe

Ingredients:
16 oz of vodka
3-5 tablespoons of floral water (orange, rose, lavender, etc.)
8 drops of Lavender EO
10 drops of Lemon EO
10 drops of Orange EO
5 drops of Bergamot EO
5 drops of Cinnamon EO
5 drops of Clove EO
3 drops of Benzoin EO
Fresh rose petals and fresh rosemary (optional)

Directions:
Add your vodka and floral water to a bowl and smell each EO before adding it to your bowl. Let your nose and spirit tell you if you should add more or less than the recipe.
Combine all ingredients in a spray bottle.
Shake well before each use.
Remove rose petals and rosemary if you wish.
Keep your customized Florida Water on hand, too.

Cascarilla Powder

Cascarilla powder is an essential ingredient in protective magic that's easy to make. The powder is made from powdered eggshells and is primarily used for spiritual cleansing and protection. Originating from Hoodoo and Santeria, it has become increasingly popular throughout America due to its accessibility. Cascarilla powder can also help create spiritual barriers similar to salt, add blessings, aid in protection, and make a great nutritional addition for plants in the garden. For added protection, try complementing the cascarilla powder with Florida water.

Tip: To make a higher-quality powder, run the eggshells under a kitchen faucet to remove the membrane before drying them.

Ingredients:
2 dozen eggshells, dried
A food processor or mortar and pestle
½ teaspoon of Florida water (see recipe)
A small glass jar or sealable container

Directions:
Bake the eggshells at 200 degrees for approximately 30 minutes to further dry them. This step allows excess moisture to cook off, making for a more delicate powder. This step is significant if you grind the shells by hand using a mortar and pestle! You might notice the color change slightly if you're using white eggshells. Don't worry - your powder will still come out white.

When the eggshells are dry, grind them into a fine powder using a mortar and pestle or food processor.

Add about 1/2 teaspoon of Florida water and process until you have a fine, sand-like consistency.

Store the cascarilla powder in a jar or pack it into chalk.

For Cascarilla Chalk:
Mix 1 tablespoon of flour and 1 tablespoon of loose cascarilla powder thoroughly.
Add a tablespoon of warm water and mix until the ingredients combine to form a ball in your hands.
Roll the mixture into sticks about 1/2 to 1 inch in diameter and let them dry for 3 to 5 days. Alternatively, you can roll the mixture into balls and place them in a small-pack paper condiment cup.
Store the chalk in a glass, plastic, or metal container to protect it from breaking, and keep it in a cool, dark place.
Note: Be careful not to add too many additional or specific herbs, as this may stop the mixture from sticking together and forming chalk. You can use cascarilla powder in spells and make sigils and magical symbols.

Salt for Magic

Himalayan/Pink Salt - ("purest salt on Earth" because of maturing for 250 million years) is used for love, removing negative blockages and curses, and cleansing.

Hawaiian Black Salt - (harvested from the evaporated water on Hawaiian Island Molokai) is used for its extra strength.

Table Salt - Used for purifying, protecting, and cleansing, and used in culinary recipes.

Kosher Salt - (blessed by a Jewish Rabbi) Used to draw out negativity or absorb negativity

Black Salt -(leftover ashes or scrapings from cast iron) Used for banishing and protection.

Alaea/Hawaiian Red Salt - (From iron-rich volcanic clay) Used for love and sex, blocks negative energy, protects aggressively to defend an area that has been set with or encircled with it, and is used in culinary recipes (high in nutrients 80+).

Sel Gris Sea Salt - Used for blessing.

Celtic Sea Salt - Used for protection and attracting financial abundance.

Sea Salt - (carries the power of the sea and water elements) Used for purification and cleansing, it helps to balance emotions.

Cyprus Black Salt - (sea water dried in lava beds mixed with charcoal) Used to evoke properties of the pyramids, energy from heaven, used in culinary recipes.

Rock Salt - Used for return to sender, used to reflect negativity to sender.

Fleur de Sel Salt - (sea salt from France) is a gentler salt used with fairies and elementals.

Gray Salt - (developed in clay pools) Used in liminal workings.

Blue Salt - (sea salt mixed with blue flowers) Used for protection from the Evil eye, justice, and healing. That being said, you can make any color salt by mixing colored herbs.

Herb Infused Salts - (Salt infused with edible herbs) Choose an herb that aligns with your intentions.

Epsom Salt - Use in the bath to reduce inflammation and muscle pain and to help you de-stress.

Pickling Salt - (purest form, no added agents) Used for purification, preservation of love, prosperity, etc., and used in culinary recipes.

CHAPTER 18

Correspondance
Flower
and Herbs

Correspondence Flowers and Herbs

These worksheets can help you organize and personalize correspondences for your Sabbat celebration. You can use them to research and document correspondences that are meaningful to you and your unique way of celebrating the Sabbat. Feel free to add other herbs and flowers to personalize your unique celebration of this Sabbat. In addition, there is a section on how to dry herbs and make an infusion oil.

Foraging Calendar

January, February, and March
Chickweed, Common Mallow Leaves, Common Sorrel, Cowberry, Crow Garlic, Dandelion Root, Garlic Mustard, Ground Elder, Hairy Bittercress, Nettles, Pignut, Sheep's Sorrel, Silver Birch Sap, Wild Garlic, Winter Cress, and Wood Sorrel

April, May, and June
Beech Leaves, Borage, Broom, Chickweed, Cleavers, Common Poppy, Dandelion Leaves and Roots, Dog Rose Flowers, Elderflower, Garlic, Mustard, Ground Elder, Hawthorn Blossom, Hops, Nettles, Pignuts, Sheep's Sorrel, Spearmint, Sweet Cicely, Watercress, Wild Garlic, Wild Thyme, Wood Sorrel, and Yarrow

July, August, and September
Acorns, Apples, Beech Nuts, Bilberries, Blackberries, Burdock, Chamomile, Chickweed, Chicory, Cleavers, Common Mallow, Dandelion Leaves and Flowers, Elderberry, Fat Hen, Garlic, Mustard, Gooseberries, Hawthorn Berries, Hazelnuts, Horseradish, Juniper Berries, Nettle, Plums, Rowan Berries, Sheep's Sorrel, Spearmint, Sweet Chestnuts, Sweet Cicely, Walnuts, Wild Cherries, Wild Strawberries, Wild Thyme, Wood Sorrel, and Yarrow

October, November, and December
Chestnuts, Chickweed, Crab Apples, Hawthorn Berries, Horseradish, Nettles, Rosehips, Sheep's Sorrel, Sloes, Spearmint, Sweet Chestnuts, and Walnuts

I live in the North Eastern United States; you may find different species depending on where you live.

Herbs by Intention: Prosperity

Basil
Bay
Calendula Cinnamon
Chamomile
Clover
Cloves
Comfrey
Dandelion
Dill
Frankincense
Honeysuckle
Lemongrass
Mint
Myrrh
Poppy Seeds
Rose Hips
Rosemary
Sandalwood
Star Anise
Thyme
Verbena

Herbs by Intention: Grounding

Ashwagandha
Basil
Cinnamon
Chamomile
Damiana
Ginger
Hawthorn
Hibiscus
Kava Kava
Lemon Balm
Lavender
Mint
Oregano
Passionflower
Rosemary
Skullcap
Thyme
Valerian

Herbs by Intention: Love

Basil
Calendula
Carnation
Cinnamon
Cumin
Daisy
Fennel
Jasmine
Lavender
Lovage
Marjoram
Mint
Mugwort
Oregano
Patchouli
Rose
Rosemary
Thyme
Vervain
Yarrow

Herbs by Intention: Healing

Basil
Lavender
Cayenne
Mint
Pepper
Lemon Balm
Chamomile
Orris Root
Cinnamon
Parsley
Cloves
Peppermint
Dill
Rose
Fennel
Rosemary
Feverfew
Sandalwood
Thyme
Turmeric

Herbs by Intention: Protection

Agrimony
Juniper
Benzoin
Lilac
Basil
Marjoram
Bay Leaf
Mugwort
Black Pepper
Mistletoe
Catnip
Mullein
Clove
Myrrh
Coriander
Rose
Dandelion
Rosemary
Dill
Rowan
Fennel
Sage
Hawthorn
Sandalwood
Holly
Vervain
Lavender
Wormwood

Indoor Herbs

Growing Schedule

January + February
Start perennial herb seeds indoors.

March + April
Start annual herb seeds indoors.
Pinch perennial herbs.

May + June
Move perennial herbs outdoors.
Pinch annual herbs.
Set overgrown annuals outdoors.
Second seeding of annual herbs.

July + August
Pinch second planting of annuals.
Take root cuttings of perennials.

September + October
Move perennial herb cuttings to soil indoors.

November + December
Grow + harvest perennial herbs.
Move large perennial herbs to larger pots.

Doorstep Rice Spell

Fill a jar with raw white rice without sealing it. Place the jar by the front door for protection. Remember that rice absorbs negative energy rather than repelling it. Replace the rice with fresh raw rice weekly. Avoid bringing old rice back into your home or cooking it. Dispose of it outside your home through burning, scattering, or throwing away.

Dehydrate Herbs

When you have more than enough fresh herbs for cooking, the BEST way to keep them is in their dehydrated form.

Sun Dry
It's called sun-dry, but do NOT dry herbs under the sun. Place in a warm spot, but avoid direct sunlight.

Air Dry
A very common method to dry herbs. It is the cheapest and most natural way of preserving your fresh herbs.

Microwave Dry
This is the fastest way, and it keeps your herbs greener.

Oven Dry
It is quicker than air and sundry, but herbs will cook a little, removing some of the potency and flavor.

Food Dehydrator
An efficient way to quickly dry and preserve the flavor and medicinal value of fresh herbs.

Infusions

Exploring the Art of Infusion: Techniques and Methods for Infusing Plant Matter
Infusion is a process that involves soaking plant matter in a liquid to create a flavored medium. This can be achieved using a variety of liquids, including water, alcohol, oil, or sweet solutions. Two primary methods of making infusions are cold and hot, each producing a unique flavor profile. Cold infusions are less bitter and have a fresh flavor, while hot infusions are more intense and offer quicker results.

How to make infused vodka, vinegar, and water. Infused vodka is made by adding flavoring agents to vodka and letting it sit for several days or weeks before straining out the solids. Infused vinegar follows the same method and can create vinaigrettes or a refreshing beverage called a "shrub." Infused water is a simple way to flavor water by adding sliced fruits or vegetables.

Several infusions include extracts, tinctures, glycerine, decoctions, and tisanes, each with a unique preparation method. Extracts, for example, are cold infusions typically concentrated and made with alcohol. Tinctures, on the other hand, are strong infusions used for medicinal purposes. Glycerine is a popular alternative to alcohol for those who are sensitive to it. Decoctions require simmering plant material for an extended period, while tisanes are hot herbal infusions used to differentiate herbal beverages from teas made exclusively with Camellia sinensis plant leaves.

There are two methods for infusing herbs or flowers into carrier oils: the solar infusion method and the slow infusion cooker method. For the solar method, fill a mason jar with herbs, cover them with carrier oil, and place them on a sunny windowsill for 2-6 weeks before straining the oil. For the slow-cooker method, fill a mason jar with herbs, cover them with carrier oil, place them in a slow cooker with water, and let the mixture infuse for 10-12 hours before straining the oil. Store the oil in a cool, dark place.

Freezing herbs is a simple method to keep them fresh throughout the year. This involves chopping the herbs, blending them with olive oil, and storing them in freezer bags or ice cube trays. This method is also suitable for making DIY baby food.

Freezing Herbs

Freezing is an excellent method to preserve herbs; you'll have fresh herbs for the whole year. You can have whatever you want whenever you want:-)

Cut up your chosen herb and add 2-3 tablespoons of olive oil.

Put in blender and blend for 3- 4 minutes.

Put in freezer storage bags to use throughout the year.

Or, if you will use them soon, you can put them in an ice cube tray for later.

My daughter does this with her DIY baby food, which works great.

Kitchen Herbs to use for Magic

Pepper: banish spells, protection

Cloves: prosperity, friendship

Rosemary: love, lust

Thyme: approval, money, purification

Garlic: healing, protection   **Cinnamon:** cleansing, success

Bay: wishes, psychic work   **Basil:** money, purification, love, protection

Mint: love, money, healing

Salt: protection, purification

DIY Terrarium

Supplies:
A clear container of your choice
Pebbles, small river stones, or expanded clay balls that are used in hydroponics
Charcoal (activated charcoal, horticultural charcoal, or lump charcoal will all work as long as the product does not contain any additives)
Potting soil (choose a well-draining soil to prevent it from getting compacted and waterlogged)
Decor (wood, rocks, or other decorations)
Plants

Planting tools: a spoon, long-handle tweezers, or even chopsticks can be useful when planting in thin-mouthed containers.

Directions:
Start by covering the bottom of the container with a 1-inch layer of pebbles or crushed stone. This drainage layer keeps the soil from becoming waterlogged and swampy.

Add chunks of charcoal to the stone or cover it with a 1/8-inch-deep layer of crushed charcoal to cover the pebbles. This helps with filtration and any odors.

Next, add 2 to 4 inches of sterilized potting soil on top of the charcoal, depending on the size of your container and the size of the plants.

Now, you get to be creative and design your miniature landscape. If your container is large enough, the soil can be molded into hills and valleys to add interest; add rocks and small logs for a natural-looking setting. You could even add lakes, paths, statues, and driftwood.

Finally, it's time to plant! Look for dwarf or low-growing plants with the same light, humidity, water, and temperature requirements. Combine different sizes, shapes, colors, and leaf textures to make things interesting.

Select plants that don't mind wet foliage, such as moss, ferns, or prayer plants.
Plant a woodland scene, use flowering alpines, get carnivorous, or go totally tropical!

Broom

Cytisus scoparius

Folk name: Link, genista, banal, Scotch broom

Magical Properties

Sacred to the Sun

Symbolize the Sun

Purification

Protection

Divination

Draw or Paste your herb here

Physical Properties & EO

It May:

Urinary support

Planet: Mars

Broom

Cytisus scoparius
Folk name: Link, genista, banal, Scotch broom

Some Suggested Uses:

Use to Sweep around areas of magic work outdoors.

Increase the wind by throwing it in the air.

Calm winds by burning.

Carry broom with you in sachets to increase psychic powers.

An infusion of Broom sprinkled in the home may exorcise poltergeists.

Irish Moss

Chondrus crispus
Folk name: Carrageen, Pearl moss,

Magical Properties
Money
Luck
Protection

Physical Properties & EO
It May:
Anti-inflammatory,
Nutritive,
Laxative
Mucilaginous

Draw or Paste your herb here

Use Caution:

Planet - Moon

Irish Moss

Chondrus crispus
Folk name: Carrageen, Pearl moss

Some Suggested Uses:

Irish Moss, also known as Carageeb or Pearl Moss, is a seaweed rich in iodine and trace minerals. It is a source of protein, amino acid, and manganese. It is known to soothe dry tissues and can be helpful for chronic dry lungs and soar throats.

It can be used to stuff luck or money poppets.

Carry some to increase your luck.

Use to have a steady flow of money.

Carry it on trips for protection.

Lemon Grass

Cymbopogon citratus
Folk name: Sweet rush, barbed wire grass, cochin grass, Malabar grass, oily heads, and silky heads.

Magical Properties
Aids communication
Openness
Protection and
Luck in love affairs.

Draw or Paste your herb here

Physical Properties
It May:
Reducing fevers
Aiding with digestive issues
Antibacterial
Antimicrobial properties
Planet - Mercury

Use Caution:

Lemon Grass

Cymbopogon citratus
Folk name: Sweet rush,barbed wire grass, cochin grass,
Malabar grass, oily heads, and silky heads.

Some Suggested Uses:

Lemongrass is a shrub-like herb commonly used in cooking and making herbal tea. It has a lemon-like, sweet flavor that works well in sweet dishes and drinks.

It can be used for curing digestive tract spasms, stomach aches, high blood pressure, convulsions, pain, vomiting, cough, and joint pains.

Lemongrass can be used in erotic potions, charm bags, and other lust rituals.

High John the Conqueror

Ipomoea jalapa
Folk name: Bindweed

Magical Properties
Love spells
Sexual Spells
Good luck
Luck at Gambling

Draw or Paste your herb here

Physical Properties
It May:
Be a strong laxative
Emetic
Planet -

Use Caution:

High John the Conqueror

Ipomoea jalapa

Folk name: Bindweed

Some Suggested Uses:

It has a pleasant, earthy smell.

Dried pieces and chips of the root are used in formulating oils and washes used in other spells.

Hold a root or a related prayer card during your meditations and spell work to help you focus on High John the Conqueror, his unbeatable spirit, his luck, and his success.

The root is often steeped into an anointing oil, which can be used to bless candles, crystals, and sachets. Anoint a green candle with this oil for success, luck, and money, a pink candle for love and devotion, a purple candle for removing obstacles and added protection.

Burn over charcoal, add to charm bags, and blends, and use as an offering.

Crocus

Crocus vernus

Folk name: spring crocus, giant crocus, snow crocus

Most forms of Crocus are extremely toxic

Magical Properties

Attracting love

Visions

Draw or Paste your herb here

Physical Properties & EO It May:

Help tumors

Rheumatoid arthritis

Gout

Essential Oil Properties It May:

Use Caution:

Most forms of Crocus are extremely toxic

Crocus

Crocus vernus
Folk name: spring crocus, giant crocus, snow crocus

Some Suggested Uses:

Saffron crocus, or autumn crocus, is the dried stigma of the plant Crocus sativus L., family Iridaceae.

It is a well-known spice and food colorant. It has been used in traditional medicine for the treatment of many diseases, including tumors.

Spring crocus is a traditional decoration for early spring festivals

Rose

Rosa spp.
Folk name:

Magical Properties
Associated with both gods of love,
Aphrodite and Eros
Attracting love
Prophetic dreams
Calm Stress
Reduce family feuds
Divination

Draw or Paste your herb here

Physical Properties & EO
Rose Essential Oil is the most
often used for mental health.
It May:
Sedative, Stress relieving, and Anti-
depressive
Planet - Venus

Use Caution:

Rose

Rosa spp.
Folk name:

Suggested Use:

Love Spell
This is a simple recipe for a spell that uses roses.

Ingredients:
2 red roses
1 teaspoon of honey
A small piece of parchment paper
A pen or marker
A small container with a tight-fitting lid
A small piece of red ribbon or string

Instructions:
Pick the petals of the 2 red roses and place them in a small container with a tight-fitting lid.
Add the honey to the container, close the lid, and shake the container to mix the ingredients well.
Write your desired outcome or intention on parchment paper.
Anoint the container with the mixture while reciting your intention or desired outcome.
Fold the parchment paper three times and tie it closed with the red ribbon or string.
Place the parchment in the container and then the whole thing in a dark and cool place for at least 24 hours.
After 24 hours, open the container and use the mixture as desired.

Note: Keep in mind that spell-casting is a personal and subjective practice, and the outcome may vary depending on your personal beliefs and intent.

Violet

Viola odorata
Folk name: Blue violet, Sweet violet

Magical Properties
Change in luck
Wishes granted
Calm tempers
Induce sleep

Draw or Paste your herb here

Physical Properties
It May:
Help chest congestion
Blocked nose, and
Dry throat.
Essential Oil Properties
It May:
Anti-inflammatory
Treat acne and eczema
Planet:

Use Caution:
This oil should not be
consumed when pregnant.

Violet

Viola odorata
Folk name: Blue violet, Sweet violet

Some Suggested Uses:

Violets are often used in spells for various purposes, such as attracting good luck, prosperity, protection, faithfulness, passion, fulfilling wishes, promoting peace, and healing emotional wounds, particularly after a relationship breakup. The leaves of violets are believed to have the ability to absorb negative energy and ill will directed toward you. According to folklore, dreaming of violets is considered a sign of positive change and good fortune in your life. Another belief is that your wish will be granted if you are the first to pick a violet in the spring.

Violets and pansies have a distinct floral taste with a hint of celery-like flavor. They can be a beautiful and delicious addition to salads or a decorative touch on cookies and cakes. To candy them, simply brush the petals with a bit of beaten egg white and sprinkle with sugar or dip them in melted syrup. The Viola odorata variety is commonly used for this purpose, but any variety of violets and pansies can be used, although the flavor may vary.

Primrose

Primula vulgaris
Folk name: Butter rose, English cowslip, Password

Magical Properties
Protection
Love
Attract fairies

Draw or Paste your herb here

Physical Properties & EO
It May:
Help to cure vertigo
Aid muscle spasms

Essential Oil Properties
It May:
Help PMS symptoms
Moisture-retaining effects
Planet: Mars

Use Caution:

Primrose

Primula vulgaris
Folk name: Butter rose, English cowslip, Password

Some Suggested Uses:

Collect the primrose morning dew on Ostara for a potent rejuvenation spell ingredient.

Primrose would be an ideal flower to offer on an altar dedicated to Jophiel, the angel of beauty. It also holds a strong connection with the energy of Azrael and could provide solace to someone who is grieving the loss of a loved one.

Rubbing the leaves on pale cheeks will add color to them.

Lilac

Syringa vulgaris
Folk name: Common lilac

Magical Properties
Keep away evil
Clear haunted houses
Blooming of new love
Banishing negative energies

Draw or Paste your herb here

Use Caution:

Physical Properties & EO
It May:
Essential Oil Properties
It May:
Be a natural anti-depressant
Ease minor pain
Reduce fever
Planet: Venus

Lilac

Syringa vulgaris
Folk name: Common lilac

Some Suggested Uses:

Create a lilac oil infusion, gather about a cup of dried lilac flowers, and place them in a large jar. Cover the flowers with a neutral carrier oil such as grapeseed, sunflower, or jojoba oil, and secure the lid on the jar. Allow the blend to infuse for six to eight weeks. Once the infusion is complete, strain out the flowers and use the resulting oil in protection magic or love spells.

Try a lilac facial toner, gather a cup or two of slightly wilted lilac flowers and place them in a jar. Fill the jar with witch hazel, making sure that the flowers are fully submerged. Allow the mixture to steep for a few days, then strain out the flowers. The resulting lilac and witch hazel blend can be used as a facial toner to help keep your skin looking healthy. Note: It's important to check for any allergic reactions before using the toner on your face.

Daisy

Chrysanthemum leucanthemum
Folk name: Bairnwort, Bruisewort, Eye of the Day

Magical Properties
Love
Protection (particularly for children)
Happiness
Joyfulness
Creativity

Draw or Paste your herb here

Use Caution:

Physical Properties & EO
It May:
Essential Oil Properties
It May help:
anti-inflammatory, analgesic,
antispasmodic, and antimicrobial
properties, ability to soothe
emotional tension,

Planet: Sun, Venus

Daisy

Chrysanthemum leucanthemum
Folk name: Bairnwort, Bruisewort, Eye of the Day, Mauldinwort

Some Suggested Uses:

The name daisy comes from "day's eye" because a daisy will open its petals in the morning and close them again at night.

It is a common belief that placing daisies under your pillow may lead to dreams about the person you are yearning for and potentially rekindle an old love affair.

Daisy Dream Poultice

Ingredients:
1 cup of fresh daisy petals (make sure they are pesticide-free)
1/4 cup of lavender flowers
1/4 cup of chamomile flowers
1 tablespoon of dried rose petals
1 tablespoon of honey
1 tablespoon of olive oil

Directions:
Combine the fresh daisy, lavender, chamomile, and dried rose petals in a small mixing bowl.
Heat the honey and olive oil over low heat in a separate small saucepan until they are well combined.
Mix the honey and olive oil with the dried flowers in the bowl.
Spread the mixture onto a clean cloth or a bandage and fold it into a small pouch.
Place the pouch under your pillow before going to sleep.
As you sleep, the poultice releases the soothing scent of the flowers and the natural oils, helping to bring about sweet dreams and potentially even rekindling an old love.

Honeysuckle

Lonicera caprifolium
Folk name: Dutch Honeysuckle, Goat's Leaf, Woodbine

Magical Properties:
Attract money
Increase psychic powers
Sweetening spells

Draw or Paste your herb here

Physical Properties & EO
It May:
Help tumors
Rheumatoid arthritis
Gout
Essential Oil Properties
It May:
 Planet: Venus, Jupiter

Use Caution:
Most varieties of Honeysuckle
are mildly toxic.

Honeysuckle
Lonicera caprifolium
Folk name: Dutch Honeysuckle, Goat's Leaf, Woodbine

Some Suggested Uses:

Honeysuckle vine can help to bind two lovers together. Some practitioners suggest using a photo, poppet, or personal item of one or both parties in combination with the vine as a way to symbolize the connection.

Fresh flowers can be gathered from a garden. Dried blossoms are available as an herbal supplement or specialty tea. And there are always scented oils, candles, and incense to draw upon Honeysuckle's seductive power.

Honeysuckle Love Bath:

Ingredients:
1 cup of dried Honeysuckle flowers
1/2 cup of dried rose petals
1/4 cup of lavender flowers
1/4 cup of chamomile flowers
1 tablespoon of honey
1 tablespoon of sea salt

Directions:
In a large mixing bowl, combine the dried Honeysuckle flowers, rose petals, lavender flowers, and chamomile flowers.
Mix the honey and sea salt in a small bowl until well combined.
Add the honey and sea salt mixture to the dried flowers and mix well.
Fill a warm bath with water and sprinkle the flower mixture into the water.
Soak in the bath for at least 20 minutes, focusing on your intention for love and attraction.
As you soak, the flowers and honey are said to release their soothing scents and energy, helping to attract love and bring you closer to your desired partner.

Daffodil

Narcissus spp.
Folk name: Asphodel, Goose leek, Lent lily

Magical Properties

Love spells
Fertility increase
Good luck
Attract fairies
Wishes

Draw or Paste your herb here

Physical Properties & EO
It May:

Induce sickness
Numbness
Hallucinations
Convulsions
Cardiac effects
Cancer treatments.
Planet - Venus

Use Caution:

Please do not consume or use daffodils in anyway as they are highly toxic

Daffodil

Narcissus spp.

Folk name: Asphodel, Goose leek, Lent lily

Some Suggested Uses:

Daffodils have long been believed to possess magic properties. To harness this power throughout the year, one can dry the flowers and use them in various spellwork, such as creating poppets, talismans, medicine bags, and rituals. The dried flowers can be used in various ways, such as:

Sprinkling on an altar to attract friendly spirits

Sprinkling on a doorstep to keep negative energy away

Adding to a bath to increase luck and attract new people into one's life

Mixing with rose petals to draw back a wandering lover"

Daffodil Luck and Success Spell

Ingredients:

3 fresh Daffodil flowers

3 small green candles

1 tablespoon of cinnamon powder

1 tablespoon of nutmeg powder

A piece of parchment paper

A pen

Directions:

Pick three fresh Daffodil flowers and place them in a small vase.

Set the three green candles around the vase and light them.

In a small bowl, mix together the cinnamon powder and nutmeg powder.

Sprinkle the powder mixture over the Daffodil flowers while focusing on your intention for luck and success.

Write down your specific goal or intention on a piece of parchment paper.

Hold the parchment paper in your hands and recite a spell or affirmation of your choice while visualizing your goal being achieved.

Place the parchment paper under the vase and let the candles burn out.

Keep the dried flowers in a safe place or carry them with you to attract good luck and success in your endeavors.

Jasmine

Jasminum grandiflorum
Folk name: Jessamin, Anbar, Yasmin

Magical Properties
Spiritual love
Wealth or money
Prophetic dreams
Aphrodisiac
Relaxation
Divination

Draw or Paste your herb here

Physical Properties & EO
It May: *Use Caution:*

Planet - Moon

Jasmine
Jasminum grandiflorum
Folk name: Jessamin, Anbar, Yasmin

Some Suggested Uses:

Jasmine tea is a popular beverage created by steeping green or white tea leaves with the petals of the Jasmine flower. It is believed to possess properties that make it useful for divination practices, such as reading tea leaves or using them in rituals.

To prepare crystals, some practitioners cleanse and charge them by placing them in a bowl filled with Jasmine flowers or passing them through the smoke of burning Jasmine incense.

Jasmine Relaxation Spell

Ingredients:
A handful of dried Jasmine flowers
A small piece of amethyst
A small glass jar with a lid
A few drops of lavender essential oil

Directions:
Mix the dried Jasmine flowers and a small piece of amethyst in a small bowl.
Add a few drops of lavender essential oil to the bowl and mix well.
Place the mixture into the small glass jar and seal it with the lid.
Hold the jar in your hands and recite a spell or affirmation of your choice while visualizing feelings of relaxation and calm.
Place the jar in your bedroom or in a place where you relax.
Every time you feel stressed or anxious, open the jar and take a deep breath in the scent of Jasmine and lavender.
Repeat the spell as often as needed.

Columbine

Aquilegia canadensis
Folk name: Lion's herb, Granny's bonnet

Magical Properties
Courage
Love
Faries
Clarity
Jealousy
Fortitude

Draw or Paste your herb here

Physical Properties & EO
It May: help sarcomas from HIV, asthma, lupus, arthritis, inflammatory bowel, multiple sclerosis, macular degeneration, and Alzheimer's

Planet - Venus

Use Caution: Columbine is Toxic and should not be ingested.

Columbine

Aquilegia canadensis
Folk name: Lion's herb

Some Suggested Uses:

Add the flowers or seeds to your bathwater to help you gain clarity in a situation.

Use leaves and flowers in magic to dispel jealousy.

The Columbine flower has the ability to assist those who struggle with finding joy and humor in life. It will aid in discovering one's own unique way of having fun and being lighthearted.

Columbine Clarity Room Spray

Ingredients:
1 handful of fresh or dried Columbine flowers
1/2 cup of distilled water
1/2 cup of witch hazel
1 small piece of amethyst
A few drops of lavender essential oil

Directions:
Bring 1/2 cup of distilled water to a boil in a small pot.
Once the water is boiling, add 1 handful of fresh or dried Columbine flowers and let steep for 10 minutes.
Remove the pot from the heat and strain the mixture into a glass spray bottle.
Add 1/2 cup of witch hazel and a few drops of lavender essential oil to the bottle, and shake well to combine.
Crush the small piece of amethyst and add it to the bottle.
Shake well to combine.
To use, spray the room with the solution while reciting a spell or affirmation of your choice, focusing on feelings of clarity and focus.

Apple Blossom

Malus communis
Folk name:

Magical Properties
Purifies emotions
Inner health
Restore hope
New dreams

Draw or Paste your herb here

Use Caution:

Physical Properties & EO
It May:
Create peace of mind and draw
happiness into your life.

Planet - Stars

Apple Blossom
Malus communis
Folk name:

Some Suggested Uses:

Blessing: May the apple blossoms, sparkling like countless stars, Guide me towards hope and faith, And help me to share their cosmic abundance, In every moment of my earthly days.

Apple Blossom Prosperity Spell

Ingredients:
1 handful of fresh or dried apple blossoms
1/2 cup of sea salt
1/2 cup of rice
1 small piece of citrine
A few drops of vanilla essential oil

Directions:
In a small bowl, Mix together 1/2 cup of sea salt and 1/2 cup of rice.
Add 1 handful of fresh or dried apple blossoms and mix well.
Crush the small piece of citrine and add it to the bowl.
Add a few drops of vanilla essential oil and mix everything together.
Sprinkle the mixture in the corners of your room or workspace, or bury it in your garden.
As you do this, recite a spell or affirmation of your choice focusing on abundance and prosperity.
Leave the mixture in place for at least a week, and then dispose of it.

Chickweed

Stelaria media

Folk name: Adder's mouth, Passerina, Starwort, Winterweed

Magical Properties
Courage
Balance
Wisdom
Inner peace
Fidelity
Healing
Love
Protection
Lunar energy
Endurance
Amplification
Safe travel
Abundance
Luck

Draw or Paste your herb here

Use Caution:

Physical Properties & EO
It May:
Help dry skin and irritating eczema
Anti-inflammatory
Antipyretic
Laxative
Planet - Moon

Chickweed
Stelaria media
Folk name: Adder's mouth, Passerina, Starwort, Winterweed

Some Suggested Uses:

Chickweed can be eaten as part of a mixed edible weed salad. It tastes much like alfalfa and has a cool, juicy crunchiness to match.

Love, Peace, and Harmony: A Magical Chickweed Potion Recipe

Ingredients:
1 cup fresh chickweed
1 cup distilled water
1 teaspoon honey
1 teaspoon dried lavender
1 teaspoon dried rose petals

Instructions:
Begin by cleaning and drying the chickweed.
In a small saucepan, bring the water to a boil.
Once boiling, remove the pan from heat and add the chickweed, lavender, and rose petals.
Allow the mixture to steep for 10-15 minutes.
Strain the mixture through a fine mesh strainer or cheesecloth.
Stir in the honey until it dissolves.
Allow the potion to cool before drinking.

This potion is said to have magical properties, such as bringing love, peace, and harmony to the person who drinks it. You can also add different dried herbs or essential oils to enhance the effects of the potion and make it your own.

CHAPTER 19

Crystals

Correspondence Crystals

I have included worksheets to familiarize you with some correspondence associated with this season. Feel free to add others to personalize your unique way of celebrating this sabbat.

Cleansing vs. Charging

Cleansing

Removes past energies
Item is restored to its natural state
Crystal-like quartz and selenite can cleanse other crystals/tools

Charging

Adds purpose or intention
Programs a tool for a specific energy
Charged crystals can be used to add energy to other items

Cleansing and Energize	**Energize and Charge**
Cleansing with Water	Quartz Points
Water Bath	Sunlight
Cleansing With Moonlight	Moonlight
Cleansing With Sound	Plants
Cleansing With Sunlight	Herbs

A few crystals never need cleansing. For example, citrine, kyanite, and selenite are self-cleansing. Clear Quartz and Carnelian cleanse other crystals.
Be sure to check which ones are safe in water.

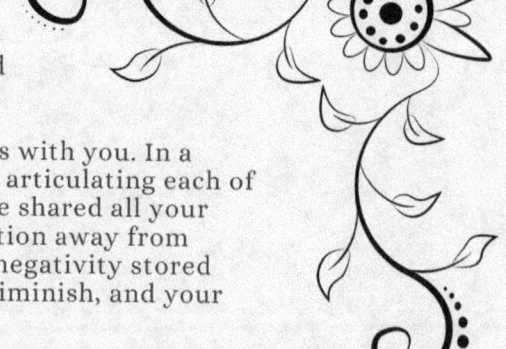

Grounding Spell with Hematite

Let Go of Troubles: Hematite serves as a versatile stone for grounding and balancing energy.

Select a hematite stone that resonates with you. In a tranquil setting, confide in the stone, articulating each of your troubles one by one. Once you've shared all your concerns, bury the hematite in a location away from your home. As the Earth absorbs the negativity stored within the stone, your troubles will diminish, and your problems will ease.

Crystal Shapes

Clusters
radiates unity
throughout the space
and
charges other crystals

Pyramids
anchoring crystal and
powerful for
manifesting desires

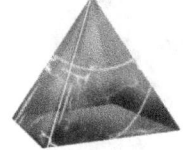

Cubes
consolidates energy,
grounding & meditation,
and connect to the
energy of the Earth

Double Terminated
absorb negative
energy,
grounding, break
down old patterns,
and
promotes psychic
ability

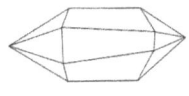

Twin
grounding &
harmonizing
energies, and
balances yin &
yang energies

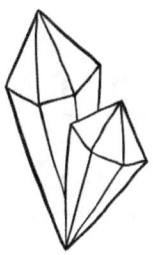

Points
concentrates &
directs energy

Crystal Shapes

Wand
healing rituals,
moving & directing
energy

Egg
healing, fertility,
and
balance

Spheres
emits energy
equally
from all direction,
and
ideal for scrying

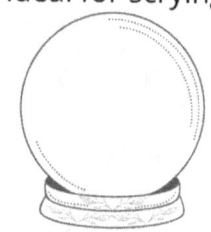

Druzy
charging, relaxation &
harmony, purify &
amplify body's
natural healing
properties

Geode
amplifies,
conserves &
releases energy,
and
Internal healing

Isis
feminine energy,
healing
emotional
hurt and distress

Choosing the Shape of Your Crystal
1 - Look up the energetic properties of your crystal.
2 - Consider the shape and if it offers benefits, such as enhancing any of the properties you are interested in.
3 - Consider if the crystal shape suits your chosen way of working with the stone.

Crystal Grids

To create a crystal grid, first, decide on your intent. You can choose from Love, Travel, Wealth, or Joy. Next, select a layout that aligns with your intent. You can choose from Health, Growth, Intuition, Flower, Connection, Seed, Balance, Metatron's Cube, Energy, Fibonacci sequence, or Abundance.

After selecting your layout, choose crystals that align with your intention. Trust your intuition when selecting the crystals, as there are no right or wrong stones. You will need a center crystal, which can be any stone, but a point will be more powerful for directing your intention straight up into the universe. Then select a selection of points or tumbles to align with your intention.

To set up the surrounding stones in your crystal grid, start from the outside and move inwards. As you place each crystal, make sure you keep your intention in mind. If you want, you can activate your grid by using a quartz point to circle each of the stones to connect them energetically.

Here are some examples of crystals and their properties that you can use:

Quartz: Master healer, Amplifier
Citrine: Happiness stone, Abundance
Tourmaline: Protective stone
Adventurine: New beginnings, Abundance
Rose Quartz: Nurturing stone, Love
Lapis/Sodalite: Communication stone, Expression
Amethyst: Healing stone, Calming, restorative.

Crystals   for Ostara
Green Aventurine
Bumblebee Jasper
Sunstone
Citrine
Amethyst
Tiger's Eye
Aquamarine
Amazonite
Serpentine
Carnelian
Moss Agate
Rose Quartz

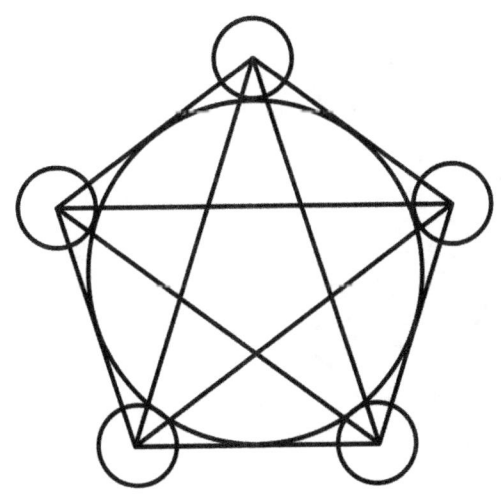

Seed of Life

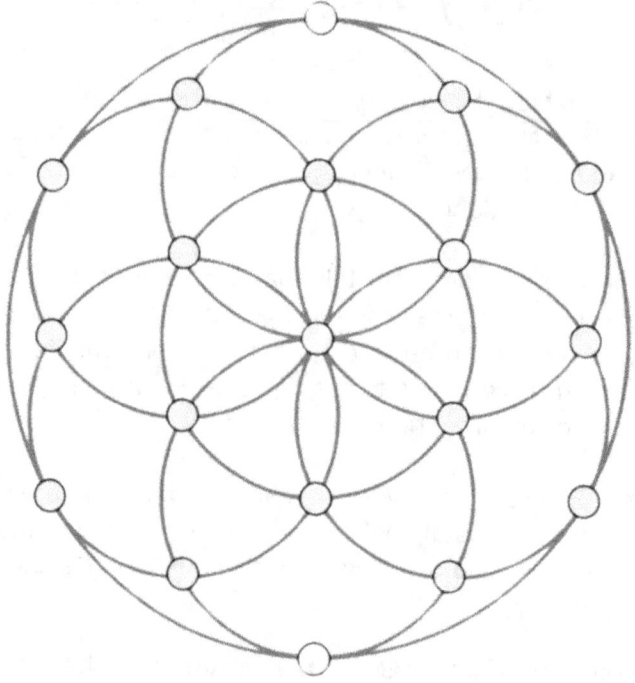

Metatron's cube

Agate

Magical Properties
Grounding
Stabilizing
Balance
Harmony
Calm
Enhance mental function
Increase energy

Classification
Origin
Rarity

Draw or Paste your crystal here

Crystal Pairs With Many
Don't Mix With
Cost

Got it from:
Notes:
Planets - Moon
Chakra - Crown
Signs - Gemini, Virgo

Identification
Color(s) Blue
Transparency
Lustre
Crystal System -
Chemical

Bloodstone

Magical Properties
Abundance
Alignment
Organisation
Smooth energy flow
Generosity
Idealism
Good fortune
Purification

Classification
Origin
Rarity

Draw or Paste your crystal here

Crystal Pairs With Many
Don't Mix With
Cost

Got it from:
Notes:
Planets - Mars
Chakra **-** Base
Signs - Aries, Libra, Pisces

Identification
Color(s) -
Transparency -
Lustre -
Crystal System -
Chemical

Aquamarine

Magical Properties

Cleansing
Meditation
Serenityeace
Prophecy
Inspiration
Tranquility
Inner power strength
Soothing
Calming
Safe travel on water

Classification
Origin
Rarity

Draw or Paste your crystal here

Crystal Pairs With Many
Don't Mix With
Cost

Got it from:
Notes:
Planets - Saturn
Chakra - Throat
Signs - Aries, Gemini, Scorpio, Aquarius, Pisces

Identification
Color(s) -
Transparency -
Lustre -
Crystal System -
Chemical

Magnesite

Magical Properties
Relaxation
Visualisation
Heartfelt love
Purification

Classification
Origin
Rarity

Crystal Pairs With
Don't Mix With
Cost

Got it from:
Notes:
Planets -
Chakra - Crown
Signs - Aries

Identification
Color(s) -
Transparency
Lustre -
Crystal System -
Chemical -

Honey Calcite

Magical Properties
Deepen intellect
Memory
Wisdom
Psychic abilities
Spirituality
Astral projection
Channeling
Higher Consciousness

Classification
Origin
Rarity

Crystal Pairs With
Don't Mix With
Cost

Got it from:
Notes:
Planets -
Chakra - Base Chakra, Solar Plexus
Chakra, Third Eye Chakra
Signs - Cancer

Identification
Color(s) -
Transparency -
Lustre -
Crystal System -
Chemical -

Iolite

Magical Properties
Power
Inner strength
Leadership
Self-confidence

Classification
Origin
Rarity

Crystal Pairs With
Don't Mix With
Cost

Got it from:
Notes:
Planets -
Chakra - Third Eye Chakra
Signs - Taurus, Libra, Sagittarius

Identification
Color(s) -
Transparency -
Lustre -
Crystal System -
Chemical -

Cobra Jasper

Magical Properties
Relaxation
Contentment
Compassion
Nurturing
Consolation
Tranquility
Healing
Completion

Classification
Origin
Rarity

Draw or Paste your crystal here

Crystal Pairs With
Don't Mix With
Cost

Got it from:
Notes:
Planets -
Chakra - Base Chakra, Heart Chakra,
Crown Chakra
Signs -Leo, Virgo, Scorpio

Identification
Color(s) -
Transparency -
Lustre -
Crystal System -
Chemical -

Rhodonite

Magical Properties
Calmness
Self-confidence
Refinement
Gratefulness
Elegance
Delicacy
Courtesy
Tact
Alternatives
Inner path

Classification
Origin
Rarity

Draw or Paste your crystal here

Crystal Pairs With
Don't Mix With
Cost

Got it from:
Notes:
Planets - Venus
Chakra - Heart Chakra
Signs -Taurus

Identification
Color(s) -
Transparency -
Lustre -
Crystal System -
Chemical -

Sugilite

Magical Properties
Transformation
Enhance meditation
Expand awareness
Grounding
Deflect negativity

Classification
Origin
Rarity

Crystal Pairs With
Don't Mix With
Cost

Got it from:
Notes:
Planets - Uranus, Neptune
Chakra - Crown, ThirdEye
Signs -Aquarius, Pisces

Draw or Paste your crystal here

Identification
Color(s)
Transparency
Lustre
Crystal System
Chemical

Unakite

Magical Properties
Love
Compassion
Kindness
Tolerance
Studying
Balance
Calming
Relationships
Marriage

Classification
Origin
Rarity

Draw or Paste your crystal here

Crystal Pairs With
Don't Mix With
Cost

Got it from:
Notes:
Planets - Venus, Moon
Chakra - Heart, Solar plexus, Navel
Signs -Taurus, Pisces, cancer

Identification
Color(s)
Transparency
Lustre
Crystal System
Chemical

Apatite

Magical Properties
Spirit guides
Ascended Masters
Clear thought
Understanding

Draw or Paste your crystal here

Classification
Origin
Rarity

Crystal Pairs With
Don't Mix With
Cost

Got it from:
Notes:
Planets - Earth
Chakra - Throat, Solar plexus
Signs -Virgo

Identification
Color(s)
Transparency
Lustre
Crystal System
Chemical

Desert Rose

Magical Properties
Intuition
Higher guidance
Spirit guardian
Mental focus
Elevate frequencies
Thinking carefully
Removes barriers to spiritual growth

Classification
Origin
Rarity

Draw or Paste your crystal here

Crystal Pairs With
Don't Mix With
Cost

Got it from:
Notes:
Planets - Earth
Chakra - Root, Crown
Signs -Capricorn, Scorpio, Taurus

Identification
Color(s)
Transparency
Lustre
Crystal System
Chemical

Ametrine

Magical Properties
Transform negativity
Confidence
Balance
Realization
Decision making
Boundaries

Classification
Origin
Rarity

Crystal Pairs With
Don't Mix With
Cost

Got it from:
Notes:
Planets - Uranus, Mercury
Chakra - Crown, Third eye, Solar plexus
Signs -Aquarius, Gemini

Identification
Color(s)
Transparency
Lustre
Crystal System
Chemical

Malachite

Draw or Paste your crystal here

Magical Properties
Healing the past
Spiritual evolution
Clear thoughts
Emotional growth
Inner peace
release negative energy

Classification
Origin
Rarity

Crystal Pairs With
Don't Mix With
Cost

Got it from:
Notes:
Planets - Saturn
Chakra - Heart, Solar plexus
Signs -Capricorn

Identification
Color(s)
Transparency
Lustre
Crystal System
Chemical

Brucite

Draw or Paste your crystal here

Magical Properties
Peacefulness
Communication
New ideas
Acknowledgment
Energy flow
Inner child work

Classification
Origin
Rarity

Crystal Pairs With
Don't Mix With
Cost

Got it from:
Notes:
Planets - Neptune
Chakra - Third eye, Navel
Signs -Pisces

Identification
Color(s)
Transparency
Lustre
Crystal System
Chemical

Sunstone

Magical Properties

Rest
Self-Healing
Humor
Cheerfulness/positivity
Self-confidence/self-esteem
Temperament
Self-love

Classification
Origin
Rarity

Draw or Paste your crystal here

Crystal Pairs With
Don't Mix With
Cost
Got it from

Notes: Sacral Chakra
Libra and Pisces Signs

Identification
Color(s)
Transparency
Lustre
Crystal System
Chemical

Selenite

Magical Properties
Resolution
Clarity
Enlightenment
Transformation
Clearingaway anger/negativity
Positivity
Past-Life regression
Psychic abilities
Calm & stress relief
Meditation
Healing
Cleanses/charges other crystals
Classification
Origin
Rarity

Draw or Paste your crystal here

Crystal Pairs With
Don't Mix With Salt and water
Cost
Got it from

Notes: Delicate

Identification
Color(s)
Transparency
Lustre
Crystal System
Chemical

Rose Quartz

Magical Properties
Peace
Harmony
Acceptance
Trust
Love
Healing
Empathy
Receptivity
Intimacy
Romance
Who doesn't need self-love

Classification
Origin
Rarity

Crystal Pairs With
Don't Mix With Sun
Cost
Got it from

Notes: Heart Chakra
Taurus and Leo Sign
Archangel Ariel

Draw or Paste your crystal here

Identification
Color(s)
Transparency
Lustre
Crystal System
Chemical

Clear Quartz

Draw or Paste your crystal here

Magical Properties
Amplify spells/crystals
Clears away stagnant energy
Cleansing
Healing
Positive vibes
Programmable
Can substitute for any crystal

Classification
Origin
Rarity

Crystal Pairs With
Don't Mix With
Cost
Got it from

Notes: Crown Chakra
Leo Sign
Archangel Raziel

Identification
Color(s)
Transparency
Lustre
Crystal System
Chemical

Lava Rock

Magical Properties
Vitality
Protection
Luck
Love
Calming

Draw or Paste your crystal here

Classification
Origin
Rarity

Crystal Pairs With
Don't Mix With
Cost
Got it from

Identification
Color(s)
Transparency
Lustre
Crystal System
Chemical

Notes: Lava beads are porous and can absorb essential oils

Moss Agate

Magical Properties
Growing Love
New beginnings
Trust
Release old fears
New lease on life
Grounding
Drawing strength from nature
Connecting with Fairie
New business/prosperity
Luck

Classification
Origin
Rarity

Draw or Paste your crystal here

Crystal Pairs With
Don't Mix With
Cost
Got it from

Notes:
Cancer and Virgo Signs

Identification
Color(s)
Transparency
Lustre
Crystal System
Chemical

Black Obsidian

Magical Properties

Truth-enhancing
Deep soul healing
Protection
Relieves stress and tension
Absorbs negative energy
Gives clarity of emotions
Blocks psychic attacks
Removes negativity influences
Helps to expose flaws, weakness &
blockages
Calming
Compassion
Strength
Prophesy
Helps with shadow self & brings them t
the forefront to be acknolgeked
Breaks through mental barriers
Dissolves mental conditioning

Draw or Paste your crystal here

Classification cooled molten lava
Origin
Rarity

Crystal Pairs With
Don't Mix With   water
Cost
Got it from
Notes: Base chakra
Scorpio Sign

Identification
Color(s)
Transparency
Lustre
Crystal System
Chemical

Put by the bed or under your pillow to draw out mental stress and tension.

Crystal Name

Draw or Paste your crystal here

Magical Properties

Classification
Origin
Rarity

Crystal Pairs With
Don't Mix With
Cost
Got it from

Notes:

Identification
Color(s)
Transparency
Lustre
Crystal System
Chemical

If you want to bring beauty and serenity into your home discreetly without drawing attention, consider crafting crystal bowls. These elegant pieces can serve as both decorative items and tools for spells and other mystical practices.

Grab and Go Combos

Insight
rosemary, lemongrass, nutmeg, orange, aquamarine, howlite, or clear citrine.

Wisdom
parsley, thyme, chamomile, cumin, yellow quartz, and, lapis lazuli

Money
ginger, patchouly, dill, spearmint, gold, malachite, moss agate, and pearl

Peace
cumin, lavender, violet, marjoram, amazonite, blue lace agate, and silver

Relations
pansy, rose, valerian, moss agate, peridot, and sapphire

Love
vanilla, apple, clove, lavender, rose, amber, calcite, moonstone, and rose quartz

Banishing
clove, dragon's blood, garlic, hot pepper, obsidian, jet, and smoky quartz

Protection
angelica, frankincense, sandalwood, amber, carnelian, citrine, and petrified wood

Travel
dill, caraway, fennel mustard, malachite, moonstone, or tiger's eye

Communication
mint, turquoise, tiger's eye, and sodalite

Success
rosemary, saffron, bay, pyrite, clear quartz, and selenite

Courage
horseradish, basil, chives, nettle, pepper, tigers eye, carnelian, and pyrite

Happiness
cinnamon, mint, thyme, lavender, rose quartz, amethyst, citrine, and clear quartz

Health
cinnamon, coriander, eucalyptus, rosemary, sage, thyme, agate, amethyst, jade, and sunstone.

Binding
spiderwort, witch hazel, knotweed, agrimony, and jet

Grab and Go Crystals

Abundance crystals
citrine
clear quartz
amazonite
pyrite
adventurine
tiger's eye

Mindfulness crystals
malachite
citrine
obsidian
turquoises
calcite
carnelian

Friendship crystals
rose quartz
lapis lazuli
emerald
carnelian
blue lace agate
unakite

Manifestation crystals
rose quartz
green jade
sodalite
citrine
selenite
amethyst

Stress Relief crystals
lepidolite
amethyst
rose quarts
fluorite
sodalite
aquamarine

Breaking Bad Habits crystals
amethyst
carnelian
garnet
hematite
lepidolite
citrine

Healing crystals
clear quartz
lapis lazuli
rose quartz
amethyst
aquamarine
garnet

Happiness crystals
amazonite
amethyst
tourmaline
citrine
clear quartz
smoky quartz

Lucky crystals
pyrite
green jade
tiger's eye
citrine
labradorite
carnelian

New Start crystals
aventurine
citrine
kyanite
rutile quartz
moonstone
labradorite

Productivity crystals
tourmaline
green aventurine
pyrite
amazonite
citrine
smoky quartz

Motivation crystals
pyrite
carnelian
amethyst
bumblebee
unakite
citrine

Protection crystals
labradorite
amethyst
tourmaline
smoky quartz
obsidian
prehnite

Work crystals
tourmaline
amethyst
rose quartz
pyrite
selenite
aventurine

Grab and Go Crystals

New Home crystals
tourmaline
amethyst
rose quartz
clear quartz
sodalite
citrine

Anxiety crystals
moonstone
labradorite
rose quartz
amethyst
clear quartz
aquamarine

Love crystals
rhodonite
garnet
moonstone
sodalite
rose quartz
selenite

Letting Go crystals
Rutilated Quartz
Fire Quartz
smoky quartz
serpentine
black obsidian
rose quartz

Student crystals
amethyst
carnelian
fluorite
howlite
tiger's eye
clear quartz

Confidence crystals
citrine
carnelian
rose quartz
red jasper
orange calcite
tiger's eye

Relaxation crystals
amethyst
celestite
fluorite
tourmaline
angelite
howlite

Spirituality crystals
Fluorite
white howlite
labradorite
aura quartz
blue obsidian
amethyst

Creativity crystals
carnelian
amethyst
smoky quartz
clear quartz
citrine
tiger's eye

Trauma crystals
amazonite
lepidolite
fluorite
black line jasper
rose quartz
mangano calcite

Mental Clarity crystals
amethyst
hematite
apatite
sodalite
fluorite
citrine

Animal crystals
amethyst
smoky quartz
selenite
rose quartz
carnelian
agate

Crystals for breakups
rose quartz
malachite
pyrite
septarian
rhodonite
amethyst

Communication crystals
fluorite
kyanite
amazonite
sodalite
smokey quartz
lapis lazuli

Good Sleep crystals
amethyst
clear quartz
hematite
howlite
agate
moonstone

Grab and Go Crystals

Energy crystals
clear quartz
ruby
orange calcite
amethyst
carnelian
fuorite

Plant crystals
moonstone
tourmaline
aventurine
amethyst
clear quartz
malachite

Driving crystals
amethyst
rose quartz
tourmaline
malachite
carnelian
jasper

Crystals for breakups
rose quartz
malachite
pyrite
septarian
rhodonite
amethyst

Crystals for the bath
rose quartz
carnelian
tiger's eye
citrine
amethyst
clear quartz

Crystals for bedroom
celestite
rose quartz
labradorite
selenite
smoky quartz
howlite

I put them in bowls and up high so the wieners don't get into them. I usually add some salt and lavender, and rose quartz to all of them, but whatever feels right or even gives comfort. So you do you, Boo.

I pair selenite and rosemary for protection and cleansing

I pair rose quartz with (duh) roses for love and forgiveness.

I pair amethyst and chamomile for anxiety and stress relief

I pair garnet and pine for commitment and longevity

I pair black tourmaline and sage for dissolving negativity

I pair citrine with bay leaf for manifestation magic

I pair green adventure and basil for good fortune

I pair carnelian and cinnamon for sparking creativity

I pair moonstone and jasmine for harnessing confidence

CHAPTER 28

Closed
Practices

Closed Practice

Misconceptions exist about "closed practice" in spirituality, particularly in witchcraft and the Occult.

In simple terms, a closed practice means participation is limited to those born into it or who have undergone initiation.

A common misconception is that only those born into the community can practice, but exceptions exist.

Closed practices require vetting and completion of initiation processes.

Some religions are closed due to specific cultural values and beliefs that outsiders like Brujería and Santería may not understand.

Closed Communities and Race-Locked Spirituality

While it's crucial to analyze specific religious practices, it's even more important to address how entire communities can become closed off. Distinguishing between closed communities and closed practices helps to avoid gatekeeping and prevent further marginalization. Examples of closed communities include the Amish, the Roma, Judaism (including Kabbalah mysticism), Hoodoo, and Haitian Vodou. Some communities close off their practices due to being perceived as "race-locked," a concept where these communities were established to unite during challenging times, shaping their beliefs around shared experiences.

Cultural Appropriation

Cultural appropriation is a complex and contentious issue that involves the borrowing, adoption, or use of elements from one culture by members of another culture. This concept often sparks debate because it can lead to misunderstandings, disrespect, and harm to marginalized communities. Here, I'll explain the concept of cultural appropriation in detail, focusing solely on factual information:

Definition:
Cultural appropriation refers to the adoption or use of elements of one culture by members of another culture, typically by a dominant culture appropriating aspects of a marginalized or minority culture. This can include clothing, hairstyles, symbols, language, rituals, music, dance, art, and more.

Examples:
Fashion: The use of Native American headdresses as fashion accessories by non-Native individuals without understanding their cultural significance or respecting their sacredness.

Cuisine:
Commercializing traditional dishes from various cultures without proper acknowledgment or understanding of their origins and significance.
Art and Music: Sampling or replicating traditional songs, dances, or artworks without giving credit to the original creators or understanding the cultural context behind them.

Religious Symbols:
Wearing religious symbols (such as bindis or crosses) as fashion statements without understanding their religious or cultural significance.

Power Dynamics:
Cultural appropriation often occurs within a framework of power dynamics, where the dominant culture appropriates elements from marginalized or oppressed cultures. This can perpetuate stereotypes, reinforce power imbalances, and contribute to the erasure of the marginalized culture's identity.

Cultural appropriation can lead to various forms of harm.

Diminishing Cultural Significance: Appropriation can strip cultural symbols or practices of their original meaning, reducing them to superficial trends or commodities.

Disrespect and Insensitivity: Appropriating sacred or meaningful elements of a culture without understanding or respect can be deeply offensive to those who belong to that culture.

Economic Exploitation: In cases where cultural products or practices are commodified without benefiting the originating culture, appropriation can perpetuate economic exploitation and inequality.

Appreciation vs. Appropriation

It's important to distinguish between cultural appreciation and appropriation. Cultural appreciation involves respectfully learning about and engaging with different cultures, often with acknowledgment and understanding of their significance. Appropriation, on the other hand, involves taking elements of a culture without proper understanding, respect, or acknowledgment.

Call for Cultural Sensitivity and Respect: Many advocates emphasize the importance of cultural sensitivity, education, and respectful engagement when interacting with cultures different from one's own. This includes listening to and learning from members of the culture, acknowledging sources, and considering the potential impact of one's actions.

Controversies and Debates: Cultural appropriation is a subject of ongoing debate and controversy, with differing perspectives on where to draw the line between appreciation and appropriation, as well as how to address instances of appropriation when they occur.

Legal and Policy Considerations: While cultural appropriation often involves ethical considerations rather than legal ones, some countries have laws or policies aimed at protecting indigenous cultures or traditional knowledge from exploitation or misuse. However, enforcement and interpretation of such laws can vary widely.

In summary, cultural appropriation involves the adoption or use of elements from one culture by members of another culture, often without proper understanding, respect, or acknowledgment. It can perpetuate stereotypes, reinforce power imbalances, and cause harm to marginalized communities. Discussions around cultural appropriation emphasize the importance of cultural sensitivity, education, and respectful engagement with diverse cultures.

Closed Communities

"Closed Communities" and "Race-Locked Spirituality" are terms that describe cultural or spiritual practices that are exclusive to specific racial or ethnic groups.

Definition: Closed communities refer to groups or societies that restrict membership based on specific criteria such as ethnicity, race, religion, nationality, or other factors. These communities often have boundaries that limit interaction with outsiders and may have strict rules or traditions governing behavior, beliefs, and social interactions within the group.

Examples: Historically, closed communities have included indigenous tribes, religious sects, ethnic enclaves, and cultural groups that maintain a sense of identity and solidarity through shared ancestry, language, customs, or beliefs.

Characteristics

Limited Access: Closed communities typically restrict access to outsiders, requiring individuals to meet certain criteria or undergo initiation rituals to become members.

Strong Group Identity: Members of closed communities often share a strong sense of identity and belonging based on common ancestry, culture, or values.

Preserving Tradition: Closed communities may prioritize the preservation of cultural or spiritual traditions by maintaining strict boundaries and resisting external influences.

Protection and Security: Closed communities may form in response to historical persecution, discrimination, or marginalization, providing a sense of safety and protection for members.

Challenges and Controversies:

Closed communities may face challenges related to inclusivity, diversity, and integration with broader society. Critics argue that strict boundaries can foster insularity, prejudice, and exclusion, while proponents emphasize the importance of preserving cultural heritage and protecting vulnerable communities.

Race-Locked Spirituality

Race-locked spirituality refers to spiritual or religious practices that are exclusive to individuals of a specific racial or ethnic group. These practices may be rooted in cultural traditions, historical experiences, or shared identities and may involve beliefs, rituals, symbols, or ceremonies that are specific to a particular racial or ethnic community.

Certain forms of African traditional religions, such as Vodou or Santería, are often associated with specific ethnic or racial groups and may be practiced predominantly by members of those groups. Similarly, some forms of indigenous spirituality or Native American religions are deeply connected to specific tribal identities and may be inaccessible to those outside the tribe.

Characteristics
Cultural Specificity: Race-locked spiritual practices are deeply intertwined with the cultural identities, histories, and worldviews of specific racial or ethnic groups.

Ancestral Connections: Practitioners of race-locked spirituality often emphasize connections to their ancestors and draw upon ancestral knowledge, rituals, and teachings in their spiritual practices.

Collective Experience: Race-locked spirituality may arise from collective experiences of oppression, resilience, and cultural survival, shaping the beliefs and practices of the community.

Resistance to Appropriation: Some practitioners of race-locked spirituality may be wary of cultural appropriation and may seek to protect their traditions from outside influence or exploitation.

Debates and Perspectives: Discussions around race-locked spirituality often intersect with debates about cultural appropriation, authenticity, and identity. While some argue for the preservation and protection of cultural heritage, others advocate for greater inclusivity and accessibility to spiritual practices across racial and ethnic boundaries.

In summary, closed communities restrict membership based on specific criteria, while race-locked spirituality involves spiritual practices exclusive to particular racial or ethnic groups. These concepts reflect complex interactions between culture, identity, tradition, and belonging, with implications for inclusivity, diversity, and cultural preservation.

Santería

Santería, also known as Lukumi or Regla de Ocha, is a syncretic religion that originated in Cuba and later spread to other parts of the Caribbean and the Americas. It combines elements of Yoruba religion (brought by enslaved Africans) with Roman Catholicism and Indigenous American traditions.

Beliefs: Santería worships a pantheon of orishas, or deities, derived from Yoruba cosmology, each representing different aspects of nature, human experience, and divine forces. Practitioners engage in rituals, ceremonies, and divination to honor the orishas, seek their guidance, and cultivate spiritual growth.

Cultural Significance: Santería is deeply rooted in Cuban culture and society, influencing various aspects of music, dance, art, and folklore. It is also practiced in other parts of the Caribbean and the Americas, particularly among Afro-Cuban and Afro-Latino communities.

Historical Context: Santería emerged among enslaved Africans in colonial Cuba as a way to preserve their cultural and religious traditions in the face of oppression and forced conversion to Christianity. It represents a blending of African, European, and Indigenous American influences, reflecting the complex history and identity of Afro-Cuban communities.

Many Native American Cultures

Native American cultures encompass a diverse array of Indigenous peoples, tribes, and nations across the Americas, each with its own unique languages, traditions, beliefs, and practices.

Cultural Diversity: Native American cultures vary significantly in their social structures, spiritual beliefs, artistic expressions, and ways of life, reflecting the rich tapestry of Indigenous identities and histories.

Spirituality: Many Native American cultures maintain spiritual traditions deeply rooted in reverence for the land, ancestors, and natural world. Practices such as ceremonies, rituals, storytelling, and sacred dances play central roles in maintaining cultural continuity and connection to the spiritual realm.

Many African Cultures

African cultures comprise a vast array of ethnic groups, societies, and civilizations across the African continent, each with its own languages, customs, traditions, and belief systems.

Diversity: African cultures exhibit remarkable diversity in their languages, religions, art forms, cuisines, and social structures, shaped by thousands of years of history, migrations, and interactions with neighboring peoples.

Religious Traditions: African religions encompass a wide range of traditional beliefs, including animism, ancestor worship, polytheism, and shamanism, often intertwined with cultural practices, rituals, and ceremonies.

Saami (in Finland)

The Saami, also known as Sámi or Sami, are Indigenous peoples inhabiting the Arctic regions of Norway, Sweden, Finland, and Russia (Sápmi).

Cultural Practices: Saami culture is characterized by reindeer herding, fishing, hunting, and a close relationship with nature. Traditional Saami practices include yoiking (a form of traditional song), handicrafts, storytelling, and shamanic rituals.

Spirituality: Saami spirituality is deeply connected to the natural world, with beliefs in spirits, deities, and the importance of maintaining harmony and balance with the environment.

Shinto

Shinto is the indigenous religion of Japan, characterized by a reverence for kami (spirits or deities) and a deep connection to nature, ancestors, and the spiritual essence of Japan.

Branches: While Shinto practices vary among different regions and communities, there are both open and closed branches of Shinto. Jinja Shinto, which revolves around the worship of kami at shrines, is one of the more open denominations.

Rituals: Shinto rituals, ceremonies, and festivals are central to communal life in Japan, often involving purification rites, offerings, prayers, and processions.

Druidism (proper, not neo)

Druidism is a modern revival of ancient Celtic spiritual and religious practices centered around reverence for nature, the cycles of the seasons, and the wisdom of the ancestors.

Historical Context: Druidism originated among the Celtic peoples of Europe, particularly in regions such as Britain, Ireland, and Gaul, where druids served as priests, scholars, and custodians of traditional knowledge.

Beliefs and Practices: Druidic beliefs encompass animism, polytheism, and a deep respect for the natural world. Practices may include rituals, ceremonies, meditation, and storytelling, often conducted in sacred groves or natural settings.

Gardnerian and Alexandrian Wicca

Gardnerian and Alexandrian Wicca are two branches of modern witchcraft that emerged in the mid-20th century, founded by Gerald Gardner and Alexander Sanders, respectively.

Beliefs: Both Gardnerian and Alexandrian Wicca draw inspiration from Western esoteric traditions, folk magic, ceremonial rituals, and pagan beliefs. They honor a pantheon of deities, practice magic, and celebrate seasonal festivals such as Sabbats and Esbats.

Initiation: Gardnerian and Alexandrian Wicca typically require initiation into a coven or lineage, with teachings passed down through oral tradition and ritual ceremonies. Each tradition has its own specific rituals, practices, and codes of ethics.

Some Parts of African Vodou

African Vodou, also known as Vodun, Voodoo, or Vodoun, is a syncretic religion practiced primarily in West Africa and the African diaspora, particularly in Haiti and parts of the Caribbean.

Beliefs and Practices: African Vodou incorporates elements of African spirituality, animism, ancestor worship, and Christian symbolism. It revolves around the veneration of spirits of loa, divination, healing, and ritual ceremonies.

Variation: Different sects, groups, or families within African Vodou may have variations in their practices, beliefs, and rituals, reflecting regional differences, cultural influences, and individual preferences.

Hinduism

Description: Hinduism is one of the world's oldest religions, originating in the Indian subcontinent and encompassing a diverse array of beliefs, practices, sects, and philosophies.

Diversity: Hinduism encompasses a wide range of beliefs, including polytheism, monotheism, pantheism, and atheism, as well as various philosophical schools such as Vedanta, Yoga, and Samkhya.

Denominations: There are numerous denominations and sects within Hinduism, each with its own theological interpretations, rituals, and practices. Some are open and inclusive, while others may be more exclusive or restrictive in their membership requirements.

Beliefs and Practices: Hinduism encompasses a vast array of beliefs and practices, including devotion (bhakti), ritual worship (puja), yoga, meditation, karma, dharma, and reincarnation.

Hopi

The Hopi are a Native American tribe located in northeastern Arizona, known for their rich cultural heritage, artistry, and spiritual traditions.

Spirituality: Hopi spirituality is deeply rooted in reverence for the land, ancestors, and cosmic forces. Central to Hopi beliefs are the concepts of balance, harmony, and interconnectedness with nature.

Kachinas: Hopi religious ceremonies often revolve around the worship of kachinas, spiritual beings believed to inhabit the natural world and serve as intermediaries between humans and the divine.

Inuit

The Inuit are Indigenous peoples inhabiting the Arctic regions of Canada, Greenland, Alaska, and Siberia, known for their resilience, adaptability, and unique cultural traditions.

Spirituality: Inuit spirituality is deeply connected to the land, sea, and animals of the Arctic environment. Beliefs often revolve around animism, shamanism, and a profound respect for the natural world.

Shamanism: Inuit religious practices may involve shamanic rituals, drumming, storytelling, and ceremonies to communicate with spirits, seek guidance, and maintain balance with the environment.

Judaism

Judaism is one of the oldest monotheistic religions, originating in the ancient land of Israel and encompassing a rich tapestry of beliefs.

Rastafari Movement

The Rastafari Movement is a religious and cultural movement that originated in Jamaica in the early 20th century. It emerged as a response to social, economic, and political conditions faced by black Jamaicans, drawing inspiration from various sources, including Christianity, Pan-Africanism, and Ethiopianism.

Beliefs: Rastafari adherents believe in the divinity of Ethiopian Emperor Haile Selassie I, whom they revere as the Messiah (or Jah), and the fulfillment of biblical prophecies regarding the return of the King of Kings. They also emphasize principles such as African liberation, social justice, and the rejection of Babylon (systemic oppression).

Cultural Practices: Rastafari culture is characterized by spiritual practices such as Nyabinghi chants, cannabis sacrament (known as ganja), natural living, dreadlocks, and a distinctive lifestyle focused on unity, love, and righteousness.

Tribal (almost all)

Indigenous tribes or tribal communities exist in various parts of the world, including Africa, the Americas, Asia, and Oceania. These communities often have distinct languages, cultures, traditions, and social structures shaped by their historical experiences and connections to the land.

Cultural Diversity: Tribal societies exhibit remarkable diversity in their beliefs, practices, and ways of life, ranging from hunter-gatherer societies to settled agricultural communities. They may practice animism, ancestor worship, shamanism, or other spiritual traditions.

Connection to the Land: Many tribal cultures maintain strong connections to their ancestral lands, viewing the natural environment as sacred and integral to their spiritual and cultural identities.

Zoroastrianism

Zoroastrianism is one of the world's oldest monotheistic religions, originating in ancient Persia (modern-day Iran) around the 6th century BCE. It was founded by the prophet Zoroaster (or Zarathustra) and served as the state religion of the Persian Empire.

Beliefs: Zoroastrianism revolves around the teachings of Zoroaster, who preached the existence of a single supreme deity, Ahura Mazda (the Wise Lord), and the dualistic struggle between good (truth, order) and evil (falsehood, chaos). It emphasizes ethical conduct, free will, and the pursuit of righteousness.

Practices: Zoroastrian rituals and practices include prayers, purification rites, fire worship, and the veneration of sacred elements such as fire, water, and earth. Death rituals, including exposure of the deceased to scavenging birds (sky burial), are also significant in Zoroastrian tradition.

Kemetic Orthodox

Kemetic Orthodoxy is a modern religious movement that seeks to reconstruct and revive the ancient Egyptian religion of Kemet (Egypt). It draws inspiration from archaeological evidence, historical texts, and scholarly research to reconstruct the beliefs, rituals, and practices of ancient Egyptian spirituality.

Beliefs: Kemetic Orthodoxy emphasizes devotion to the gods and goddesses of ancient Egypt, including deities such as Ra, Osiris, Isis, and Anubis. It incorporates rituals, offerings, prayers, and meditative practices aimed at honoring the divine and fostering personal spiritual growth.

Initiation and Training: Kemetic Orthodoxy does not require formal initiation in the traditional sense, but it does involve a process of study, learning, and engagement with the religion's teachings and practices. Practitioners may undertake a series of coursework and rites of passage as part of their spiritual development.

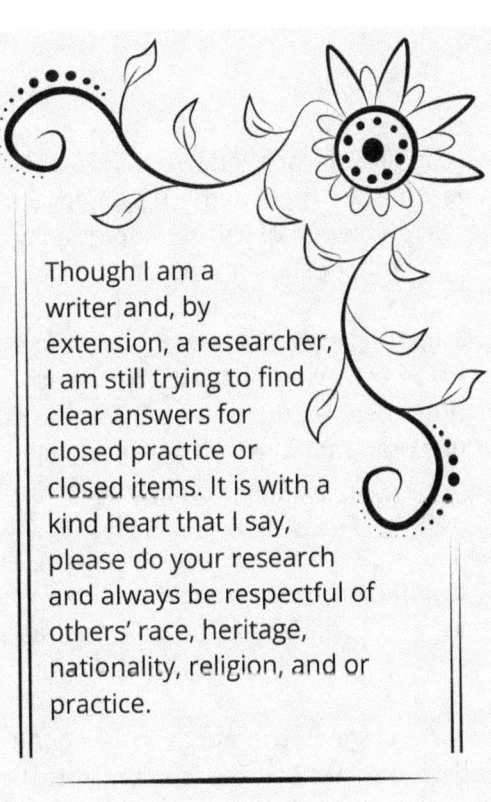

Though I am a writer and, by extension, a researcher, I am still trying to find clear answers for closed practice or closed items. It is with a kind heart that I say, please do your research and always be respectful of others' race, heritage, nationality, religion, and or practice.

Haitian Vodou

Haitian Vodou is a syncretic religion that developed in Haiti among Afro-Haitian communities during the Atlantic slave trade. It combines elements of traditional West African religions (such as Yoruba and Fon), Roman Catholicism, and indigenous Caribbean beliefs.

Beliefs: Haitian Vodou is polytheistic, with a pantheon of spirits, each associated with different aspects of life, nature, and human experience. Practitioners believe in the interconnectedness of the spiritual and physical worlds and the importance of rituals, offerings, and ancestor veneration.

Cultural Significance: Haitian Vodou is deeply ingrained in Haitian culture and identity, serving as a source of spiritual guidance, communal solidarity, and resistance against oppression. It is recognized as one of the main religions in Haiti, alongside Catholicism, and influences various aspects of daily life, art, music, and literature.

Historical Context: Haitian Vodou emerged as a survival mechanism and form of cultural preservation among enslaved Africans in Haiti, who faced harsh conditions and brutal treatment under French colonial rule. It provided a means of resistance, empowerment, and cultural resilience against oppression.

Hoodoo

Hoodoo, also known as conjure or rootwork, is a syncretic folk tradition practiced primarily by African Americans in the Southern United States, as well as in the Caribbean. It incorporates elements of African spirituality, Indigenous American beliefs, European folk magic, and Christian mysticism.

Beliefs and Practices: Hoodoo encompasses a wide range of spiritual practices, rituals, and beliefs aimed at achieving specific goals, such as protection, healing, prosperity, and love. It often involves the use of herbs, candles, roots, charms, and rituals passed down through oral traditions and family lineages.

Cultural Significance: Hoodoo has played a significant role in African American culture and history, serving as a means of empowerment, survival, and resistance against oppression. It has influenced various cultural expressions, including music, folklore, literature, and art, and continues to be practiced as a form of spiritual and cultural heritage.

Historical Context: Hoodoo originated among enslaved Africans in the Southern United States, who adapted and syncretized spiritual practices from their diverse cultural backgrounds to navigate the challenges of slavery and maintain connections to their ancestral traditions.

Closed Objects

Objects that carry cultural or spiritual significance for certain communities, emphasizing their value, as well as addressing issues related to their preservation and respectful use.

White Sage

Description: White sage (Salvia apiana) is a sacred herb traditionally used by various Indigenous American tribes in smudging rituals to cleanse spaces, objects, and individuals of negative energy.

Cultural Significance: White sage holds deep cultural and spiritual significance for Indigenous American communities, who have used it for ceremonial purposes for centuries.

Endangerment: Due to over-harvesting, habitat destruction, and climate change, white sage populations are currently declining, leading to concerns about its sustainability and conservation.

Appropriation Concerns: The commercialization and widespread use of white sage by non-Indigenous individuals or communities have sparked concerns about cultural appropriation and the exploitation of sacred traditions.

Palo Santo

Description: Palo Santo is a type of aged wood from the Bursera graveolens tree, native to South America, particularly regions like Peru and Ecuador. It is burned for its aromatic scent and spiritual properties.

Cultural Significance: Palo Santo holds cultural and spiritual significance for Hispanic/Latino communities in South America, where it is used in rituals, ceremonies, and healing practices.

Endangerment: Like white sage, Palo Santo is facing endangerment due to over-harvesting and habitat loss, leading to efforts to regulate its trade and promote sustainable harvesting practices.

Appropriation Concerns: The commercial buying and widespread use of Palo Santo by those outside of Hispanic/Latino communities have raised concerns about cultural appropriation and the unethical exploitation of natural resources.

Dream Catchers

Dream catchers are hand-made woven hoops, traditionally crafted by Indigenous American artisans and adorned with sacred items such as feathers and beads. They are believed to protect the sleeper from negative dreams.

Cultural Significance: Dream catchers are deeply rooted in Indigenous American cultures, particularly among tribes like the Ojibwe, Lakota, and Anishinaabe, where they hold spiritual significance and are considered sacred objects.

Authenticity: There is a belief among some Indigenous communities that only dream catchers made by Indigenous artisans are authentic and hold spiritual power, while mass-produced versions may lack cultural integrity.

Appropriation Concerns: The commercialization and mass production of dream catchers by non-Indigenous individuals or companies has led to concerns about cultural appropriation and the commodification of Indigenous spiritual practices.

Sweetgrass

Sweetgrass (Hierochloe odorata) is a fragrant grass native to North America, traditionally used by Indigenous American tribes in smudging rituals and ceremonies for its pleasant aroma and spiritual properties.

Cultural Significance: Sweetgrass holds cultural and spiritual significance for many Indigenous American tribes, symbolizing healing, purification, and connection to the Earth.

Appropriation Concerns: Concerns about cultural appropriation arise when non-Indigenous individuals or communities commercially exploit sweetgrass without understanding or respecting its cultural significance, leading to calls for sustainable harvesting practices and cultural sensitivity.

In summary, these "closed objects" hold deep cultural, spiritual, and ecological significance for the communities from which they originate. However, they are also facing endangerment due to over-harvesting, habitat loss, and commercial exploitation, leading to concerns about cultural appropriation and the need for sustainable conservation efforts.

Egg limpia

Egg limpia, also known as "egg cleansing," is a South American folk practice used for spiritual cleansing and healing. It involves the use of a raw egg to absorb negative energies or illnesses from a person's aura or energy field.

Cultural Significance: Egg limpia is deeply rooted in the cultural and spiritual traditions of South American folk medicine and shamanic practices, where it is believed to restore balance and remove blockages in the body's energy system.

Geographical and Cultural Context: Egg limpia is primarily associated with South American cultures and is part of their indigenous healing traditions and folk practices.

Karma

Karma is a concept originating from Hinduism and later adopted by Buddhism, referring to the law of cause and effect. It suggests that the intentions and actions of an individual influence their future experiences and circumstances, either positively or negatively.

Cultural Origin: Karma is deeply rooted in Hindu and Buddhist philosophy and spirituality, where it serves as a moral and spiritual principle guiding ethical behavior, personal development, and the cycle of reincarnation.

Belief System:

Karma is central to the belief systems of Hinduism and Buddhism, shaping notions of morality, justice, and spiritual evolution within these religions.

Spirituality For Beginners

Spirituality is about experiencing what's beyond the physical and using that knowledge to improve your life and the lives of others. It's not about relying on second-hand information but finding the truth for yourself.

As you develop spiritually, you'll gain psychic abilities, expand your existence beyond the mundane, and make better decisions. With intention and visualization, you'll be able to fight whatever holds you back directly. Start today and experience the excitement and meaning true spirituality brings to your life.

Smudging

Smudging is a sacred ritual practiced by various Indigenous American tribes, involving the burning of specific herbs (such as white sage, cedar, or sweetgrass) to cleanse and purify spaces, objects, and individuals.

Cultural Significance: Smudging holds deep spiritual and cultural significance for Indigenous American communities, who believe it helps to dispel negative energies, promote healing, and maintain balance and harmony.

Differentiation: It's important to note that smudging is distinct from "smoke cleansing," which is a more general practice used in various spiritual and cultural traditions for similar purposes but may not necessarily involve the same rituals, beliefs, or cultural contexts.

Spirit Animals

Description: Spirit animals are an integral part of the spiritual beliefs and practices of many Indigenous American tribes. They are believed to be guides, protectors, or sources of wisdom and strength for individuals and communities.

Cultural Specificity: The concept of spirit animals is deeply rooted in the cultural and religious traditions of certain Indigenous American tribes. While other cultures may have similar beliefs about animal symbolism, the specific practice of connecting with spirit animals is exclusive to these Indigenous communities.

Belief Exclusivity: According to Indigenous American beliefs, one's spirit animal is determined by their ancestry, personal experiences, and spiritual connections within the tribe. It is not something that individuals outside of these communities typically have or claim.

Chakras

Description: Chakras are energy centers or focal points within the subtle body, according to Hindu and Buddhist spiritual traditions. They are believed to be located along the spine and correspond to different aspects of physical, emotional, and spiritual well-being.

Cultural Significance: The concept of chakras is integral to Hindu and Buddhist spiritual practices, including yoga, meditation, and energy healing. Each chakra is associated with specific qualities, elements, colors, sounds, and spiritual lessons.

Practices and Techniques: Within Kundalini yoga and other spiritual disciplines, various practices such as breathwork, visualization, meditation, mantra chanting, and mudras are used to balance and activate the chakras, promoting physical health, emotional harmony, and spiritual awakening.

CHAPTER 32

Ostara
Journaling

Journal Prompts for Self-Reflection and Shadow Work

Journaling prompts can be an excellent tool for self-reflection by helping you delve into your thoughts and emotions. Expressing yourself through journaling can be therapeutic and provide clarity and understanding of your experiences without fear of judgment.

The versatility of journaling prompts is a significant advantage. You can customize them to your unique needs and interests and use them to explore any aspect of your life. Whether it's your relationships, career goals, personal values, or simply gaining a better understanding of yourself, there's a prompt that's perfect for you. You're free to choose the prompts that speak to you and follow your authentic path.

Remember, there's no right or wrong way to engage in self-reflection. This is a personal journey, and the insights you gain are unique to you. Embrace the process, trust your instincts, and allow yourself to be vulnerable. Your journaling practice will mature over time, and each entry will bring you closer to a deeper connection with yourself.

Self-Reflections

How have I grown or changed since the beginning of the year?

Self-Reflections

In what areas of my life do I feel a sense of renewal and rebirth?

Self-Reflections

What seeds of intention have I planted, and how are they beginning to manifest?

_____

_____

_____

_____

_____

_____

_____

_____

_____

_____

_____

_____

_____

_____

_____

_____

_____

_____

_____

_____

_____

_____

_____

_____

Self-Reflections

How can I embrace balance in my life, aligning with the equal lengths of day and night?

Self-Reflections

What aspects of my life am I ready to let go of to make room for new growth?

Self-Reflections

How can I nurture and care for myself, just as I would care for a budding plant?

_____
_____
_____
_____
_____
_____
_____
_____
_____
_____
_____
_____
_____
_____
_____
_____
_____
_____
_____
_____
_____
_____
_____
_____
_____
_____
_____
_____
_____
_____
_____
_____

Self-Reflections

What creative projects or ideas am I excited to bring to fruition during this season?

_____
_____
_____
_____
_____
_____
_____
_____
_____
_____
_____
_____
_____
_____
_____
_____
_____
_____
_____
_____
_____
_____
_____
_____
_____
_____
_____

Self-Reflections

In what ways can I celebrate and honor the natural world around me?

Self-Reflections

What rituals or practices can I incorporate into my daily life to connect with the energy of spring?

Self-Reflections

How do I cultivate a sense of gratitude for the abundance in my life?

Self-Reflections

What relationships or connections am I ready to foster and strengthen?

Self-Reflections

What old habits or thought patterns am I willing to release to invite positive change?

Self-Reflections

How can I bring more lightness and joy into my everyday experiences?

Self-Reflections

What intentions do I set for my personal and spiritual growth during this season?

Self-Reflections

In what ways can I contribute positively to my community and the world around me?

Self-Reflections

How do I honor the duality of light and dark within myself?

Self-Reflections

What steps can I take to create a more harmonious and balanced living space?

Self-Reflections

How can I infuse more mindfulness into my daily activities?

Self-Reflections

What symbols of renewal and growth resonate with me, and how can 1 incorporate them into my surroundings?

Self-Reflections

How can I express gratitude for the interconnectedness of all life during this season of Ostara?

Cutting Energy Cords

If you're looking for ways to cut energy cords, try these techniques:

Visualize All the Cords Coming Back to You

When trying to cut cords, you're often thinking about yourself or someone or something else. To test this exercise, visualize yourself calling back your golden light from what you're trying to cut cords. Imagine all of these golden threads entering your core. When you're finished, do something empowering to seal the energy, such as doing at-home exercises or enjoying a nourishing snack.

Intuitively Ask the Holder of the Cord to Let Go

Center your energy field and identify where you feel the most energetic cord is coming from. Ask this source, with claircognizant or clairaudient inner thought, to release this cord from you, watch it be let go, and come back to you. Some people like to imagine a golden energy scissor cutting the cord, with the cord on your end coiling back to you. Do something nourishing to seal the energy after seeing the cord entirely return to you clairvoyantly, like visualizing a light ball surrounding your energy field. If you're doing this technique for a client, ask your Spirit or Guides for one nourishing thing they can do.

Blue Grid Visualization

This technique seals your energy field with healing light. Imagine a blue electric field cage glowing around you, then visualize any old links or dangling cords twisting or dropping from the energy field. Imagine the old cord pieces breaking off and washing away at your feet, back to the nearest waterway. Then, visualize a glowing blue light grid across your energy field until you feel clear.

When you're finished, visualize a golden light in your core, your Solar Plexus. Bow to yourself or your guides, and offer gratitude for the energy you used to visualize, sense, or think through these shamanic energy exercises. Finally, imagine your palm chakras and heart shining golden light.

Did it Work?

After cord-cutting, you should experience a sense of balance and inner peace. You may feel more focused on a particular project and experience contentment, which is the typical energy state of most soul bodies on Earth.

However, if you continually think about a certain person or situation even after cord-cutting, you may have a karmic relationship with them. In this case, deeper energy work may be needed.

To achieve longer-lasting results after cord-cutting, repeat the above process for up to 21 days or explore other techniques such as "How To Cut Cords Energetically" or "3 Easy Steps To Spiritual Cords Cutting."

For optimal results, try cord-cutting during a full or new moon, representing release and setting new intentions.

Usually, energy entanglements sort themselves out with continued intent, deeper energy work, or when doing energy boundary work. Give yourself and the other person or situation three days to settle after using any cord-cutting technique.

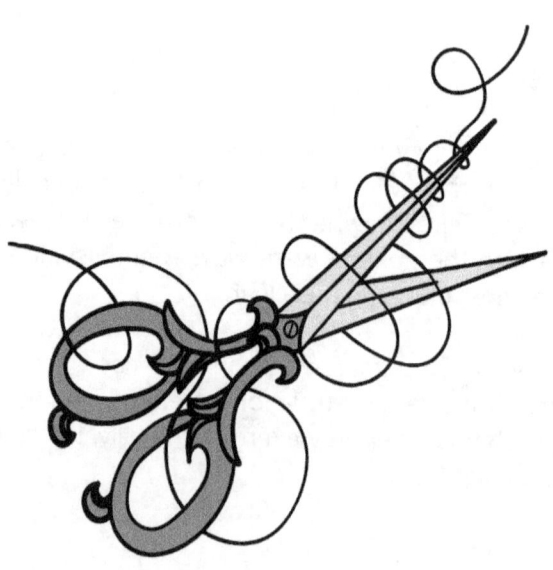

A Mantra for Cord Cutting

With a full heart, I release you from your place in my life – forever grateful for our shared memories. May your chosen path bring happiness and joy.

I now reclaim the energy that was taken from me and release any energy that I gave away. May I be free from any lingering attachments that bind us.

May all cords be cut, transmuted, and dissolved, and may all energy return to its rightful sender with power, peace, and forgiveness.

Let this process be completed and sealed now with the comforting power of acceptance. So it is.

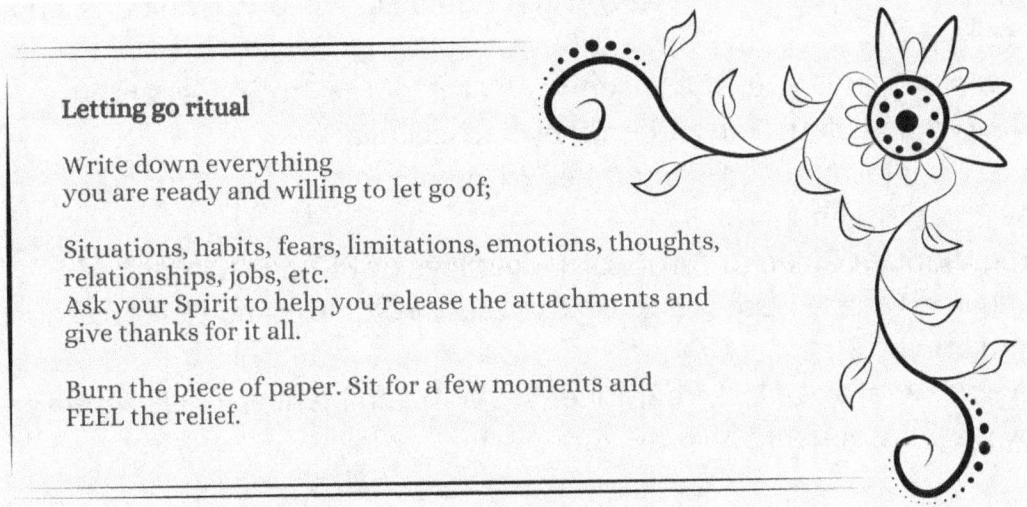

Letting go ritual

Write down everything
you are ready and willing to let go of;

Situations, habits, fears, limitations, emotions, thoughts, relationships, jobs, etc.
Ask your Spirit to help you release the attachments and give thanks for it all.

Burn the piece of paper. Sit for a few moments and FEEL the relief.

Reference

The Complete Book of Correspondences Sandra Kynes

The White Goddess Graves, Robert Guiley, Rosemary Ellen. The Encyclopedia of Witches and Witchcraft

The Complete Grimoire: Magickal Practices and Spells for Awakening Your Inner Witch by Lidia Pradas

Heal the Witch Wound: Reclaim Your Magic and Step Into Your Power by Celeste Larsen

Cunningham's Encyclopedia of Magical Herbs (Llewellyn's Sourcebook Series) (Cunningham's Encyclopedia Series, 1) by Scott Cunningham

Psychic Witch: A Metaphysical Guide to Meditation, Magick & Manifestation Mat Auryn

Llewellyn's Practical Magick (11 books)

Encyclopedia of World Mythology and Legend

The Encyclopedia of Celtic Mythology and Folklore Monaghan, Patricia. Astronomer's Stars Moore, Patrick

Self Care for Witches: The Art of Healing and Self Love through Witchcraft by Blair Blackmore

The Door to Witchcraft: A New Witch's Guide to History, Traditions, and Modern-Day Spells by Tonya A. Brown

Seventy-Eight Degrees of Wisdom: A Tarot Journey to Self-Awareness (A New Edition of the Tarot Classic) by Rachel Pollack

Everyday Tarot: Unlock Your Inner Wisdom and Manifest Your Future by Brigit Esselmont

The Ultimate Guide to Tarot Card Meanings by Brigit Esselmont

Intuitive Tarot: 31 Days to Learn to Read Tarot Cards and Develop Your Intuition by Brigit Esselmont

Everyday Tarot: Unlock Your Inner Wisdom and Manifest Your Future by Brigit Esselmont

Reference

A History of Magic, Witchcraft, and the Occult DK

The Modern-Day Witch (11 books) by Shawn Robbins, Leanna Greenaway, Lisa Chamberlain

Witchcraft for Daily Self-Care: Nourishing Rituals and Spells for a More Balanced Life by Michael Herkes

The Untamed Witch: Reclaim Your Instincts. Rewild Your Craft. Create Your Most Powerful Magick. Lidia Pradas

Paganism: Pagan holidays, beliefs, gods and goddesses, symbols, rituals, practices, and much more! An Introductory Guide by Riley Star

Buckland's Complete Book of Witchcraft   Raymond Buckland

The Modern Witchcraft Spell Book: Your Complete Guide to Crafting and Casting Spells (Modern Witchcraft Magic, Spells, Rituals) by Skye Alexander

Scott Cunningham—The Path Taken: Honoring the Life and Legacy of a Wiccan Trailblazer by Christine Cunningham Ashworth

Herbalism for Witches: 3 Books In 1-Guide to Herbal Apothecary and Plant Witchery+Magical Herbs for Spiritual Healing and Sacred Heart+Manifest Your Spiritual Wellness with Spells and Herbal Magic by Ruby Goldwin

Protection and Reversal Spells: The Witch's Self-Defense Guide Against Curses, Hexes, Negative Energies, Harmful Spirits, and Psychic Attacks. Create Your Own Shield with the Most Powerful Magic! by Alyssa Vera

Book Reviewing for Independent Authors: A Personal Experience
As part of my company, I have been reviewing books for Independent authors for five years. I've had the opportunity to meet and interact with some really incredible people. One of those individuals was Rev. Pamela Irene Flowerday, who reached out to me with her book, "Ask Yourself: Understand and Unlock Your Psychic Power for Personal & Planetary Healing." Her writing style was absolutely incredible, and I was blown away by the content. I highly recommend this book, and if you're interested, check out my reviewer page at Robinsreview.com for a short Q&A with the author. (sorry not a shameless plug)

The author, <u>Rev. Pamela Irene Flowerday</u>,, wrote Ask Yourself: Understand and Unlock Your Psychic Power for Personal and planetary Healing.

After completing some of the exercises in the book, I was astounded by the wealth of knowledge I had gained. The book helped me to identify and trust my inner knowing, and I was inspired by Rev. Flowerday's insightful content. With this newfound understanding of my intuitive abilities, I was able to embark on a path of profound spiritual growth and personal transformation.

Another author I've had the opportunity to meet and interact with some really incredible people. One of those individuals was Alexx Shaw, who reached out to me with her book, "The Soul Family: a Guide to Karmic relationships, Soulmates, Soul Tribes, and Twin Flames"

She offers practical guidance infused with spiritual wisdom and scientific perspectives and it absolutely made sense. I highly recommend this book, and if you're interested, check out my reviewer page at Robinsreview.com for a short Q&A with the author. (sorry another shameless plug)

The author, Alexx Shaw,
wrote The Soul Family: a Guide to Karmic relationships, Soulmates, Soul Tribes, and Twin Flames

THE
SOUL
FAMILY

A GUIDE TO KARMIC RELATIONSHIPS, SOULMATES,
SOUL TRIBES, AND TWIN FLAMES

Ms. Shaw offers practical guidance infused with spiritual wisdom and scientific perspectives. This book is a transformative journey of self-discovery, providing tools to navigate relationships more effectively and heal from past experiences.

ALEXX SHAW

With clarity and depth, Shaw's exploration of existence, purpose, and relationships challenges conventional notions and illuminates the intricate dynamics of ego, karma, and soul connections. Through insightful reflections on core karmic lessons, readers are empowered to understand the significance of the individuals in their lives and embrace the journey of self-discovery. "The Soul Family" is a must-read for anyone seeking deeper insights into their existence and the connections that bind us all.

If you read only one book in 2024, let this be that book.

Mystic Mind Community

Why Join The Mystic MindCommunity?

We bring together spiritual people who are seeking more connection, the ability to share their own experiences, and learn from online Challenges, Live Events, Courses, and each other!

The concept for building this Spiritual Social Network is so we can grow together in a supportive, inclusive, and fun Spiritual Metaverse covering a wide range of spiritual resources.

The Mystic Mind Podcast

The Mystic Mind Podcast is a creative exploration to help support you in your intuitive and spiritual development journey and add a little fun!

I mean, we have to have fun on this journey, right?

As a professional Energy Healer and Spiritual Teacher, I share some of what I've learned along the way during my spiritual development journey for over a decade. In this podcast, you will find shows on Intuitive Development and/or reflections, Angels, Divination, Energy Work, special guests, interviews, and more.

Also, have you joined our Mystic Mind Community?
Mystic Mind is available on
Spotify
Anchor fm
Amazon Music
Apple Musi
DCNW Podcast:
Spotify:

Colby Parrish

(727) 831-8077

Facebook: The Wondering Fool - Spiritual Advisor
Instagram: Thewonderingfool333
TikTok: TheWonderingFool333

Hours of Availability
Tuesday through Saturday 11 am - 8 pm EST

Service Menu
General Psychic Readings
30 min/$60
45min/$90
60min/$120

Tarot - Oracle - Lithomancy
3 Card Single Message
Pull/ $20
Couples Readings
40min/$80
Personal Monthly
Forecast/$120
Numerological
Chart/$150

Available for private parties and events!

He is my spiritual adviser, so I highly recommend him and his services!

Jamie Wareham

www.lightworkerpath.com
Email: lightworkerpathsite@gmail.com

Service Menu
Reiki + Sound Healing Sessions
Soul Coaching Sessions (spiritual life coaching)
Intuitive Development
Mentorship Programs
Reiki Level 1,2 & 3 Attunement
Certification Courses
Spiritual/Energy Development Classes

She is a fellow writer who co-authored "The Voyage & The Return: The Path to Self Discovery." Moreover, I've taken her classes, and they were interesting and helpful. She's super knowledgeable about energy work, angel spirit guides, meditation, and reiki healing.

Here is a profound quote from her book "Some of the best teachers are ones who have journeyed into the heart of darkness and come through it all like the powerful Phoenix they are! A rebirth into something else, something stronger, something that yearns to help others through their own forms of darkness."

SEWICKLEY, PA

Elemental Magic
For all of your metaphysical needs

elemental-magick-inc.myshopify.com
948 4th Avenue Coraopolis, PA 15108
Phone Number: (412) 741-1428

Facebook Group Elemental Magick
Instagram Elemental Magick Inc

We are a women-owned metaphysical business that has been operating since 2015! Located in Coraopolis, Pennsylvania, we provide some of the best quality crystals in Pittsburgh with a personal service guarantee every time you shop. Our products include candles, books, incense, and items from local artisans, including Gaias Grace.

Hours of Operation
Sunday: CLOSED (Sunday Funday Facebook Live 7:00 pm EST)
Monday: CLOSED
Tuesday: CLOSED
Wednesday: CLOSED (Witchy Wednesday Facebook Live 7:00 pm EST)
Thursday: 12 pm - 6 pm
Friday: 12 pm - 6 pm
Saturday: 12 pm - 6 pm

Odie's Curiosities

Handmade High-Quality Jewelry Available on Facebook

Discover beautifully crafted handmade items, including reiki-charged jewelry that is hand-strung with care. With a specialty in Mala beads, this Facebook store offers stunning and unique pieces you won't find anywhere else.

Contact through Facebook Messenger

Whimsical Cauldron and Crafts

www.whimsicalcauldronandcrafts.com
Email: Whimsicalcauldron2019@gmail.com
Facebook: Whimsical Cauldron and Crafts, LLC

They sell crystals, minerals, specimens, jewelry, herbs, sage, etc.
They also feature other vendors and their merchandise.

I have purchased almost everything they have for sale and can confidently say they are a great small business for high-quality crystal needs. They have always been kind and patient, especially when I first learned about crystals. If they didn't have something I was looking for, they would get it for me.

Emerald Coast Alternatives

emeraldcoastalternatives.com

Welcome to Emerald Coast Alternatives, your online herbal tea shop. We aim to provide accessible, effective, and affordable herbal tea blends that help you feel better and enjoy life more. Our teas are delicious and effective in managing symptoms of anxiety, PTSD, PMS, insomnia, inflammation, and headaches. We donate one Herbal Tea "Care Package" monthly to a Recovery Center in the USA. Thank you for choosing Emerald Coast Alternatives as your trusted herbal teas and self-healing tools source.

Follow them and learn more about what their products can provide on TikTok @freespirit.beauTEA

Enhance your Health with The Plant Cemetery Herbal Subscription Box!
MONTHLY HERBAL HEALTH & BEAU-TEA SUBSCRIPTION BOX
$10 OFF YOUR FIRST BOX with Code: PlantBox10
FREE SHIPPING ON ALL PRODUCTS!

Although I am not typically a tea fan, I absolutely adore the tea from this company. I purchase it frequently and have even signed up for their monthly subscription box.

Thank you immensely for your ongoing support. Sharing all this with you has been a delight, and I hope you found it as enjoyable as I did. I genuinely appreciate every like, follow, share, and review. If you're inclined, please take a moment to share your experience by leaving an honest review to help spread the word about my book! Together, we can contribute to making the world a better place. Once more, thank you from the depths of our hearts.

Thank you!!

Robin

Explore a realm of opportunities with KIPS Publishing LLC. Books possess the ability to change lives and broaden perspectives. We are delighted to present you with a selection of engaging, educational, and motivating books beyond your wildest dreams. By simply scanning our QR code, you can delve into a vast library of KIPS books and explore the finest content we have to offer. Don't miss out on this thrilling chance to elevate your reading experience. Scan now and unlock a gateway to a world filled with knowledge, creativity, and motivation!

I'm excited to announce that my next book in the self-help series based on shadow work and inner child healing is coming soon. So stay tuned for more information.

 Scan here for the latest release
from Robin Ginther Venneri
and KIPS Publishing

Thank you so much for your support!

If you enjoyed this book, then kindly leave a review on Amazon and on any of your social media accounts, and please tag me on them.

Thank You so much!
Blessings to You and Yours,
Robin Ginther-Venneri

Questions, concerns, and ideas can be directed to
KIPSPublishingllc@gmail.com

How to Support Indie (Independent) Authors

Review their books;
Like & comment on their posts;
Share their in-story or about pages;
Preorder their books. You know you are going to buy them anyway!
Recommend them to other readers;
Email or message about a book of theirs you loved;
Follow them on social media.

www.ingramcontent.com/pod-product-compliance
Lightning Source LLC
Chambersburg PA
CBHW080836120626
46553CB00009B/2451